THE DEALMAKER'S WILL

The Story of One Deal–
And the 7 Rules That Made It Happen

by

WALKER THRASH

First published in the United States of America, November 2025 by
Left Field Publishing.

ISBN: 9781966883036 (paperback)
ISBN: 9781966883043 (ebook)
ISBN: 9781966883050 (audiobook)

The story, all names, characters, and incidents portrayed in this production are fictitious. No identification with actual persons (living or deceased), places, buildings, and products is intended or should be inferred.

Library of Congress Control Number: 2025918902

Book Cover by Brandon Gratton
Printed in the United States of America

Dedication

To Katie, my wife, my mom-to-our-four, and my sharpest negotiator—thank you for keeping me on my toes and proving I'm lucky.

To my Dad, the most creative man I know, for early access to the boardroom.

To my Mom, for loving us enough to read the placard at every landmark along the way.

And to Annabelle, Marie, Lizzie, and Turner: you are our happiness. Stop growing up.

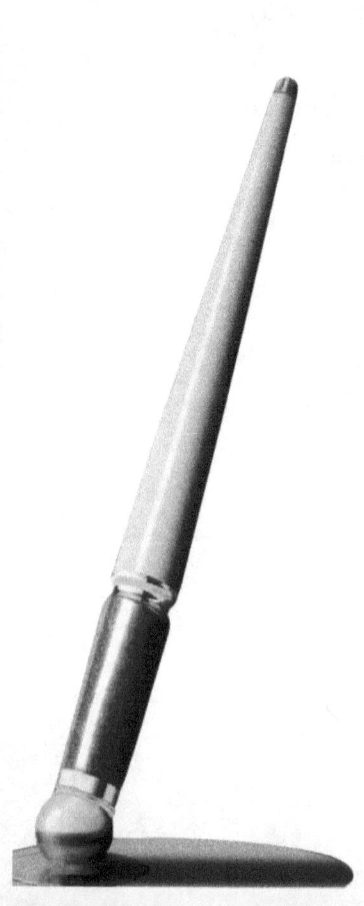

Chapter 1

"…so that his place shall never be with those cold and timid souls who know neither victory nor defeat."

—Theodore Roosevelt

Will felt his hands; they were wet. He rubbed them inconspicuously on his dark jeans, hoping no one noticed. Any tell that he was flappable could waft through the room like pheromones. In a space packed with forty bidders, that would be fatal.

"One million...now one-and-a-half...now one-and-a-half. Who will give me one-and-a-half?" The auctioneer's chant was rhythmic and practiced.

He forced his eyes up, scanning the crowd. Sharon Peyton was there. Their eyes locked. A faint smile flickered across her lips. Will froze. She didn't know his name, but he knew exactly who she was and why she was so interested in this particular auction item.

"One-and-a-half...now two...somebody go two...Will you give me two?"

The numbers rattled around his skull. The room pressed in tighter. On the first Thursday of each month, the cramped conference room in the Jefferson County, Colorado Trustees' Building transformed into an auction house. Occasionally, there was something special on the auction block.

Like today.

"Two million...now two-and-a-half...now two-and-a-half...who wants to be at two-and-a-half?"

Calm, he told himself. But calm was slipping away with each chant.

Will watched as Don Andino—seated near the front—gave a slight head nod that caught the eye of the auctioneer. It was as if to say, "Hello, everyone. I'm now mildly interested." It also signaled that Don was on the bid at $2.5 million and triggered a collective sigh from the room. There would be no stealing today, and by that sigh it was obvious the crowd's idea of a steal lay somewhere between $2 and $2.5 million. Will surveyed the room: shaking heads and folded arms were appearing in droves. A smattering of interested parties began to emerge as the disinterested faces seemed to blur from Will's vision.

"Alright, we have two-and-a-half...now three...now three...come on folks...who will be at three million?"

Silence ensued. Don Andino looked over his shoulder. He stared right through Will without recognition and scanned back and forth to see who was still in. To Will, it looked like a nonverbal taunt, and it had some impact. Eyes darted left and right. Only a handful of attendees met his gaze: Sharon Peyton, a middle-aged man in a boring blue blazer two rows from the back, and a slightly older gentleman with silver hair curiously sitting in the very back row scribbling in a small leather notebook. Sharon Peyton shot Don a look—not baiting him, but close to it. The man in the blue blazer looked like he wanted to disappear. The silver-haired gentleman assessed the scene but offered no facial cues. He didn't appear to be interested in the auctioneer, just the bidders.

"A pretty price at three...give me three million...now three...give me three..."

Will raised his hand sheepishly. He could feel his heartbeat thumping in his chest. The auctioneer fired an imaginary shot at Will with his thumb and forefinger, thus recognizing his bid, and seamlessly moved through his chant. Will had done it. Though he told himself before the auction he would stop at $2.5 million, he had officially bid

$3 million and now gained the focus of the room. "Okay, three...now three-and-a-half." Don Andino looked over his shoulder again, shaking his head. The man in the blue blazer stared darts at the auctioneer. The silver-haired gentleman in back swapped his focus between Will and Don with the look of a bystander simply entertained by the scene.

"Now three-and-a-half...give me three-and-a-half...somebody give me three-and-a-half. Come on folks, three-and-a-half-million."

The auctioneer paused. The room was silent. The reality that he could end up with the winning bid quickly sank into Will's consciousness, along with the gravity of what that entailed. He planted his sweaty hands firmly on his thighs and scanned the crowd, then Don Andino, then Sharon Peyton, then the boring blue blazer, then the silver-haired gentleman in back. Will did his best to signal confidence—he even sat up a little in his chair—yet at that particular moment he was anything but confident. His bid was at $3 million, and he was only prepared to raise the ante another $250,000. Unfortunately, the bidding had moved more quickly than he anticipated and the sharks were still circling.

"Okay, can I get three-and-a-quarter...now three-and-a-quarter...somebody give me three-and-a-quarter."

The break in cadence was quick, but this incremental adjustment of math was telltale that the winning bid was approaching. Nobody bid $3.5 million, so $3.25 million was the first concession the auctioneer would try.

"Three-and-a-quarter-million...somebody give me three-and-a-quarter...GOING ONCE."

Will was now frozen in silence. Sharon Peyton raised her eyebrows and her head ever so slightly, signaling her first bid of the afternoon. The auctioneer winked at her and nodded. Will exhaled deeply, now grappling with the idea of stretching his bid to $3.5 million.

"We got three-and-a-quarter...now three-and-a-half...now three-and-a-half...give me three-and-a-half."

The auctioneer reintroduced the price without hesitation; it was obvious he'd been in this situation before. Then, pointing to the back of the room, he acknowledged a bid quickly and moved to his familiar verse with new numbers.

"Alright, three-and-a-half...now four...a steal at four million...now four...now four."

Will glanced back. Was the silver-haired gentleman in back finally bidding? If he did, Will missed it. Sharon Peyton craned her neck, looked back and then promptly returned her focus to the auctioneer with a scowl.

"Somebody go four...now four...now four. Hey...we got four million...now four-and-a-quarter."

The numbers were piling up quickly. Will was outbid handily and, for him, the auction turned purely academic. He looked over at Don Andino who was now checking emails on his phone, unamused. He turned to Sharon Peyton, already outbid by three-quarters-of-a-million, reading the entire room and looking for any action.

"Okay, we're at four...now four-and-a-quarter...now four-and-a-quarter...somebody give me four-and-a-quarter."

Nobody flinched.

"GOING ONCE...GOING TWICE," the auctioneer paused for effect. "SOLD for four million dollars to the gentleman in back."

Chapter 2

"You have to learn to be a follower before you become a leader."
—Charlie Munger

"Damn," Will murmured to himself as the crowd began to disperse with the low buzz of whispers and snide comments. The auction was over. Don Andino shoved his phone in his pocket, stood, and gestured at Sharon Peyton to wait for him. Will turned to offer the silver-haired gentleman a defeated wave, but the silver-haired gentleman was sitting stoically in the back row still watching the activity; he was not the victor. The man in the boring blue blazer ambled toward the auctioneer. He shook the auctioneer's hand, signed a piece of paper, and worked his way out of the room.

And with that signature, the man in the blue blazer laid claim to the $4 million dollar prize: a one-acre parking lot in charming and wealthy Golden, Colorado. Will stood up and checked his jeans to make sure nothing had fallen out. His throat burned just above his chest, reminding him of his chronic battle with acid reflux. His pocket was vibrating. He reached in and retrieved his phone. There was a new text message. It was Farrah Parks.

We need to talk.

Will shoved his phone back in his pocket. "Shit," he said to himself.

Maybe that day, maybe the next, but she would be reaching out again soon. He side-stepped through the aisle of chairs and slinked toward the back door.

"Did you think you had it, young man?" the silver-haired gentleman said as Will passed. The gentleman adjusted the gray wool scarf around his neck, which complemented his crisp, white-collared shirt and red cashmere sweater. Will stopped a few steps past him. The gentleman was facing forward, not looking at Will, with the leather notebook resting in his lap and pen in his left hand.

"You looked nervous."

"Do I know you?" Will said flippantly. He was not in the mood for heckling.

"You do not." The silver-haired gentleman extended his hand. "Julian Darrow."

"Will Powell," Will replied, meeting the gesture with a practiced grip. As Will let go, he noticed the name "Will Powell" smudged in red ink on the inside of Julian's palm. He temporarily dismissed the notion of being a target. "You thought I looked nervous, huh?"

"Perhaps constipated?"

Will smiled. "And you. Did you think you would win the bid? I didn't see your hand go up."

"I wasn't here to bid," Julian remarked.

Will rolled his eyes. "Yes. That makes sense. You came to the auction for fun, right? Are you heading to the assessor's office next to watch people pay taxes?" he prodded.

Visibly annoyed by the tone, Julian stood up. "Would you like me to explain the theater you missed, son?"

"Excuse me?" Will was growing angry now.

"The play that just unfolded around you. The one to which your $3 million ticket did not gain you admission."

Will shook his head. "It was nice meeting you, Julian, but I have to get going." He turned and stepped toward the back door again.

Undeterred, Julian continued, "The man in the blue blazer. The one you think won the bid. Did he look like a developer to you? Or perhaps a contractor looking for a steal?" Julian spoke loud enough for Will to hear from a few feet away.

Will froze and turned around. He knew in that moment Julian was not a mere spectator. "No, he didn't," Will replied, now intrigued.

"And the woman, Sharon Peyton. She finished second best today," Julian continued. There was a formality to his speech that commanded Will's attention.

"No, she bid three-and-a-quarter. Someone in the back bid three-and-a-half," Will replied, his accurate recalling of the events bringing about an accomplished grin.

"Did you happen to see who that was?"

"No, I missed it. I was looking at a guy up front. He'd already bid once. I thought he'd be next. Plus, after the bid passed $3 million I knew I was screwed."

"There was no bidder at $3.5 million. It was a ghost, Will. An auctioneer's trick." Julian paused. "So that leaves us with Ms. Sharon Peyton. What if I told you she will get the deal? Not today, but she will end up with this parking lot." Julian moved closer to Will.

"I'd ask how you know that?" Will replied, still not catching on.

Julian looked over at the ten or so people remaining in the room, breaking eye contact with Will. "Let's start with the facts. What was the outstanding balance of the loan before today, Will?" Julian continued. "Do you know?"

"Right at $4 million," Will answered.

"Excellent. You aren't as lazy as you dress. And the final price today?"

"$4 million," Will answered.

"An outrageous coincidence, wouldn't you say?" Julian mused. "So, who then is the man you saw signing the documents? The one in the blue blazer that bid the exact amount of the outstanding loan balance?" Julian probed on.

"The bank," Will replied solemnly, as if he should have known that answer.

"Correct. And in the sea of people here, few understood the importance of being the second highest bidder. And thus, they were spectators like you," Julian proclaimed.

"Okay, I get that you understand this better than me but tell me why she automatically gets the deal. The bank won the bid. Sure, they weren't going to let it go for less than the loan. But now they own it outright. They can do what they want. That isn't how an auction works."

Julian sighed. "Isn't it? Tell me, Will Powell, after this charade, who will receive the first phone call from the bank?" He paused. "I'll answer that for you. It will be Ms. Sharon Peyton. And when she receives the call, she will close this deal."

"How can you be so sure?" Will asked.

"Because she has honed her craft," Julian replied simply.

"Okay. I'll just take for granted you're right," Will said, now fully intrigued. "But the short guy up front didn't know. He was bidding, too."

"He did indeed," Julian quickly responded. "That is Don Andino. He owns Sabre Construction. He's far too shrewd to be here on a whim. I suspect his ploy was twofold." Julian pressed on. "What did he bid?"

"Two-and-a-half. I was the one who outbid him," Will shot back.

"Precisely. And that ended his hopes of snatching the land at a ridiculous price. You eliminated his first option."

"And his second option?" Will asked.

"He is exploring it now," Julian gestured toward Sharon Peyton and Don Andino locked in conversation. "As I said, he is shrewd. Don expressed his interest in the deal by bidding. Now he is deducing if Ms. Peyton will go forward with the land purchase. If she does," Julian added, "It will be much closer to the $3.25 million she last bid."

"And if she buys it, Don is out?" Will questioned.

"Most likely he'll end up with the contract to build whatever she develops there."

Will and Julian stopped talking for a few seconds. They watched Don Andino and Sharon Peyton chat. Don gave a loud belly laugh and put his hand on Sharon's shoulder to steady himself. She returned an exaggerated smile. They were standing very near the auctioneer, who was still packing his things away. It now seemed to Will that all were indeed complicit, players in a game for which he did not have the rulebook.

"So why are we talking, Julian?" Will broke the silence.

"Because you raised your hand to bid," Julian answered. "And I have an urgent matter that requires action."

He reached into the inside pocket of his jacket and produced a business card, handing it to Will. "My address is on the card. We need to meet by next Friday."

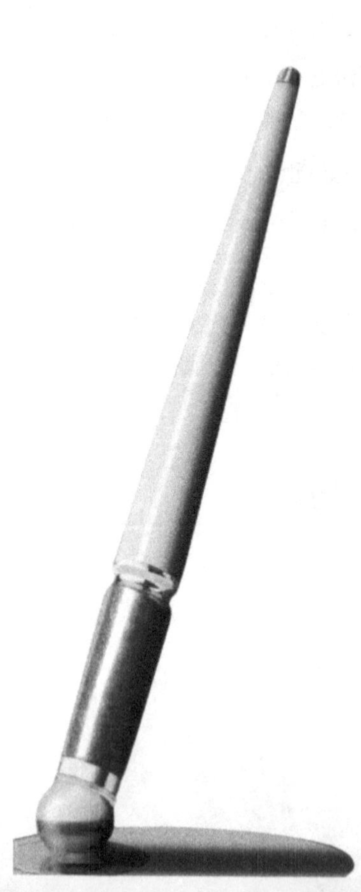

Chapter 3

"A good companion shortens the longest road."

—Turkish Proverb

Kirsty Powell was sitting in the dining room sipping coffee and reading a self-help book when Will lumbered in from the hallway. His eyes were still adjusting to the morning sun as if he'd suffered a long night. In truth, he hadn't slept. It was Saturday, two days since the auction was held. Both nights were spent pondering his encounter with Julian and the possibilities it presented.

"Need some more coffee?"

"If you're offering." She lifted her cup high in the air, still reading.

Will walked up slowly behind her and leaned over the top of the chair. He reached down with his right hand and closed the book in her lap.

"What the eff?" she said playfully, yet genuinely annoyed.

"You're going to have to give me a kiss first."

"You didn't say that," she replied. "Would've gotten it myself."

He leaned down, delivering a cordial kiss on the lips.

She winced, creating immediate space by pulling back her head. "Your breath smells like farts. Now you owe me some more coffee. And by the way, you made me lose my place. I didn't have the page marked."

"You're at the part where she says to be fierce," Will quipped, snagging Kirsty's mug while walking toward the kitchen.

"Cute."

It was a fine start to this Saturday, better than many had been lately. Will loved Kirsty deeply, yet at present they ran circles around each other, chasing daylight to dark with the pace of their own lives. Nothing alarming or foundational, just distracted. They were comfortable companions raising a teenage daughter and trudging through their days, occasionally bothered by the lack of concern for each other's workload. Will knew she sometimes felt unnoticed; Kirsty had said as much. He would concede she was unnoticed more than he cared to admit. But she was not unloved, far from it. The two-way street of disregard simply ruled the present day.

Their careers were still front and center. Will had traded his job as VP of commercial lending at Grand Bank Colorado for the glamorous life of an entrepreneur, which, in hindsight, felt more like a sleep-deprived, stress-induced trap. Banks, he had realized, were full of VPs, but entrepreneurs got to dream up big ideas—ideas that bore his signature. So, he left. Now, he found himself juggling unmanageable schedules, sleepless nights, and oxidative stress in exchange for...less money than his toothless electrician. Not exactly the freedom and wealth he had imagined. Meanwhile, Kirsty, blissfully unaware of his financial woes, kept offering overly chipper advice, spouting buzzwords like "pivot" and "lean-in" as if they could solve everything. Will would rather keep the problems than solve them with her buzzwords.

Will returned from the kitchen, handed Kirsty a fresh cup of coffee, and pulled out his phone to check emails. "You got any plans today, Boo?" he said, not looking up from his phone. "Boo" was a holdover term from the '90s and '00s R&B songs he listened to as a teenager. They both appreciated its significance in the music genre, though Kirsty, at forty-three (and four years older than Will), dismissed anything after 2002 as being "New Age trash".

"No, we're pretty much caught up at the office. All of our Friday closings miraculously funded on time, so I'm gonna work out in a bit. Sela and I may go shopping after." Kirsty was the proprietress of Promontory Title Company, which she co-owned with a female business partner.

"You looking for anything in particular?" Will asked.

"Nah, just gonna mess around. You have to work?"

"I told Dex I'd run by Westminster to check on the apartments. They're supposed to be laying the wood flooring today. Want to make sure it's the right one." Dexter Mathis was Will's best friend, which led to his investment in the apartments.

"Honey, I'm sure Dexter doesn't care what floors get installed."

"You're right. But I do. And I promised him I'd stay on top of these guys."

"Can't they just send you a picture?"

Those kinds of comments irked him; partially because they were always accurate and partially because he knew she did it on purpose. But this Saturday had started smoothly, and he was not going to venture off the path. Will adjusted his seat and leaned onto the arm of the chair closest to Kirsty.

"I met an interesting guy on Thursday."

"Really?" she replied half-heartedly while still reading.

"Yeah, he was a trip."

Kirsty, possibly sensing that Saturday's smooth vibe as well, looked up and closed her book over her hand, so as not to lose her place.

"Who was he?"

"He was at the auction. I'm telling you, Kirsty, I think he came there just for me. He wasn't there to bid."

"Why'd you think that?"

"Because he sat in the back row and watched me, kinda like my dad would watch me play Little League. Just sat there quietly. And when it was over, he walked past everyone, didn't even look at them. He came straight up to me, like he'd been waiting for the right time. And, Kirsty, he..."

"What?"

"Nothing."

"What?" she persisted.

"When we shook hands...I swear he had my name written on his palm."

"That's weird, honey."

"It was crazy. And I'm pretty sure I saw it. But I'm telling you, what he knew was crazier. He explained the entire auction process."

Kirsty scrunched up one side of her mouth, "Hadn't you just sat through the auction? What's the point of recapping?"

"Because the process he explained was totally different from what I thought I saw. And I worked at a damn bank. I should've seen it, too. I'm telling you, this guy's sharp. He knew everyone's move before they made them."

Will's phone dinged the factory setting tone for a text message. He raised his hand up to see the text clearly. It was from his fifteen-year-old daughter, Sela. She was in her room upstairs.

Will often made breakfast on Saturday mornings for the family. This was typically followed by him walking upstairs and waking Sela. His trademark salutation was, "The sun is shining. You should be awake."

On the off chance she woke up early, Sela would use his phrase against him, goading him into making breakfast quickly.

Will was a sucker for Sela. She was not technically his daughter—although he called her that without hesitation. Sela was part of a package deal. She had just turned six when Will and Kirsty tied the knot. Now at fifteen, the precocious Sela Cole was an astonishingly bright young woman who maintained her childish charm. Will adored her, even if at times he didn't understand her.

He stood up and started to walk into the kitchen.

"What? That's it? You were telling me about this guy at the auction, the mystery man," Kirsty said accusingly. "You actually had me intrigued."

"Sela just texted me. She wants breakfast," he said, shaking his head and smiling. Part of him was just happy she was waking up before 11:00 a.m.

"She'll be fine for a few minutes."

Will turned around. "Yeah, sorry. So this guy, Julian, comes up to me, explains that the entire auction was a charade and that everyone was really just bidding for second place."

"Second place? That's silly," Kirsty challenged.

"Okay, maybe not that simple, but the story gets longer if I get into detail. Essentially, I didn't have a shot of getting the property and this guy knew it."

"Julian sounds like a pro. Anything come of it?"

Will nodded. "I'm meeting him at his house in Evergreen on Monday night. Said he had to meet by Friday."

"Why?"

"I have no idea."

"He also sounds shady."

"Kirsty, I'm gonna be honest. I don't care. There's something different about him. He knows things I need to know. I can't stop thinking about it. I'm telling you, he singled me out. And I know it's probably a shitty idea to get involved with him, but I swear I need somebody like this guy."

"For what?"

"That's just it. I have no idea."

"Well, don't get yourself in trouble."

Will cocked his head to the side with a half-hearted smile, signaling he heard Kirsty. "I'm gonna be in trouble if I don't make those pancakes."

Chapter 4

"Most powerful is he who has himself in his own power."

—Seneca the Younger

On that same Saturday, Will's ex-brother-in-law and solitary real estate investor, had a very different experience. Dexter Mathis woke to the sun rising into his open master bedroom window as it shone on his fifth-floor River North Art District (RiNO for short) condo in Denver. If money was all that mattered, he could have awoken anywhere in the city. But money had little to do with Dexter's choice to exist on the outskirts of the hustling downtown core. After his divorce from Will's sister, Dexter developed an allergy to anything that hinted at permanence. RiNO had become the place for food, drink, art, and unscripted nightlife. It was edgy with a gentle spirit. Dexter didn't disappear there—he simply became nameless. To be nameless was most people's fear; for Dexter, it was an ambition. RiNO possessed a grittiness that had become foreign to Denver, now chock-full of dress shoes, messenger bags, and the proud young professionals toting them. Once a raw industrial area—and an excellent spot to be mugged after dark—RiNO had transformed into a place to escape, to breathe, just steps away from the labyrinth of tall buildings and convention spaces necessitated by Denver's explosive growth.

The beautiful woman he had courted the night before now glowed in the bright Denver morning light. Her sculpted arms lay atop the thick blue-gray comforter; her body tucked beneath in a show of newfound modesty.

"Would you like some coffee?"

"What time is it?" she responded groggily.

"Six-thirty."

"Do we have to get up now? Kind of a late night."

"I'll make you some," he said with a gentle smile.

Dexter sat up, pulled a black T-shirt over his head, and swung his feet over the edge of the bed until they rested on the ground next to a pair of black snakeskin boots, which he kept either on or near him at all times, like beloved pets. The T-shirt partially covered the large tattoo that ran from his left shoulder down to just above his elbow. It was a series of graphics and symbols and read "Never Live Someone Else's Life." Dexter used both hands to pull his long black hair free of his shirt. He reached to the nightstand for the hairband lying on the stack of heavily dog-eared books. The gray at his temples was visible as he tugged his hair into a tight ponytail. Dexter then stood up, slipped on his jeans, and headed to the kitchen.

After brewing two cups at the wall-mounted espresso machine, he reappeared to find the young woman still under the covers.

"You're making me get up, aren't you?"

"No. Don't worry about me," he said. "I'm going out on my bike. Gonna start my weekend with a long ride. Need to clear my head."

"Seriously?" she said with a dry throat.

Dexter didn't answer; his handful of leather bracelets slid on his wrist as he took a sip from a thick orange mug with "Breckenridge" written in cursive. He handed the young woman her coffee in a clean, white cup.

"Make yourself at home. If you want to curl up or watch a movie, go for it. If I'm not back when you leave, don't worry about locking up; I'll do it from my phone later. Had an awesome time last night." He grabbed the remote from a nook in the modern headboard wall and tossed it to her. "Here. Enjoy your morning. Seriously."

Dexter continued to drink from his mug. The young woman—a couple of decades younger than the forty-eight-year-old Dexter—sat up. Her hair was a mess, but despite the dishevelment she was a sight to behold. She started to gather the comforter around her body, but then apparently thought better of it. She stood up, fully naked, walked over to Dexter and shared a long, closed-mouth kiss; her soft lips first warmed by the morning sun, and then by a sip of hot coffee. His gentle hands rested on her tight hips. It was not the drunken passion from the previous night; it was genuine. Dexter had received similar before.

"Thanks."

"You're very welcome," she replied sheepishly. "I should go."

The young woman gathered her things and headed into the Carrera marble master bathroom. She was not the first and was not destined to be last. Dexter had several women in orbit and considered the constellation healthy and liberating. In his mind, it was a stable system. The conversations were stimulating, the passion ever-present, and the pressure nonexistent.

Dexter headed to the closet, grabbed his mountain biking clothes and his keys, and walked to the master bedroom door.

"Are we going to do this again?" she asked.

"Your call," he said with a wink and exited the room.

Dexter filled a squeeze bottle with ice and water, grabbed the dual suspension Yeti mountain bike from the rack in the living room and was out the door before the young woman had even finished changing. He made it to the parking garage below the five-story building via the stairs, loaded the bike on the matte gray Range Rover, and jumped into the firm leather driver's seat. A faint smell of marijuana still lingered from the night before. With the push of the ignition button

Dexter Mathis was on his way into the Rockies.

His phone rang. The name Preston Lowden appeared on the screen. Dexter touched the green phone icon on his center console. "Good morning, Preston. Surprised you're up this early. You make any decisions?"

"Honestly, I didn't sleep last night. We'll take your offer." There would be no small talk. The usual business deal foreplay eluded the young Mr. Lowden. The wannabe entrepreneur's voice was audibly nervous.

Dexter turned the volume up two notches higher. "Which one? There were two offers on the table."

"$350,000 for 40%."

Dexter smiled. "Awesome, man. Good choice. I'll circle up with the attorneys and get drafts over to you by midweek. We'll get it all signed and I'll take you to that restaurant over by Union Station; the one with the flight of steaks I was telling you about."

And with that, Dexter bought 40% of RevMax—a nascent real estate management software company he knew he could scale. Preston Lowden developed the software merely to manage the eight-plex apartment building he and his single mother owned in Denver's Sunnyside area. With the advent of AirBnB, Sonder, Stay Alfred, and a host of other nightly-rental companies, Preston saw an opportunity to use a dynamic pricing strategy. Dexter, impressed with the young man's talent, saw a bold future for RevMax.

Dexter allowed Preston to hang up as he eased onto C-470 on his way to the Matthews Winters trails. Dexter reached into the cup holder and picked up his phone. Without looking, he slid his thumbnail to the side of the phone and toggled the manual ringer off switch. He would not be taking any more calls on this beautiful September morning.

Chapter 5

"Men willingly believe what they wish to be true."

—Julius Caesar

Evergreen, Colorado, was a bucolic haven just inside the foothills of the Rocky Mountains. People traveled to Evergreen to escape their urban jungle. People lived in Evergreen to escape Denver and its neighboring suburbs. It was a short, thirty-minute commute to downtown Denver, and yet Evergreen felt detached. There was an invisible line on I-70 West where Denver's explosive charge of capitalism paused, the world slowed down, and the feeling of winding through the mountains began.

Will Powell's black Toyota 4Runner sped quickly west on I-70. He was running a few minutes behind. His right hand rested atop the steering wheel while holding Julian Darrow's business card. The term "business card" was a stretch; there was no company name or professional designation, just his physical address in Evergreen. He rested the card vertically in his cupholder and reached for his phone. A message was visible on the home screen:

It was from Farrah Parks, the head loan officer at Grand Bank Colorado. With no answers to give her, Will ignored Farrah's message yet again. After all, he had worked there for seven years. He knew the steps. She was being too proactive; it took sixty days for a past due payment to hit the red flag list at the bank. Will was only forty-five days behind. He had fifteen days to figure something out before he felt the full heat of being late on his payment on the Westminster apartments. Farrah could text him all she wanted, but that wouldn't change anything. He had options; or more accurately, he had fifteen days to come up with an option that worked.

After exiting and a few twists and turns, Will followed Siri's voice commands to a gravel driveway. It was nearly 7:00 p.m.; he was supposed to be there by 6:45. Though he was in a hurry, the gravel driveway pitch was steep, more suitable for hiking than driving. His only option was to roll slowly through a series of switchback turns up to a modest but stunning home nestled on the side of the mountain. It was mainly floor-to-ceiling glass with a thin, flat roof structure pitching slightly front to back and appearing to originate from the shards of stone behind.

Will walked to the front door and rang the doorbell. A series of deep melodic tones bounced against the concrete floors and expansive glass walls. "You found me," Julian said as he answered the door. He wore a crisp white dress shirt paired with a tailored sweater and well-fitting slacks. Julian was a slender man, a byproduct of either exercise or stress. His sharp angular features and taut skin gave way to soft blue eyes. Time had stripped away any remaining weight, giving his athletic frame a certain avian quality. Perched comfortably at the stoop of his doorway, his blue eyes welcomed Will with unclear intention.

"Sorry, I'm late. Thought it wouldn't take as long to get here."

"Imagine if you had thought correctly."

"Your place is impressive."

"It's quiet. And don't be sorry. Simply don't be late in the future." Julian stepped aside, allowing Will to enter. The views of the aspens stretched out in every direction, stunning even in the dimming light of dusk.

Will took the space in. Upon deeper inspection he could see the interior was a bit outdated. The furnishings were gently worn and the kitchen appliances, visible from the living area, were high-end but tired. The architecture, however, was truly amazing. Beams danced across the ceiling intertwined with taut steel cables, the materials masterfully connected by hand-forged steel plates. It was as if the house was so precisely conceived it would simply collapse if a cable snapped. Twenty years before, it must have been a sight.

"Did you build this place, Julian?"

"No, I've been here only…" He paused for a few seconds, then smiled. "fifteen years, come to think of it."

"That's a pretty long time to me."

"Not at my age. Son, I invited you out here for a reason. Shall we just cut to the chase, then?" Julian said with eyebrows raised.

"Sure," Will replied. "I'm thinking you're not much for small talk anyway."

Julian led Will to the other side of the living room, down a short hall to what was obviously a home office. The room stood in stark contrast to the rest of the house. Books of every color filled the shelves. Some were stacked, some upright with bookends, and several were strewn about the shelves in no particular order. It looked as if Julian had feverishly run through them more than once, sifting and sorting information. At first glance there appeared to be no rhyme or reason to the order, and yet the longer Will stared at the colorful jackets, the more he started to see a pattern. Although the arrangement was unclear, he had a sense Julian could commandeer any specific title with a single effort.

In the center of the room was a large round coffee table with deep cognac leather chairs on either side. Atop the coffee table were a handful of books and a tattered legal pad full of handwritten notes with many of the pages folded over the back. Julian reached down and gathered the items, walking over to place them on one of the few open bookshelves.

"Let's have a seat, Will." Julian motioned to the chairs. Will eased into the leather chair. It made the rubbing sound only genuine rawhide leather could. It was as comfortable as it was deep. "May I offer you a drink?"

"Um, sure. How about a Miller Lite?" Will asked.

Julian stood stoically as if Will were not done speaking. Will perceived immediately that Miller Lite was not on the menu. "A bourbon?" he fished.

"Bourbon it is." Julian left the room, returning shortly with the glass of bourbon in hand, and what appeared to be a glass of water for himself.

"Nothing for you?" Will asked, a touch of curiosity in his voice.

"Not tonight," Julian replied, settling into the other cognac chair with an air of quiet finality. He leaned forward, his gaze sharpening. "Do you know why I asked you here, Will?"

"I haven't the slightest idea. I assume you have a development for me to look at?"

"Of sorts," Julian answered. "I trust it's appropriate for me to be direct with you. I find it simpler."

"Sure."

"You bid $3 million at the auction on Thursday, correct?"

"Yes, I did."

"And I presume you do not have $3 million dollars?"

Will shrugged his shoulders. He wanted to rebut, yet had a distinct feeling Julian had done his homework.

"Let me ask you this, son. What do you want?"

The query landed heavy with Will, along with the straight bourbon he was sipping, and he looked dead into Julian's eyes. "That's a loaded question."

"Indeed. What do you want to achieve? Is it money?" Julian pressed.

Will sat silently for a minute and took another sip from his glass. He leaned forward, folded his hands, and put his elbows on his knees. "Julian, I drove out here because you asked me to, because I assumed you had a project for me to do. And to be honest, right now I could use a deal that worked. If we're going to sit here and play games, I have a wife and daughter at home. And with everything I have going on, I don't see them enough as it is. So why don't we just—"

"Then why attend the auction?" Julian interrupted.

"Why was I at the auction?" Will repeated, visibly annoyed.

"Yes, if your affairs are so pressing, why attend the auction on Thursday? Surely landing that deal would only add to the stress," Julian pushed.

Will leaned his head back and closed his eyes. He slowly rolled his head to one side as if to release the tension he was holding.

"I guess I was just looking for a steal. If I could've gotten it cheap enough, I probably would've just flipped the land for a profit."

"And what suffered on Thursday as you spectated at the auction? I am aware of forty apartments in Westminster that are slow to lease up, a small hotel you purchased in a foreclosure sale, fifteen townhomes in Wheat Ridge for which you've already pulled the building permit. And what pays for it all? That is the question I struggle to answer, Will."

"I'm selling a condo near Jefferson Park in Denver this month," Will answered reluctantly. The accuracy of Julian's recap teetered on intrusive.

"Ah yes, congratulations. Your brother-in-law Dexter Mathis invested a small amount in that deal, correct?"

That comment startled Will. It was one thing to know the handful of projects on which he was working; there are multiple ways of associating someone's name with a project and compiling a list if that person has some basic real estate knowledge. But to know that Dexter put up money and that they were friends elevated Julian's level of detail knowledge to scary.

"Ex-brother-in-law," Will said coldly.

"Yes. I assumed the accuracy was not needed."

"Are you stalking me? Really...Dexter? And how do you know about the hotel?"

"I am thorough, Will," Julian said unapologetically. "That leaves you with two condos free and clear of any debt."

"That's right."

"You do sound busy. And all of this, is it performing near the level you've underwritten?" Julian queried. "To justify the time you're expending?"

Will paused for a few seconds. And then with a sigh he said, "Honestly, Julian, I'm up to my ass in loans. My phone rings every five minutes. I'm eating Nexium like candy because my stomach is in knots. And that condo sale I just mentioned mainly goes to cover the note on the apartments for the next three months until I can get them cash flowing." Will was now finding this a bit cathartic. It wasn't every day he could speak to someone who understood his plight.

"Ah, my former life." Julian smiled. "I did arrange this meeting because of a project. But there's a catch. You must approach this project differently."

"I'm all ears."

"At the auction, you revealed something to the crowd. Do you know what that was?"

"That I don't understand what's going on?" Will said sarcastically.

"Action," Julian announced. "We are similar beasts, you and me. It's action that ultimately gets deals done. Raising your hand at the auction without a penny in your pocket, that's pure action. But action for action's sake is unproductive, and in this line of work it's downright dangerous. If unchecked, you'll be stuck in an endless loop. The loop of needing the next deal to pay for the last. Am I on the mark, Will? Are you not in that loop today?"

"What are you proposing?" Will asked, signaling Julian was spot-on.

"Put off the groundbreaking in Wheat Ridge. For the next ninety days, I'll pay you $20,000 per month and cover your debt payments on your properties. In that time, you'll learn a different path to dealmaking...a set of rules."

"What rules?"

"My rules, son. There are seven in all."

"Why seven?"

"Because I said there are seven. You'll understand that point as you learn the rules."

"What if I say no?"

"Consider this. If you wish to resign your post after ninety days, we'll part ways and you owe me nothing." Julian looked Will sternly in the eyes. "If you've learned nothing in ninety days, it will most assuredly be time for you to go."

"My post?" Will said curtly.

"Indeed. I'll get to that. There's an RFP being issued by the City of Golden. Are you familiar with that term?"

"A 'Request for Proposal'," Will responded. "The city sends out a request for proposals on a project they want to see get done. I'm oh-for-two on responding to those. Both times I did, they just picked the developer they had a relationship with. I never had a chance."

"Excellent. You understand they aren't easy to win. That's a fortuitous start."

"I understand they're impossible to win if you don't have an in," Will said dismissively.

Julian moved right along, unperturbed.

"The auction was your introduction, your shot across the bow."

"The city didn't have anything to do with that," Will remarked.

"Correct, yet their two main targets for the RFP undoubtedly took notice." Julian smiled. "I have it on good authority that Sharon Peyton and Don Andino are the lead candidates."

"Of course you do." Will sat back in his chair and prepared for more new information. "So what is the RFP for?"

"An office building. To be exact, a fifty-thousand-square-foot office building. The city is buying it because the company that headquartered there is leaving."

"Ouch. What's the price tag on a project that size?" Will said quickly.

"Hard to say. The terms have not been discussed. There are several ways we could put this together. And remember, the city is putting out the request."

Julian stood up and walked over to his desk. He reached for a neatly stacked set of printed papers contrasting with the dark gray soapstone top. Along with the printed pages was a large-format white calendar filled with small handwritten notes in each day of the week. Julian was obviously a fastidious notetaker. And there were a few ubiquitous desk items: pens standing upright in a sleek wooden stand, a metal box of paper clips, rubber bands, a staple remover, and one picture. The picture was in a frame with a small stand propping it upright on the desk. It was not visible from Will's vantage point. It faced at an angle toward the single chair at the other side, where Julian presumably would sit alone. Will was tempted to get up and turn the picture around. Julian was mysterious to the point of not being real. A photo could shed light into his humanity. He had not mentioned his family, nor a significant other, and it seemed as if Julian lived alone. Will surmised the picture could just as easily be of Winston Churchill, Abraham Lincoln, Martin Luther King Jr., or some other lofty personality. Next time, he thought.

"The city is holding a Q&A meeting on Monday at 3:00 p.m. You will need to be there," Julian said while handing the printed papers to Will. "This is the RFP. Read it thoroughly. We'll review your thoughts after the meeting."

"Slow down. I haven't accepted the offer, and I still don't know what you're asking me to do," Will said plainly. "Why don't you just do it yourself? You've obviously prepared. Why dump this in my lap if you could just show up and do the deal?"

"It would be wiser for me to send a proxy," Julian said cryptically.

"Bullshit! You can't go, can you?"

"Your perceptiveness is encouraging," Julian said without explanation.

"And I'm guessing it's not because you have a doctor's appointment on Monday."

Julian nodded. Will sat bemused for a moment, letting the silence take over. He folded his hands and rested his chin, his elbows steady against his knees. Will was noticeably weighing the options in his head. He took an audible deep breath and said, "I'm in."

"Then it's settled," Julian acknowledged.

"Yep. If you're that tainted then you can't screw me."

"Indeed." Julian smiled warmly and proffered his hand. Will reached across the coffee table, sealing the deal. The two men stood and gathered the glasses.

"Will?"

"Yeah?"

"Be on time Monday."

"Julian?" Will replied.

"Yes."

"Be on time with my money."

Chapter 6

*"It's okay to have your eggs in one basket as long as
you control what's in that basket."*
—Elon Musk

The gilded, initialed cufflinks held back a thick fold of fabric on Nick Spencer's crisp white shirt. It was 8:00 a.m. and Nick was on his phone sifting through myriad newsfeeds in his office in the South Congress area of Austin. Two oversized, glossy black screens had yet to awaken on the desktop before him. In the dark reflection he could see a few hairs out of place; he would address those immediately.

"Nick, James Patridge is on Line 1," Michael said over the speakerphone. Michael's official title was chief investment officer, yet he more often played the unglamorous role of Nick's administrative assistant. It was a small firm.

"Is he on my calendar?"

"Not that I can see."

"Not that you can see? Michael, do you have your glasses on?"

"Yeah."

"Can you see your calendar on the screen?"

"Yeah, Nick."

"Is Jimmy on the fucking calendar?"

"No," Michael said reluctantly.

"This is why you still drive a Civic. Put him on hold. I'll get to him." Nick sensed his protégé was rolling his eyes in the other room. That was good, all part of his mentoring.

Nick, with Line 1 on hold, returned his focus to his desktop screens, now fully lit and swarming with the early newsfeeds. Social media was abuzz with talk of inflation, foreign wars, partisan politics, and a host of disquieting issues that threatened to destabilize the most stable markets on earth. Nick swiped left on his phone to reveal the accounting app he used to keep up with his investments. In the dashboard a bold number sat at the top: $128,114,387.23. This was the total capital he had under management. Five years earlier, the dashboard would have revealed a mere $54,305,991.82 ($50 million of that coming from Nick's uncle, who owned a sizable pipeline business in Houston, though that tidbit was not part of Nick's pitch). The more telling and troubling figure would be that, six months prior, the dashboard read $127,820,714.24. The minor shift was of no consequence; it accounted for an infinitesimally small percent of gain. The inactivity that number revealed was the troubling data point. Nick had ridden the markets up, but then pulled much of the money when interest rates soared, opting for bonds and other safe havens. Idle dollars do not purchase gold cufflinks. And to his cadre of wealthy investors, there was only one fate worse than death: inactivity.

Nick's income, as was the case with many private equity structures, was dependent on the returns generated from the cash he managed. While the dollars sat idle in an account, Nick earned a measly half a percent. Half a percent in this case would yield Nick Spencer roughly $640,000 for the year. Of course, that was pre-tax, pre-country club, pre-luxury SUV, pre-911 Turbo S, pre-Class A office space, pre-condo in South Congress, and pre-alimony. After all living expenses, that income would be tight—really tight.

More importantly, his clients were not looking for their money to collect low interest returns trapped in CDs or money market accounts. No dinner party banter could celebrate the prudence of parking cash in such mundane shelters. Nick wanted to put the money to work. He had to put the money to work. He could place the cash in the markets at returns of 12 to 15%, sometimes even a few basis points higher, of which he could net in the neighborhood of 5% for himself. His personal return on those invested dollars could literally be ten times what he made on the dollars sitting idle in the bank. If the money sat there long enough, his capital sources would surely move the funds elsewhere. Some occasionally reminded him, "anybody can watch over money that sits in the bank."

This had become the lopsided game for private equity. "Smart" money flooded into private equity firms to combat the stock market volatility and the low interest rate environment. At the end of that flowing stream sat people like Nick Spencer, sitting atop a pile of cash, with the burning desire to send it out the door.

The recent uncertainty in the world afforded him some time, but time was running out and a big portion of the $128,114,387.23 needed to be put to work. Idle money triggered anxiety, but there was an obvious other scenario: bad investing. Losing money was a surefire path from managing millions to managing an Outback Steakhouse, and the painful descent for those unfortunate souls was swift.

Nick's hair, shirt, cufflinks, cars all served to reinforce a character that he had played long enough to become reality. It might have ended his marriage, but it would be the force that took Nick Spencer to his ultimate goal: a billion-dollar private equity firm.

"Nick?" Michael interrupted the silence again. "You want me to have Mr. Patridge call you back?"

"No. I got it." Nick let out an audible sigh while shaking his head at his CIO/assistant's impatience. He pressed Line 1 on his desktop speakerphone. "Jimmy," Nick said with a swagger. "How's it going watching oil prices dance around?" James—who did not go by "Jimmy"—was a client of Nick's and a friend of a friend to his uncle.

"I'm calling to check in. Wanted to get your take on the current environment. It's crazy out there."

"My take," Nick replied. "My take is you pay me to worry about that. If we need to discuss it, I'm not the right guy. There are a bunch of zombies out there. Some of them are dead and don't know it yet. Opportunities are everywhere; we're just vetting them now to see where we go." Nick's reluctance to take investment advice was purely a defense mechanism. He had watched other investment firms fail and believed wholeheartedly that one telltale sign of failure was to start taking investment advice from their clients.

"Anything specifically?"

"Everything specifically. Pick a sector, it's overvalued, and there's opportunity coming."

"The smart move was to take it out of the market when you did, Nick. Can't argue with that. The hogs have gotten fat. Now, when do you see putting my money back to work?" James inquired. He accounted for nearly $10 million dollars of the fund. As was the case with many of Nick's clients, that question had become ubiquitous.

"When it's the right move. And that's coming. You do realize, Jimmy, I don't make shit sitting on your money, right?"

"Yes, and I appreciate that."

"Good, because I take it seriously. And I appreciate the fact that you're a riverboat gambler, I do. It's what makes us different from most. I'll let you know when I make a move, and it'll be soon." Nick's demeanor with his clients was consistent; when he was on the phone with one of them, they were the only two people in the world who really knew what was going on.

"Good, Nick. I want to get this money moving again."

"Great, because I have my eye on an Aston Martin Vantage and I can't make myself buy it sitting on all this cash like Ebenezer Fucking

Scrooge. I gotta go, Jimmy. I have a call in ten minutes. We can line up a time to talk about some specific moves...after I've made them."

Nick didn't wait for goodbyes as he pushed the speaker button on his phone to end the call. He glanced at the home screen to his left. There were several folders—more than thirty—scattered randomly across a picture of Aspen, Colorado, during ski season. Alongside managing a billion-dollar fund, owning in Aspen was a goal. And lucky for Nick, he was goal-oriented. Somewhere toward the right-hand side of the smattering of folders, covering the faces of the unsuspecting Aspen skiers, was a folder labeled Launch Pad Hotel.

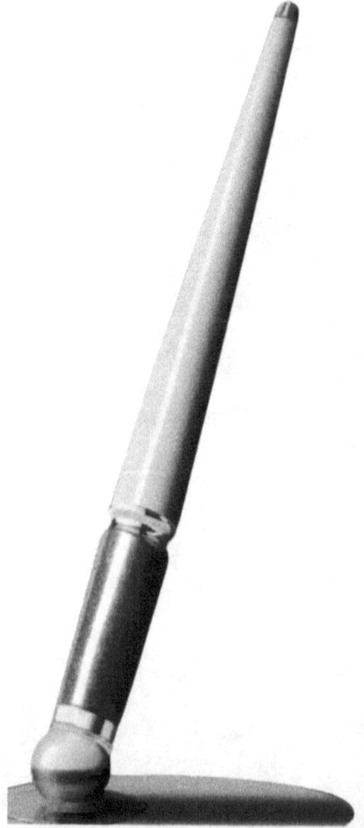

Chapter 7

*"You can't truly know how good you are
until you're tested against others."*
—Serena Williams

The City Hall in Golden used the clever address of 911 10th Street. It sat in an idyllic spot just above a small rushing river aptly named Clear Creek. Encircling that section of Clear Creek was a mostly shaded walking trail with a small shed at its origin, known as the Bike Library, that was open all day and run by volunteers who generously loaned out bikes for a leisurely ride. If clean air had a smell, it smelled like a bike ride down Clear Creek trail on a Golden summer day. Washington Avenue, the main drag of downtown, was at the edge of the bike trail and a block up from City Hall. It was the quintessential mining town, settled in 1859 during the gold rush, and ironically named not for the ore the miners coveted, but after one of its early settlers: Thomas L. Golden. The large arch over the entrance to Washington Avenue proudly stated, "Howdy Folks, WELCOME TO GOLDEN, Where the West Lives." That welcoming spirit was sincere.

Founded just a few years later in 1873, and standing in stark contrast to the insulated downtown, was Coors Brewery. After moving its headquarters to the periphery of downtown, the gargantuan MillerCoors campus now sprawled along Highway 58 directly en route from Denver. The compound of drab concrete and metal buildings was a statement of industry—the largest brewery in the world—and only revealed itself to the speeding cars by way of a red

Coors sign and a two-story model of a beer can representing the "banquet beer" itself.

Golden's dichotomy of natural beauty and pure capitalism fostered the mindset of the town. A portion of its citizenry would gladly see businesses like MillerCoors shuttered, yet they would sooner die than decrease funding for the parks and events held regularly.

"Welcome, everyone," Jessica Dews, Golden's deputy manager, said to the small group of onlookers, "to our meeting regarding the soon-to-be-released Request for Proposal for an exciting new mixed-use development of a building the city has recently acquired." Jessica was a consummate professional. She began passing out the flawlessly stapled pages to the five potential developers seated at the table and circulating a contact list. "Each of you has expressed an interest in this project. Some of you as late as this morning." She shot a look at Will. They were roughly the same age and knew each other from a small townhome project Will had developed in the area two years before.

"This project is extremely important for our city. If you're here, you already know that we're in the process of purchasing a large building downtown currently being vacated by Teleprime Companies. In the ever changing landscape of telecommunications, they are consolidating their offices into a single headquarters in Broomfield. The fifty-thousand-square-foot, four-story facility is zoned industrial, but the city will likely consider a special-use permit in order to attract the most dynamic development we can."

"Jessica, this doesn't tell me what the city wants." Don Andino, who had also bid at the parking lot auction, was already dissecting the document and making it clear he was on a first-name basis with the deputy manager. Don, a quintessential capitalist, was visibly ill, eyes glazed and nose red from sniffling. Another man at the table, in a pressed blazer, was noticeably perturbed at the sight of Don's lackadaisical approach to not infecting everyone.

"There is some guidance, but we didn't want to be too prescriptive," Jessica responded.

"So anything is on the table? And we have…" he paused to look down at the document again while clearing some potentially deadly congestion, "six weeks to submit a concept for approval?" The manner in which Don asked the question left Will thinking he was already well aware of the terms.

"If you read the document you'll find some suggestions," Jessica responded.

The perturbed man at the table chimed in. He was well-dressed and nervous. "What about apartments? Would the city consider that?"

Don could not contain a small chuckle, which turned into a cough. "That's not going to happen, friend." He looked at Jessica for backup.

"We do currently have a moratorium on dense multifamily. And truly, apartments do not provide a platform for sustainable job creation."

Sharon Peyton was dressed in her signature denim jacket. She conscientiously enjoyed a slow pull of coffee from her large, custom-branded "The Peyton Team" insulated cup. "So would you say job creation is the number one objective for the project?"

Will liked her question. He assumed Julian would approve. It put Jessica directly on the spot to deliver some specificity.

"I wouldn't necessarily say we ranked the objectives for the project, Sharon. Our interest is bringing a project that feels like it belongs in downtown Golden."

Will sighed. It seemed Jessica was on a first name basis with his two most worthy opponents, and he had six weeks to present a project that would beat them out. He was starting to doubt Julian's sanity. Of course, Julian had produced no compelling evidence to the contrary.

"Who decides the winner here?" A woman dressed in a forgettable pantsuit felt it was her time to shine.

Jessica turned and smiled gently. "Well, the fact that you're all here means we've already won. I'm confident a fitting proposal will surface. The planning department will be instrumental in the process, but the city manager will be tasked with the final decision."

"Is Paul in planning working on this?" Sharon inquired.

"He's terrible," Don said under his breath.

"Yes, he's working on it," Jessica offered a tight-lipped smile. It was apologetic and unclear as to which comment she was really addressing.

"Oh, fff...." Sharon moaned quietly, swallowing a hard 'f' sound.

Will worked with Paul Tollison on a townhome project two years earlier. He submitted the designs seven times before Paul finally approved the project. After rounds of site plan changes, architectural notes, and color suggestions, it was clear that Will was not in the driver's seat. Eventually, eight months later than expected, Will broke ground on the townhomes. In Will's mind, it was Paul's townhome project. Will just put up the money, got the loan, took all the risk, and did all the work.

"Can you give us any guidance as to what the city would like to see here?" Sharon was back on track with her professionalism.

"We really don't want to push an agenda, Sharon. Golden attracts the best and brightest, and we want to put that foot forward. Whatever development you suggest should keep in mind the ideals of the city and its current economic development initiatives."

Sharon nodded and seemed to take that information as satisfactory.

"How will we be notified?" Will finally spoke.

"Please make sure your contact info is filled out today and that you include it as requested in the document."

Feeling more confident, he spoke again. "So then what level of concept design should we present in six weeks?"

"You don't have to go the route of an artist rendering, but I would think a descriptive narrative about the project is a must."

"Yeah, that sounds about right," Don chimed in. In a move far beyond what the crowd was comfortable witnessing, Don put a fist to his mouth and deeply cleared his throat. The combination of movements added gravitas to what would come out of his mouth next, as if to say, "I'm clearing the way for something big." The perturbed man cringed and sucked his face down and in, as if he were attempting to tuck it into his neck. Don said, "You know, it would be hard to develop a full project concept and rendering in this short window of time." He was talking down to the group. He winked at Will, signaling Don Andino was definitely going to have a rendering produced in six weeks.

"How about a microbrewery?" The perturbed man spoke again. Apparently, he had moved on from apartments into an entirely different business venture, possibly roused to action by Don's lack of regard for his well-being.

"Jesus Christ," Don said with a dismissive chuckle. "How about a marijuana dispensary? Or another Starbucks? I'll just go ahead and pitch those for you, friend."

The blow had been dealt. The perturbed and now nervous man moved his gaze down to the table in defeat and looked to the lady wearing the pantsuit for comfort. She also appeared to be an outsider, and Will's guess was that she would not be submitting a proposal at all. Will was somewhere in the gray area, closer to outside than in. His bid at the recent auction must have signaled to Don and Sharon that he should be taken seriously. The bid represented his financial wherewithal to play, and any person with enough money was a potential threat.

Jessica realized the meeting was going a bit off the rails. "Let's talk process. Are there any specific questions regarding process?"

"If we have a specific user for the space already in mind, is there someone we can reach out to in order to talk about a potential use? I'd hate to go down the road with a group that doesn't fit the city's vision." Sharon was back on task as well.

"There won't be any real dialogue with regard to a specific company, but do you have a possible use in mind, Sharon?"

Sharon's eyes darted back and forth, and she coyly kept quiet. Her look prompted Jessica's quick response. "If you want to run a use by me, you can send an email, Sharon. But please no specific company info. I will have to share it with the group. I want to make sure we're holding to process here."

"And how many copies of the proposal should we supply? Is there a platform available to upload a digital submittal?" Sharon continued to put out signals that she should be taken seriously.

"Yes, the file-sharing link is in the document, and you will provide two hard copies to our office."

Don Andino pulled his chair closer to the table and leaned in over his elbows. He placed his five fingertips on the sign-in sheet in the middle of the table and slowly rotated it so he could read the names. His dominant posture was not subtle. "And you, Will Powell," he said while peering at the list, obviously signaling he had to look Will's name up. "What's your interest in this project?"

Great question, Will thought. He would soon be asking Julian the same thing. Though he had no idea exactly why he was at the RFP meeting, Will was not about to be bullied. He leaned in slowly over his elbows in a similar posture to Don.

"We'll see, Don. I just hope Sharon and I don't have the same user in mind." He winked at Don and shot Jessica a smile as he stood up.

Will's pocket buzzed once as he exited the room, alerting him of a new message. Farrah Parks was incessant.

He wanted to disregard her note, but like a stress fracture, ignoring the problem was undoubtedly going to make it worse. After all, he had a few more days, and if needed, he would push Julian to make good on his first installment into the Will Powell education fund.

Five minutes seemed sensible to hear Farrah's diatribe on late fees, her career ambitions, and her reluctance to go out on a limb for him. And all of that would be easier to stomach now, after establishing himself with Don and Sharon as a legitimate contender for the RFP. Less than thirty seconds ticked by before his phone rang. "Will? You alriiight? You been getting my texts?" The youngish-sounding Farrah Parks delivered the lines with a loose Texas panhandle drawl.

"Yeah, I got them. Look, I know it's…"

"Don't be mad at me. It wouldn't be riiight."

"What do you mean, mad?"

"I didn't realize you had a new company paying the note on Westminster."

"What are you…" He stopped short, processing as he spoke. "I mean, how did you not know?" He had no idea what company she was referencing, but Will was not stupid. He would let this play out long enough to see if there was an advantage for him.

"Aimless Action LLC? Kind of a weird name, Will. Didn't know it was paying your note. I accidentally posted it to the wrong account for a few days. Matter of fact, when I texted you the other day, I didn't realize I had it. I've got it corrected now. You're all square."

"You bet," Will said, willingly taking credit for the deposit. "Wait, Farrah, how many days have you had the payment?"

There was silence on the other end while she considered the timeline. "It was last Thursday."

Will immediately felt the burn of acid reflux in the back of this throat. The payment on his Westminster loan—which he did not make—came the day of the auction, before he and Julian agreed on anything. The silver-haired gentleman had acted swiftly, and prematurely. A peculiar and weighty feeling ensued. His heart raced and he swallowed hard. The dissonance was disorienting. On one hand, Julian's actions showed remarkable faith in Will; on the other hand, he displayed a level of control that was terrifying.

Chapter 8

"Leadership is an intangible that involves a constant interplay between the leader and the led...Another element to be considered is the Man to be led, and with whose morale we are concerned."

—General Omar N. Bradley

To: Will Powell
From Julian Darrow
Date: Tuesday, September 10, 2025, 19:27:31 MDT

Subject: Tomorrow morning at corner of 13th and Washington in downtown Golden at 6:45 a.m.

Cheers, Julian

At 6:35 a.m. on Wednesday morning, Will was barreling down I-70, amused by the curt subject-only email Julian had sent the night before, which he almost replied to with a sarcastic reminder about email etiquette. By 6:43 a.m., his black 4Runner rolled into downtown Golden, where he parked near Indulge Bistro and Wine Bar, tugging on a light sweater against the crisp fall air as he prepared to locate Julian's address and avoid the inevitable chiding for tardiness.

"Where the hell are you, Julian," he said under his breath, a smidge perturbed at the early hour. His hands were buried in his pockets and his eyes darted askance down the cross streets of 13th and Washington, just as the email said.

6:45 a.m. Nobody.

Come on, old man. Will started to pull out his phone. After the handshake deal at the silver-haired gentleman's house, he had added the name Julian Darrow in his phone. As Will began to peck the letter J into his phone, he heard a car coming down 13th Street. He did not pay it much attention until the black Lincoln Town Car pulled up to the corner. The heavily tinted rear window rolled down slowly, revealing an empty seat, as if the Town Car was acting alone and out of habit.

"You've got to be kidding me," he muttered again, barely audible. "Of course he's got a driver."

"Good morning," Julian offered from across the back seat. "Let's take a ride, shall we?" The freshly waxed black Town Car purred in front of him. Its hubcaps glistened with a sparkle that could only be manipulated by a specific product and diligent hands. The driver, an olive-skinned man in his fifties, exited the front and proceeded to open the rear door, stepping aside with an expressionless face to let Will pass. The man was thin, his skin revealing an unnatural leathery quality—the kind that is not innate, only earned through effort; if he furnished his hand quickly it would just as likely be brandishing a knife as a stiff handshake. Will stood motionless for a moment. The absurdity of the scene took him aback. It was comically similar to every mob movie he had ever seen—comical, unless you are the person asked to get in the vehicle.

"It's cold out there, son." Julian sat in the back seat in collared shirt, red cashmere sweater and dark slacks peering over the morning's edition of *The New York Times* and clutching a gold fountain pen. The morning's crossword puzzle, held firmly in his slender hands, was half conquered without so much as a smudge on the letters. Two steaming to-go cups sat in the cup holders to his left. He reached to the one farthest away and held it up toward Will. "I assume you enjoy coffee? There's cream and sugar up front with Vince, if you're so inclined."

"Appreciate it." Will finally spoke. He climbed into the roomy back seat. "A driver, huh?"

"Vince? He's more than a driver." The silver-haired gentleman smirked. "A man of many talents."

"So, is that a newspaper? I didn't know people still did that."

"Reading? You should attempt it more often. It's informative."

Julian wrapped the newspaper with both arms, a gesture indicative of times gone by, and began to read again. "Vince," he said plainly, offering a single nod as if to a horse. The order resonated with the wiry driver, who eased out into the vacant street and slowly began to accelerate.

"I didn't fancy you a man for crossword puzzles," Will chided.

"An exercise in humility," Julian responded.

"Was it your humility that paid my note in Westminster before we had a deal? You didn't have any right to do that, Julian."

"Consider it a gift among partners. If it's unwelcome, I can take it back. Is that what you'd prefer?"

Will's silence answered that question. He reached for the coffee and brought it to his lips. There would be time to figure out Julian's motives. The strong dark roast beneath his nose masked the overwhelming odors of leather polish and cigar smoke in the meticulously kept vehicle. The black leather seats had noticeable gray cracks, the heavy veining a foolproof marker of their age. The dark woodgrain doors held chrome-tipped buttons, impeccably clean despite the years of toggling. The seatback pockets were heavily pleated and looked like two old purses stitched onto the fabric. Nothing in view was digital, and nothing was short of pristine condition. "Where are we going?" Will asked.

Julian let out a dismissive "humph" and said, "We're simply riding. Vince will drop you off when we're done."

"Are you going to kill me?" Will said, half-jokingly.

Julian looked up from his paper and shook his head indifferently. "If we succeed, there's no reason for your demise." Will smiled uncomfortably at Julian's humor. "Tell me, Will, what did you learn yesterday? I trust the RFP meeting was enlightening."

"Tell you what I think. I think I'm running a fool's errand here. There's no chance the city will pick me to do this project. I think Don Andino and Sharon Peyton were literally having a name-dropping contest. And, Julian, I can't compete with that kind of—"

"Rubbish," Julian rebuked, taking an abruptly harsh tone, still peering into the newspaper and appearing to continue reading a column of print at the top of the next page. "Anyone can compete. If you don't believe that, I'd invite you to return to the predictable loop of disheartening events you call your business. Your mindset is unproductive." He returned his focus to his newspaper and reached for his cup of coffee.

Taken aback, Will groused, "Quite frankly, Julian, I don't have time either. I've got some great projects to develop that I'm not willing to put aside just so I can chase rainbows with you."

"Rainbows? I stopped chasing rainbows years ago, son. If you want to call it quits, do it now. Spare me the misfortune of wasting my time."

"That's what I'm trying to tell you; this is a waste of time. You weren't at the RFP meeting. I'm screwed on this one. They aren't going to pick me over Don or Sharon. You picked the wrong horse here."

"Now I'd agree with that." Julian took another slow sip of his black coffee and began to scan his newspaper with deliberate precision. "A six-letter word for UPSET, Vince?" Vince's gaze flicked briefly to the rearview mirror. His eyes darted up, then back to the road, his silence a predictable reply.

"The city is certainly not going to pick you over Don or Sharon if you don't bring them anything of value," Julian continued, his attention still fixed on the paper. Then, with a theatrical sigh, he tapped the crossword with his gold fountain pen. "It starts with an M. Six letters, Vince. Surely you can manage that." Vince remained mute, his expression unchanged, which only seemed to amuse Julian further.

The Town Car lurched as Vince took a hard right onto Highway 6 and began to accelerate into the morning traffic. The view of Table Mountain was crystal clear in the full brilliance of morning sunlight. Julian gazed out the window, appearing to take in the majesty of the view.

"Okay, what's the punchline? Is this another game, like the auction? Am I playing for second or third here?"

"I was uncertain whether you were playing at all. No. There's no punchline. But understand, every successful deal relies on meticulous execution of the proper steps. If you start your dealings with the wrong foot forward, you'll fail."

"Alright but I need to see some movement here pretty quickly, Julian," Will huffed.

Julian crossed his ankle over his thigh and glanced ahead, as if scouting their next destination. "Your demands are interesting. To continue making them, you need to understand how to listen." Julian broke his focus and squinted as he said, "Take us on the loop and then head back, Vince."

The driver offered no response but applied the blinker and eased into the right lane.

"Let me explain why you're here, Will. I selected you because of one thing: action. We've discussed that. Action is the cornerstone of dealmaking. There are countless people in the world right now who have read and absorbed volumes on dealmaking and negotiation. Tonight they will dream of the day they can use the tools. And tomorrow they will cower when the situation presents itself. Tools without activity are useless. Why forge the iron sword only to watch it rust in the corner? You, on the other hand, wage war with bare hands, Will."

"Bare hands?"

"MIFFED!," Julian said with some excitement. "You continue to amaze, Vince." He began scratching the word down with his golden pen, shaking his head at the length of time it had taken him.

Will glanced up at Vince who stared vacantly at the road ahead. Will was reasonably sure Vince had not contributed in the least to Julian's epiphany, or any other previous crossword answers. "Julian?" Will prodded.

"Ah, yes, where were we?" Julian stopped briefly, collecting his thoughts. "Bare hands indeed. But we are at the beautiful intersection of a deal. My interests conveniently align with yours. I need your action, and in return I will arm you with the proper tools. The money is a secondary item, not central to this deal. It will be there, you have my word, but let the focus be on perfecting your craft...its shelf life is longer."

"Okay, let's not focus on the money?" Will asked facetiously. "You're legitimately crazy. I can see that now. And what's with this car and driver bit? Nobody does this anymore, Julian. It's not normal. And the crossword puzzles..."

Julian sat still, peering down at the newspaper in his lap. He was no doubt more comfortable with the ensuing silence as Will examined him, waiting with bated breath for some reaction. After a deep inhale—the length of which he appeared to relish—Julian turned and faced Will with a cold, predatory stare and said, "An athlete's first effort."

"What?" Will responded.

"Six letters again. Starts with an R."

"ROOKIE," Will offered immediately. "And there's no damn way that's in your newspaper."

"ROOKIE," Julian repeated as he began scribbling the answer. "Indeed. Quick on the draw—and refreshingly self-aware."

"Alright, look. I'm willing to trust you understand what you're talking about...for a minute," Will said. "But we need to get somewhere. This whole show isn't doing it for me."

"Excellent. Thought you'd never ask. For today, we'll start with some fundamental truths of dealmaking. And before you slick back your hair and attempt to summon a superhuman quick wit, please understand that negotiation is no different from any true craft. It is honed over time and with great effort. It does not require a natural talent beyond your own, yet it is not simplistic enough to come naturally. I will make you this one promise," Julian said, now pointing at Will. "If you commit to all seven rules, you will no doubt see the world of dealmaking in a different light."

"What are they?" Will asked with piquing interest.

"For sake of clarification, we'll get into many more topics beyond these first few, I'm sure. But here's number one, and you won't see this in a textbook.

"RULE NUMBER ONE: BE ACTIVE...AND TAKE ACTION."

"Okay, wait, you kinda said that before. And that's too general. You're beating a dead horse...next," Will said dismissively.

"Vince, perhaps this will be a shorter ride than I thought," Julian sighed. Vince sat stoically in the driver's seat, a maestro of dignified quiet. "If I'm beating a dead horse, then please hand me a club. Let's ensure this horse is dead. You need to absorb this, son. Action is a religion. Why think? Why read? Why lie in bed and dream? If you come to a conclusion and do not act on it, you have shamed yourself. If you can only pray for one thing, pray for the courage to act."

"Okay, I'm all square on that one. You said it yourself. It's why I'm here. And that's still not a rule."

"It's the almighty rule. And don't just have the courage to act; be intentional with your action. Don't simply find a piece of land to develop...work to make its development inevitable. Action creates opportunity within opportunity. It gives insight. Action wraps its tentacles around every successful deal. Act intentionally."

"I've got it. Give me something strategic. I'll act on it...if it's good enough. You have my word." Will turned, leaning his elbow on the center console, engaged.

"Fair enough. Perhaps you have an innate proclivity to act. Now, can you learn? Can you listen? Let's skip to number two, for now."

"Alright, what is it?"

"Rule Number Two: Everyone is Self-Interested. Serve Their Interests to Achieve Yours."

"Seems pretty straightforward," Will replied.

"Doesn't it?" Julian said with a smirk, his tone dry as ever. "And yet, it's the hardest rule to follow. Let's unpack it with a little scenario. Suppose you're an artist—an extraordinary stretch, I admit—and you've just completed the first piece in a series. I offer you $1,000, but you want $2,000. We're at an impasse, doomed to the common fate of a dead deal. What next?"

Will leaned in, triumphant. "Simple. You're a cheap old bastard trying to underpay me. I'll wait for the next offer."

"But you want to sell it, don't you? And it's the first in a series. Let's say I start arguing value—comparable sales, market conditions, and so on. How would you respond?"

Will shrugged. "I'd tell you why my piece is unique and why your price isn't good enough."

"Indeed," Julian said, fingers steepled with gravitas. "We'd spiral into the rabbit hole of defending positions. Either I pay more than I want, you take less than you want, or we walk away. But what if I tried another approach? Say I tell you I'm a restaurateur and want to feature your piece in my restaurant, complete with a biography of you. My clientele, I explain, are top-tier art collectors."

Will chuckled. "So now you're appealing to my interests. Clever, but your imaginary scenario is too convenient."

"Will, you poor, ignorant artist." Julian took another slow sip of coffee, letting the comment settle with Will first. "The principle remains—understanding interests moves mountains where positions merely build walls. Everyone has interests, every single person on God's earth. You can operate in a world you wish to be true, or you can navigate the human condition as it is. You are self-interested. It drives you. Why should your counterpart be any different? And do you know the magic pill for finding out the other party's interests?"

"Humor me."

"You simply ask. You ask questions. You get answers, and you ask more questions."

"What if I can't think of any good questions?"

"Then simply repeat a snippet of what they say verbatim and be quiet. They'll fill the silence with more information. You will eventually find a line of questioning."

"That sounds stupid," Will argued.

"Sounds stupid?" Julian asked.

"Yeah, you can't just repeat stuff and expect me...oh shit. You got me," Will admitted, shaking his head at the simplicity. "Alright, but what if they are tight-lipped about it? The people I deal with don't give you all the information. They hold on to their cards. They're trying to get the very best deal possible."

Julian paused, looking up to the rearview mirror. Vince had eased to the right lane and was quickly approaching the next exit. "Give us a bit more time," he said, returning his focus to Will. "Son, that is a reflection on you, not them. Ask better questions, and you'll receive better answers. These reticent dealmakers you describe, the ones that won't reveal any information. They go home and bore their spouses with every minute detail or pay psychiatrists when their spouses won't listen. We know what we know from warriors of the past because, for lack of anyone to listen, they kept journals, telling the world their innermost thoughts. People want an open ear. They yearn to impart knowledge. If you convey a genuine interest in them, in their plight, they will return the favor with valuable information. You simply need to tease the proper details that reveal their true interests." Julian paused to redirect. "Currently, the city is not interested in you. If you had a track record, you could start this RFP process by selling yourself, but you don't. Starting with you is the wrong move in this deal. And that is perfectly alright. We will get to your value in this equation. For now, we need another tack. They have interests and we need to tease them out. I'm assuming Jessica Dews presided over the meeting?"

"Yes, she did. And how do you know Jessica?"

"Research is a form of listening, son. And knowing the parties involved is part of doing business," Julian deflected. "Jessica's a smart woman, and logical. She'll be helpful." Julian sat back in his seat. The worn, dark gray leather made a rubbing sound as he folded his arms and leaned into it. "So you tell me, where do we start on this one, Will?"

"I don't think it matters. This game that you're trying to win, putting me out there while you play puppeteer, it doesn't translate at this level, even if I know every dealmaking secret you can give me. These people are legitimate developers."

"At this level?" Julian repeated Will's words. "And what experience do you possess at this level?"

"Okay, I may not——"

"That was rhetorical," Julian interrupted again. "Humor me. If this was all a game and you had to make a next move, what would it be? Forget the rules."

Will sighed and shifted his jaw to the side, biting on his lip. He paused a bit longer in thought and took another sip of his coffee. "Alright, my first move would be to come up with a project that makes sense."

"Excellent. And to whom should it make sense?"

Will's face lit up. "To us. We're the ones that need to make money here," he said tersely.

"Most definitely we'll need to make money. That's a critical step in this process. You're right to focus on profitability." Julian, now sitting comfortably, stuck his left hand out from folded arms and pointed at Will—shaking his golden pen. "Never forget it. I've worked with countless failures who forgot its importance. However, we can't make money if you're not chosen to do the project. If you must go up against others, let's hope they start by focusing on their own needs. Set profitability aside for a moment, it will have its place. Profitability follows mastery. It's the other party's interest you need to suss out. Often they haven't explored their own interests. It's a thing of beauty when you arrive at them together."

"Are you suggesting you can make any project profitable?"

"Not at all. That's foolish. But profitability is a touchstone by which you measure your decisions. It is not a step in the process, nor a decision. Profitability is an outcome. It is downstream of understanding interests."

Will relaxed his posture and folded his hands around his coffee cup. He took a sip. "Are you going to tell me the next step here, Julian?"

"If I thought I needed to tell you, I wouldn't have picked you up."

"And why did you pick me up, Julian?"

Julian's neck craned forward, his gaze shifting to the curb as the car slowed. He unfolded the newspaper, his brow furrowed in thought. "Vince, nine-letter word for 'item from one's past'."

Chapter 9

"When the gods wish to punish us, they answer our prayers."

—Oscar Wilde

41 DAYS TO RFP

"I need to ask you a question," Will said to a closed bathroom door.

"I'M ON THE TOILET."

"Remember the old man I met? The one at the auction?"

"GIVE ME FIVE MINUTES."

Will returned to the bed, granting Kirsty her request. After two minutes of dead silence, and while clenching the comforter tightly in two aggravated fists, he said, "Jesus, are your legs falling asleep in there?"

"THAT JUST GOT YOU FIVE MORE MINUTES!" Kirsty shouted from the toilet, a short distance through the closed door. "I'M SHOPPING IN HERE."

After what seemed to Will like ten minutes, Kirsty appeared from the bathroom. She walked to her side of the bed and stared at Will with raised eyebrows, her head cocked to the side. "Next time, leave me alone. That's my safe space. Got it?"

"Nobody takes that long," he shot back. "It's important."

"Oh, now you're upset. Okay," Kirsty said as she climbed into bed. "I'll remember that next time you're in there."

Will grabbed each side of her face deeply in his palms and kissed her. She failed to return the gesture—not moving a single muscle in her lips.

As he pulled back, he could see her eyebrows perched at the highest possible point on her forehead; her entire face signaling him: You have to say you're sorry first.

"I don't know how to say this," Will offered, undeterred. "But you forgot to turn out the lights."

Kirsty's eyebrows remained unchanged.

"Alright, I'll turn 'em off myself. But I need you to do a title search, land records, corporate filings, anything you can find on Julian Darrow."

"Nice try. That'll cost you," Kirsty said. She sat up in bed, freeing her ponytail before returning to the pillow. "But why are you so hellbent on hanging around this guy?"

"Remember when I went to his house?"

"Yeah...and?"

"I agreed to work with him."

"I think we both saw that coming," she said, feigning a yawn.

"Well, I need to know who I'm working with. So what's the price?" he said gamely.

"For what?"

"For finding out who this guy is."

Kirsty rolled her head over on the pillow to face Will. "If you really want to know, why don't you just ask him?" she offered in her signature style: honest, simple, and sometimes searing.

Will pressed on. "He's not the type to talk, and you're the best stalker I know."

"I am good," she boasted. "But sounds like you want to know more than the basics on him. If you want me to do a deeper dive, it's gonna cost you. I'll have to get creative. I'm guessing this old codger has zero digital footprint."

"Just let me know how much," Will said again. They both knew he had no intention of paying for her services, but she could undoubtedly collect in innumerable ways.

"Wait. What's he look like?"

"What's that matter?" Will asked.

"Maybe I could sleep with him. You just said he has a driver, right? He's gotta be rich. Just for a little while, until I get the info I need...and maybe some diamonds."

Will squinted in disapproval. "I'm serious."

"And why exactly am I digging up dirt on him? If he knows his stuff, and his money's good, what's it matter?"

"Because it doesn't make any sense," Will replied. "I'm telling you, he singled me out. I need to understand why."

"Okay." She rolled onto her back and pulled the covers up. "I'll dig up the dirt on Julian, but it will cost you. Now stop talking."

Will, having received an affirmative from his head PI, leaned over and kissed her on the head. "Don't know why I love you so much," he whispered before rolling over and tugging the comforter up under his arm.

"Don't know why I love you more," Kirsty responded. She, too, rolled over, pressed her back against his, and instinctively slid her leg closer until the bottoms of their feet touched. "Diamonds," she said slowly, as if entering a dream.

Will shrugged in playful disapproval. He reached to the nightstand for one last scroll through text and email on his phone before placing it on the charging station for the night.

To: Will Powell
From: Julian Darrow
Date: Thursday, September 12, 2025, 6:09:15 MDT

Subject: Pick you up at your house 6:45 p.m. tomorrow.

Cheers,
Julian

Will laid the phone down as his head canted toward the pillow. He was sleepy. That was not the norm. Tired? Yes. His nights were spent on the edge of tired and restless. But sleepiness was elusive, setting in with the rare moments of contentment, when his throat didn't burn from acid and his head wasn't full of problems. For tonight, he was sleepy.

Chapter 10

40 DAYS TO RFP

It was 8:30 a.m. sharp the next morning when Will walked down a drab, carpeted hallway at the City of Golden offices. The front desk of the planning department was vacant, but the lipstick-stained Diet Coke can suggested someone was there the day before, or from the looks of it, maybe the day before that. He craned his neck around the corner; only one office light was on, the sound of typing originating from it.

"Hello?" he said in a loud talking voice.

"Back here!" a nasally voice shouted.

Will walked toward the lighted office and knocked on the already open door labeled "Paul Tollison." A diminutive man in his mid-forties sat at his computer wearing a loud floral-print collared shirt. The roots of his hair were dark, working their way to an unnatural platinum color at the extremities. The stark transformation of color was reminiscent of a coiffed skunk, but the brilliance of the platinum hue connoted this skunk had the help of a professional colorist. Paul looked nothing like the image Will had been carrying around in his mind.

"Can I help you?" Paul's nasally tone was now less intimidating, but no less irritating. He was still facing the computer and pounding out the last few keystrokes.

"I'm Will Powell. We spoke on the phone."

"Oh, right. I have thirty minutes, Mr. Powell," Paul said as he turned around, revealing the cavalier decision to freely unbutton the top two buttons of his floral-print shirt. And it would have been a shame if he hadn't, as Paul possessed a rather impressive gold necklace.

Hanging on the wall adjacent to the desk was a montage of a little boy playing various sports and posing with multiple people.

"Who's the baseball player?" Will inquired, pointing at the photo and attempting to use Julian's method of questioning.

"Oh, that's my little nephew, Trevor," Paul shot back proudly—still bitchy, but proud.

"Well, he looks like quite a T-ball player," Will said, trying to talk about anything other than the potential project first. "Looks like he's got quite a swing."

Paul sat back in his chair and looked up to the right as if he were imagining Trevor swinging a bat. "Yeah, he thinks he's a little switch hitter."

"Well, he must be awfully good then." Will looked at Paul, who lacked any semblance of athletic ability.

"For Trevor, switch hitting is like being illiterate in two languages. The poor little guy couldn't hit a basketball. He keeps wanting me to come over and play with him, but I don't know the first thing about baseball. I was a track star in high school."

Will swallowed hard, looking at Paul in amazement. He was short and wiry. His sleeves were rolled up enough to expose the slightness of his forearms as he crossed them on his chest. Will appreciated the term "track star," which he assumed Paul carefully chose as a clever test. Any hesitation on Will's part—even the smallest inkling of disbelief—

would most assuredly send Paul recoiling back to his customary standoffish demeanor.

"Well, look, I don't want to waste your time here, Paul. I know you're busy and I appreciate you meeting me this morning. Here's the thing, I'm taking a real run at this RFP for the Teleprime office building, and I want to pick your brain for just a minute about possible uses."

"Will, as I told you on the phone, I don't make the final decisions on that. I'm a planner. I make other people's ideas work within our current infrastructure and our codes."

Will stopped and parsed through what Paul said. "Okay, that makes sense. But Paul, I know you carry some pull around here and this building is right down the street. Knowing the city was going to buy it, you must've passed by the building and given some thought as to what it should be?"

"If you want my honest opinion," Paul looked in both directions as if to make sure no one was listening in, "it's ugly as hell. They ought to tear it down."

Will laughed.

Paul continued, "Half the people in this town think preservation means you have to save everything. They built the Teleprime office in the late seventies. I was built in the late seventies. Nothing built in the seventies or eighties was meant to last forever. Have you looked at the windows on the top floors? They're all tiny, and single pane...in Colorado! You would freeze to death in there in the winter. And if you did freeze to death, your corpse would rot in there because nobody could see your body through those tiny windows."

Will did not want to stop Paul's rant but feared he would run out of time if he didn't. "Okay, I get that it's ugly, but you wouldn't really tear it down, would you?"

"If they'd let me I would," Paul snapped back, still worked up from his tirade. The more he talked, the more sassiness emanated from him.

"What keeps them from letting you?" Will probed.

"Nothing really. There is no ordinance against razing a building in downtown if it doesn't have historical significance."

Will, now armed with Paul's sentiments about the physical building, decided to change course back to the original subject. He was firing on all cylinders, channeling Julian's vibe for purposeful questioning. "What about uses, Paul? Does the city need anything in particular?"

"Again, this isn't my department, but I know Golden is thirsty for some tech."

"You mean a technology company?" Will said, puzzled.

"Yeah, tech. I don't know how you'd do it, but you'd have the city council eating out of your hands if you could bring a growing tech company. There's even a city grant available for a tech company that moves their headquarters here. It's what we're missing. We don't want more residential, there's no tax basis in that. We only released our growth control measures because of the new state law."

By "growth control measures," Paul was talking about the restrictions on residential permits. Until two years ago, Golden would not allow itself to grow more than 1% a year.

"Is there any tax generator other than tech they would want to see?" Will was being coy.

"You could go office or maybe lodging," Paul answered.

"Lodging?" Will delved deeper, deploying Julian's tactic for repeating words for lack of a more defined question.

"Sure, we could use some more hotel beds downtown. But you can't put them behind those tiny windows. You'd have to blow the building up first." Paul sat up straight, unfolded his arms, and placed his hands on the armrests of his chair as if he were about to stand up. "I'm afraid I've got to get back to work, Will. I have a stack of civil drawings to review."

"I really appreciate it, Paul. This has definitely been helpful."

Paul smiled an awkward smile, exposing both his top and bottom teeth in a movement that seemed to be foreign to him, and then said, "You know Sharon Peyton is taking a hard look at this project too?" The words threatened to take away all the morning's momentum.

"Yes, I assumed she was. Saw her at the RFP meeting," Will replied.

"I just didn't want you to get your hopes up too high."

And there it was...momentum stifled.

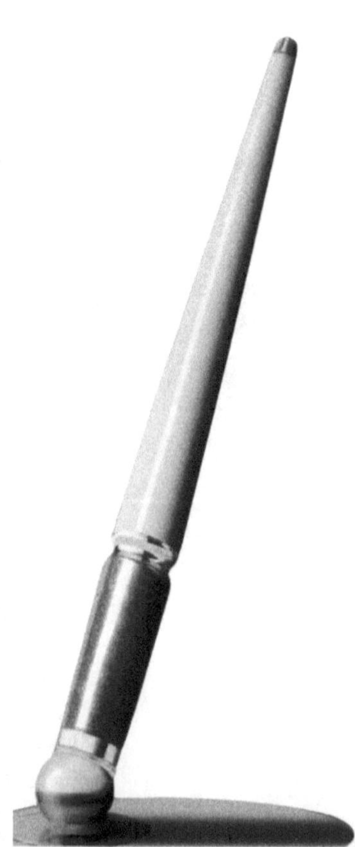

Chapter 11

"Business is a cobweb of human relationships."

—Ross Perot

39 DAYS TO RFP

His heavily-salted glass held a well-executed, classic margarita. Not the drink one would typically order to complement a flight of steaks. At times, it appeared Dexter Mathis chose to be uncommon through some rebellious effort. His dark gray Metallica T-shirt and black jeans, which covered the tops of his snakeskin boots, failed to conform with any predictable norm associated with an investor of his caliber. He dressed as if perpetually preparing to ride a Ducati motorcycle and kept a salt-and-pepper stubble of beard, eschewing any notion he kept his appearance up for others.

Unlike his dear friend Will, Dexter was habitually mellow. His soft, blue eyes seemed to listen on their own as he held someone's gaze, giving way to a genuine smile that seldom faded. Dexter was the kind of guy you could speak with for an entire evening and later realize you had not asked him a single question. You would be the subject of conversation, and he would learn more than you anticipated sharing. On occasion, you might even learn something about yourself. To decipher what portion of his being was innate and what traits had developed over years of study was impossible; he would disregard that question as irrelevant. He was Dexter Mathis, however he came to be.

Preston Lowden, RevMax's CEO and Dexter's newly anointed

partner, approached the table to find two sets of steaks, six miniature cuts in all. Their partnership agreement sat between the unused place setting to his right in a small, tight stack of stark white pages.

"Promised you a flight of steaks," Dexter said, straightening up his posture and allowing his snakeskin boot to drop off the opposite thigh. "Always keep my promises."

Preston was a nervous guy, but his uneasiness was noticeably elevated as he awkwardly scooted his chair back and released a long sigh as he sat down. Dexter watched his shoulders sink in the exhale, as if there was too much pressure within his body.

"My mom...ummm...she said...she said I should get five hundred." The words simply escaped his mouth as he tried to breathe. He was too green to have the moxie to demand it, but too afraid of his mother not to carry out her message. He had tossed the statement out there to dance above the table, hoping it would not land too hard on Dexter.

"Your mother was a high school math teacher. She's never tried to grow a company like I'm proposing. But she is right about the upfront money. You could get more. In fact, you could get even more than $500,000 for RevMax right now, Preston. I'd say possibly $750,000. But you're gonna have to give up some more ownership to do it."

"Really?" The young entrepreneur was thrown, and wide-eyed.

"Absolutely," Dexter said coolly. "I mean, I'm not offering you that kind of deal, man. I want you to own more of your company and work like hell to make it successful. But I do think you could get the other deal." He glanced over at the neat stack of papers representing the deal to which the two men had already agreed. He shoved it a little farther away, physically setting their deal aside for the moment. "Let's deal with this later."

The young entrepreneur was dejected. "Why not you, Dexter?"

"People don't come to me for money, man."

"They don't?" he paused. "I think I did."

"I don't think so." Dexter paused and took a slow sip from his margarita. He did not appear the least bit turned off by Preston's flagrant disregard for their agreed upon terms. "And that's not what you need. Money's not your problem. People come to me to connect the dots that need connecting. If you want money, there are investors out there who will gladly pay you more, but they'll expect you to perform on your own, they'll take a bigger slice, and the product will suffer for it. That's the tradeoff. You need to ask yourself if you want more money today, or if you want to build a company that pays for tomorrow."

"So you're saying taking more money today is a bad idea? Not sure that makes sense, Dexter."

"Okay. Let's play it out. What would you do with it...if I gave you the extra $150,000 you suggested? Or if somebody else gave you more for that matter, what would you do with it?" Dexter's soft, listening eyes looked directly into Preston's. He waited for a few silent seconds as it became evident Preston had no formalized plan. "I'm not pressing you, man. I'm curious. You know this product better than anyone. I might learn something. What would you spend it on?"

"I'd need to scale the company."

Dexter nodded. "That's a solid idea, dude. I agree. We're on the same page there. Scaling your company's more important than the nickels you could stick in your pocket today. But you didn't answer my question." Dexter's genuine smile morphed into a grin. He picked up the weighty silverware and began to slice through the first piece of meat: a small grass-fed filet. "We better dig in while it's still warm." He separated a small bite on his plate and raised the meat up to inspect it. Dexter closed his eyes as the first bite entered his mouth, shaking his head with utter acceptance. There was no semblance of aggression or discontent in his mannerisms; he was enjoying the first bite.

"I'd invest it in the company."

"In *your* company…" Dexter said, looking down longingly now at his second target: the aged filet in the middle of his plate. He said nothing else.

Preston, obviously at the end of his empty investment plan, cocked his head to the side and bit his lip. He fiddled with the food on his plate, though not appearing to have an appetite. "I…I don't know. I guess you're about to tell me, though."

Dexter shook his head. "I'm not gonna tell you to do anything, dude. It's your product. If we're partners, I'm gonna let you handle the software. And while you do, I'll highlight the problems we need to address along the ride to scaling this company. And I'll make sure we fix 'em."

Preston sat back abruptly. "What problems?"

"For starters, distribution, pricing structures and user engagement. I'll have a bunch of meetings with people whose job descriptions you don't care about. My part will be making sure your product gets in the hands of paying customers. There's no scale without users, man. Those are the dots I'll connect with you. It's what I do." Dexter stopped and looked down at his classic margarita. He rubbed his thumb across the condensation on the outside of the glass. "And we'll address your current problem too, dude."

"What?"

"Your mom."

"Excuse me?"

"Look. I've got gray hairs because I've been doing this a while. I see the problems you've got. Taking a company all the way means making tough decisions. Before you get too crazy on me, I'm not talking about getting your mom out of the partnership. We need her. She helped get you here. But she needs to be on board with what you're wanting, or you can't do it, man. Your mom's outlook is a problem. You guys got two different things: an eight-plex in Denver, and a software company that should be worth millions. I can get you users. But I can also be at the table to help you address your other issues."

"How do you know she's a problem?"

"You told me, dude."

"No, I didn't."

"The eight-plex. You said you wanted to lease them by the night, and she demanded half of them be long-term leases. You said it the first time we talked. You're thinking in two different worlds. That's a problem, man. I can help you with that. Scale doesn't have to be risky, but it takes some big moves. That's why you need a partner sitting next to you, not a bigger pile of cash."

"So where do we go from here?" Preston asked.

"Sleep on it. Ask yourself if you want more money up front and if you want to tackle this thing alone. If so, nothing I tell you is going to change that. And you deserve it. You built a great product. You and your mom could move into a nicer place, buy some more rental property, and upgrade your lifestyles a bit. You can do that now. And if you want to, then your mom's right, you need to ask for more money up front. I'll introduce you to an investor I know that would like this deal. And there's nothing wrong with that decision." Dexter watched as he could see the young entrepreneur considering that possibility. "But if you want RevMax to be a multimillion-dollar company...one that changes your lives...then our partnership is more important than a little more money on the front end."

Preston rubbed his lower lip with his thumb and forefinger, narrowing his eyes as he looked at Dexter, who was still thumbing his glass and looking back at him with soft blue eyes. Dexter smiled as he lifted the glass for another sip. "Funny, isn't it? You would've killed to have this decision to make a year ago, and here we are. Be proud of that, man. You're a talented dude."

The young entrepreneur took a deep breath and slowly reached for the stack of papers. "Give me the damn contract. I don't need to sleep on it," he said with newfound confidence. Dexter leaned far back in his seat and plowed his hand into his black jeans pocket, where there just happened to be a pen.

Chapter 12

"If you're the village blacksmith and the Model T comes along,
you better become a mechanic."
—Jim Barksdale

38 DAYS TO RFP

In what had proven to be a rare event on a Friday evening, Will, Kirsty, and Sela were seated at the kitchen table enjoying a homemade pizza. Will, though enjoying the gift of time with his family, instinctively glanced past Kirsty's head at the digital clock on the oven. As the digits reached closer to 6:45 p.m., he regrettably lost his family focus in anticipation of the Town Car's arrival.

Sure enough, at 6:45 p.m. sharp, a beam of light appeared and grew quickly across the kitchen wall through the windows of Kirsty's sitting room. "I need to go," Will said.

Kirsty raised both eyebrows and scrunched her lips to one side in an expression that said both "good luck" and "you got yourself into this" simultaneously.

Sela, seeing the odd expression, popped up and walked over to the sitting room window like the curious teenager she was. "Is this car here to pick you up, Dad? Strong move by whoever that is," she said with a hint of sarcasm. "Badass car...that's old school."

Will didn't answer but shot Sela a look of disapproval from across the room for her language, though undoubtedly she used worse in his absence. He stood up, grabbed the jacket he had hung on the back of his chair and offered, "I'll see you ladies in a bit."

"Be careful, Honey," Kirsty warned.

He was pulling his jacket on as he walked out the front door. Will headed down the short sidewalk connecting to the curb while Vince exited the driver's side and worked his way over to stand at attention by the rear door, his hands folded in front of him. "Thanks," Will said, as Vince leaned over and opened the polished black door for entry. The driver coldly offered nothing in return. Will looked instinctively back at his home before passing Vince and climbing down into the vehicle. Vince waited for Will to scoot safely beyond the edge of his seat and then closed the door behind him.

Julian sat with a green folder partially concealed beneath a leather notebook and fastidiously legible crossword puzzle in his lap. The sweet-scented smoke from a cigar dominated the interior and materialized in a faint haze only visible inches below the rich yellow of the overhead lights.

"Is that a Cuban?" Will asked.

Julian looked at him pityingly and said, "He's Italian." Vince peered in the review with a curled lip, shook his head and said nothing. Julian returned his focus to the crossword puzzle in his lap. "Do you possess an eight-letter word for ILL-TEMPERED in your lexicon?"

"I don't play newspaper games. And I meant the cigar. Don't be an ass. Is it a Cuban?"

Julian inspected it in his hand. "I should hope so. Promised my doctor I'd start smoking them in the evenings to relax."

"Is that a thing?" Will asked. "Doesn't sound like medical advice."

"Take it up with my doctor," Julian said before enjoying a pull of the cigar, the effortless inhale barely glowing the embers at the tip. "The young girl in the window...that's your daughter?" Julian asked, moving on.

Will was still settling in, pulling off his jacket and attempting to shake a petulant shiver that followed him in from the cold. "Yes. Her name is Sela," he said uncomfortably, again reminded of Julian's invasive understanding of his affairs.

"You must be proud," he said flashing a smile as warm as he could muster. He offered Vince a nod, and the black Town Car began its journey to nowhere. "Time to get to work, son."

"Good. Was beginning to think we were just riding around."

"Your daughter, Sela. I imagine she's a firecracker."

"Julian, I really don't want to sit and talk about my—"

"I gather it's challenging to extract information from her," Julian interrupted. "A queer scenario. She's your daughter, and I trust you want to connect with her." He paused and leaned over his elbow. "Why, then, is she a mystery to you?"

"Listen, you don't know shit about our relationship."

"Am I off base?"

Silence.

"Does she purposely conceal things? Or, perhaps you ask the wrong questions?" Julian's complete dismissal of Will's reaction was evident yet again. "I hear you met with Paul Tollison. Is he still a mystery as well?"

"Tell you what, let's stick to Paul. For the record, we had a great meeting."

"What enlightening information did you glean?"

"It was good. I got him talking. He's fine with office, hotel, or retail. As long as I put bigger windows in it, I think he'd be on board with whatever we want."

"Excellent. And I assume your impression of Paul Tollison has changed since you connected. That's a lesson to hold on to, son. It's a piece of gold. People want to share. They long to share. We just ask the wrong questions. Your daughter. Your wife. Paul Tollison. It doesn't matter who. If you want to deepen your relationship with them, be inquisitive. You'll find that people want to share, and when they do, you start to learn their personal motivation...their interests."

"Wait, are we back on the lesson plan? Rule Number Two? We've already covered that one," Will said.

"And yet it's overlooked far too often. You can't arrive at interests if you can't extract information. You have a natural proclivity to connect, Will...just like Vince. Don't squander it."

Vince, in a pattern becoming familiar to Will, had no response.

"Allow me to disabuse you of a notion carried by the masses. They assume people want to hear about their life, their kids, their hobbies. It's a grave mistake." Julian put his pointer finger in the air and turned slightly toward Will. "I regret to inform you, but they don't give a damn about you, Will. And they don't give a damn about your kids. You're a means to an end. Small talk is harmless, but it's inert."

"You need to tighten up your delivery, Julian. Those two ideas contradict themselves. Why try to connect if it serves no purpose?"

"He challenges me, Vince. It's why I like him. Full of piss and vinegar." Julian turned to Will. "Connecting is infinitely important. It's just not about you, and it's not about aimless chatter. The masses walk around feeling misunderstood. Even those at the top of their game can have a wife or husband at home brimming with discontent...a resentful child...a debt unpaid." Julian paused for a moment and looked down toward his lap, breaking eye contact. Will looked at him, and for the first time, thought he saw a man tormented. In what appeared to Will as a personal reflection, Julian had—for lack of better terms—checked out.

"Julian?" Will said, bringing him back to the task at hand.

He looked up, snapping back into the moment. "Indeed, where was I?"

"People are screwed up," Will responded.

"Precisely," Julian continued. "They have thoughts and ideas bottled up, ready to share with whomever will pay the proper attention. The rapport is built when you begin asking questions about their thoughts and ideas. Real questions. Inquisitive questions."

"What questions should I ask?"

"You don't need a list of prescribed questions, Will. Take a genuine interest in what they do for a few moments. Afford them that satisfaction. Allow them some autonomy and watch them light up. Reap the reward of unguarded conversation. As interests are revealed the questions take a more direct path to the deal at hand."

"That makes sense," Will remarked. "So is that Rule Number Three...autonomy?"

"No. Offering autonomy is not a rule of dealmaking, Will, it's an underlying thread of the entire process. We're still on number two, talking about interests over positions. Allow someone to speak for a few seconds and you'll hear their position. But allow them to freely offer their ideas...allow them that autonomy, and you'll hear their interests. Deals are made by satisfying interests. And Will," Julian leaned in, "occasionally they're made by realizing your positions are incongruent with your own interests."

"Okay, but Julian, the pace of this discussion needs to speed up," he said airily. "We've covered this already. If you're asking me to win this RFP, I need a strategy to overcome Don and Sharon."

"And that's why I've allowed you admittance into my car tonight. I come bearing a gift."

Will noticed the large green folder beneath the newspaper in Julian's lap. "Is it in that folder?"

"We shall see." Julian looked forward. "Vince, give us a full twenty-minute route. Will, here, needs a strategy. And I need an eight-letter word for ILL-TEMPERED. He looked down and studied the paper.

"Starts with the letter P." Will saw Vince's eyes dart up to the rearview mirror and focus quickly on Julian, then immediately turned back again to the road.

Will, still unsure of the full breadth of his relationship with Julian, leaned over to look out the front windshield—taking mental note of the change in course. After nearly forty-five seconds, Will turned to the silver-haired gentleman and nudged him. "Julian?"

Julian faced Will again and curiously said, "Yes, now where were we?" Something was eating at Julian, causing him to sway in and out of conversation. Will could easily see it. Anyone could have seen it.

"My strategy to beat Don and Sharon," Will repeated.

"Hmmm. Are you ready for that stage? Do you understand the parties' interests? You haven't spoken with Don or Sharon yet, correct?"

"No."

"Excellent. Because it's time to explore the most important interests of all...yours. As my proxy, you would love to see the Telemark Building transformed into a boutique hotel."

"Oh man. I'm hardly qualified to own the hotel I have."

"And Vince was hardly qualified to drive me around when we met. Lucky for him, I had some experience driving. Vince didn't own a car. You already own a hotel. Therefore, you're uniquely qualified, and I have some experience in this department as well. As for interests, this is your deal to execute, is it not? You need to make decisions based on your interests. I'm content to inherit the result."

"You're making this seem easier than it is."

"I make light out of things that aren't heavy," Julian said. "You need to realize an important rule of dealmaking. It works in tandem with understanding the interests of both parties."

Will saw the look in Julian's eyes. Imparting wisdom had become a mainstay of their visits, but landing on hard and fast rules produced a gleam in Julian's eyes, a certain fire Will imagined was present only in the realization of a successful deal and in teaching moments with his new pupil. "And what is that rule?" Will said, egging him on.

"RULE NUMBER THREE: KNOW YOUR VALUE. YOUR VALUE MAKES THE DEAL UNIQUE."

Julian continued, "I see it constantly. Poor negotiators start to second-guess their value. They begin to see the other party as the prize. And, in doing so, they commoditize themselves. You must always be the prize, a collaborative prize. You are the unique conduit by which the other party achieves their needs and interests. So, in essence, you become part of the product."

"I know I'm valuable, don't need an old bird to tell me that. But I'm not the product here, Julian." Will challenged. At present, he felt more like a pawn than a product. There was a bigger game at play, and he was the rookie. Though he trusted Julian's authority, trusting Julian's motive was a different question altogether.

"Son, you would not be at the table if you did not have a value. I saw value in you, and I consider myself an astute judge of such. You operate with a certain air of confidence, so I suppose you should see it in yourself. However, the negotiations you have successfully completed to date do not reflect your value. They are a result of lazy practice, hence the unending miserable loop of events. As you understand interests, as you bring value and authority in your given field, you become a part of the unique product. And you will garner more value by understanding this."

Will paused. "You just said bring value and authority. You touched on value, but what do you mean by bringing authority?"

"Ah, indeed. Authority is a highly important concept. We will save the authority rule for a later date."

Will, satisfied with leaving the concept of authority alone, continued, "If I'm the product, you mind telling me what that product is?" Will's question of trust was still looming.

"Part of the product," Julian reminded him. "You still need the underlying asset. That's where my gift comes into play." Julian produced the green folder from beneath the crossword puzzle. He pulled out the first few pages, leaving several inside. "My gift."

Will thumbed through the sheets. They were images of a hotel, looking more like edgy, loft-style condos than hotel rooms. "Impressive. Different...but impressive. Where's this hotel?"

"It's called Launch Pad and it's in Raleigh, North Carolina. It's not simply a hotel. The rooms sell by the night or the week, and a portion of guests stay there for months. Apparently, the youth fancy themselves nomads...vagabonds with six-figure salaries. These properties run almost touch-free. Very little service. A dash quirky for my taste, but your generation loves this sort of nonsense. Apparently eliminating any semblance of luxury increases asset value in the new world," Julian remarked with disdain.

"Julian, one problem. I'm not a hotel guy."

"Was my information incorrect? Do you not own a hotel you plucked from the foreclosure rolls while working at the bank? Quite industrious of you." He paused. "Though, some would say unscrupulous."

"Own...yes. Run...no. I pay a management company to run it. I don't know hotels. The real estate was worth more than I paid for the hotel."

"If you pay the bills, I assume you know more than you think. But don't be too caught up in that thought. Your new partner is well equipped to run the hotel. She owns two more of these: one in Charlotte, North Carolina and one in Austin, Texas."

"MY PARTNER?" Will said with a furrowed brow and tinge of discontent. "You didn't say anything about a partner."

"Her name is Charlotte Teague, yet unfortunately, she's chosen to be called Char in the articles I've read." Julian reached into the green folder and produced a bound dossier on the subject. "Ms. Teague is the gift, son."

Will exhaled audibly through his nose while opening the dossier. He stared at her image. "She looks...interesting."

Julian nodded. "Interesting indeed. There are numerous articles on her story. Take a few minutes and read the snippets."

Will began to read silently. As the articles suggested, Char (pronounced "Shar") Teague was twenty-seven when she started purchasing houses in the Raleigh area and renting them out nightly. Though the business journals focused on the dollars and cents, the local newspaper highlighted Char's apparent struggle with autism and her disorder (lexical-gustatory synesthesia) as a human-interest story—though Will did not recognize the condition. Regardless of the impetus, in three short years her inventory grew to fifteen houses. Much to her chagrin, the zoning and city ordinances in Raleigh were too restrictive and Char began to take heat from the local government, which was beginning to crack down on nightly rental infringements due to the bellyaching of older residents in the city's neighborhoods. As they threatened to shut her down, a dingy thirty-unit apartment building on the west side of the city (near the university) became available.

While convincing the zoning authorities that they were unjustly targeting a female-owned business—there were dozens of homes on platforms like AirBnB on any given night in Raleigh—she successfully convinced them to rezone the apartments so she could convert them to a hotel. Char sold the fifteen homes, netting approximately $815,000 of pure profit. That gave her the capital she needed to completely transform the property.

Launch Pad Hotel epitomized the idea of an edgy neighborhood hangout and drew attention for its unique offering. It was gritty, but thoughtful. As the Triangle Business Journal put it: "It's as if a chic Brooklyn apartment was transplanted to Raleigh, NC, as a hotel room."

"I'll admit, this really is an awesome property. But how'd you get this woman, Char, to commit to the Golden project?" Will asked.

"You haven't done that yet," Julian chided.

"I'm sorry. I'm not following you. Please don't tell me you haven't even—"

Julian interrupted. "I'm not in the business of silver-platter service. Winning the RFP means nothing if it doesn't satisfy your underlying interests. Winning for winning's sake is positional. You don't need an empty building; you said it yourself, Paul Tollison wants to see a new development. Bringing the right tenant, like Char Teague, serves both the city and yourself, does it not? Therefore, it is time to attract the tenant you want. You did not expect me to find a partner in the newspaper, did you?" Julian said wryly.

"This is nonsense. You can't read a few articles from a business journal and magically decide that this lady is going to say yes to a site in Golden...a building I don't even control." Will was visibly upset. His face was flushed and his eyebrows raised to form an expression of surprise and anger at Julian's unfounded assertion. "How am I supposed to pull her onto my team?"

"Have you not paid attention to any of the rules thus far?"

"You know I have, but—"

"Then apply them," Julian said sharply.

"And what makes you think this Char Teague is even willing to listen?"

"Math," Julian answered.

"You're going to have to be more specific than that."

"I've been active, Will. Rule Number One. As I explained, Char Teague has three Launch Pad properties, each one slightly larger than the last, proving the size of our building is not an issue. Her third Launch Pad, in Austin, is in a market with which she was unfamiliar. By all accounts, Colorado emerges as the most obvious and elegant next move."

"Okay. None of that proves anything. And that's not math," Will declared.

"Your impatience is off-putting," Julian responded, deadpan. He reached into the green folder and produced the rest of its contents for Will, which totaled roughly twenty-five pages. "Here's the math. As I said before, research and preparation is a form of listening."

"What am I looking at?" Will quizzed as he began scanning the first pages.

"Loan documents, company operating agreements, and profit and loss statements for each of the three hotels," Julian responded. "There's something afoot...a trend. I believe it will help you recruit Ms. Teague onto the team. I simply can't put my finger directly on it."

"Well, that puts us in an awkward position, doesn't it?" Will said sarcastically.

"Your former relative, Dexter, the one who presents himself as middle-aged hippie. Do you think we could enlist his help?" Julian asked.

Will held the papers upright in both hands. He tapped them against the tops of his legs to straighten the stack and then reached across the console, all but snatching the green file folder. After tucking the papers inside, he said, "This is perfect. I'm running all over town trying to put this project together and now you're asking Dex to join the fun. Tell you what, he's the best I've ever seen at sizing up a deal, and if he calls this a dead end, how about we just call it quits?"

"PETULANT. That's it. Eight letters. Thank you, Vince. The word is PETULANT indeed." Julian leaned down and filled in the squares of his crossword puzzle while Will again questioned the origin of his inquiries. "I agree with your proposition. Let's exercise some patience and see what Dexter thinks, shall we?" Julian asked rhetorically while scribbling. He kept his head down, seemingly entranced by the puzzle. Will began to open his mouth, to elicit more information about Char Teague, but stopped himself short. He sat quietly as Julian mumbled clues to himself, occasionally stopping to pen the answer. In mere minutes they were back at the streetlight in front of Will's home. Julian said nothing as Vince pulled to a stop. Will shook his head, gathered the documents from the green folder, and exited the Town Car.

Chapter 13

"What you aim at determines what you see."

—Jordan Peterson

36 DAYS TO RFP

"Don't be a douchebag, Ron," Nick Spencer barked into the speakerphone, his polished black loafers resting on his desk. Michael, his CIO/assistant, could easily hear him from the other office. The reality that Michael could hear him seemed to fuel Nick's volume level when he was being his most assertive. "I'm seriously tired of answering questions like this. No, I don't know how to predict the theoretical effects of the next pandemic on the economy. Nostra-fucking-damus couldn't predict that, except that it would suck in the short run. But, tell you what, I can tell you I see opportunity right now in the real world. Winter is coming, and there's a shitload of guys out there with no winter coat. It's time to move some money."

The clichés were flowing like wine in recent conversations, and so was the pressure. His stockpile of investors, mainly consisting of wealthy Texas tycoons, was growing restless; their fortunes were not built by sitting on the sidelines, and even though many were semi-retired, they were a feisty bunch willing to take reasonable risk.

Nick had proven savvy in the face of financial decline. That was admirable, but the real litmus test would be on the other end of the cycle. That was obvious. If the $128 million under his watch was going to turn into a cool billion, then his calculated moves in the uncharted waters of a rising interest rate would need to be smart, and more importantly, noticeable. Being noticeable would attract more investors and more money.

"How do you feel about hotels?" the voice on the other end queried.

"There's upside. But I think it's in a newer wave of hotels. I've already made a measured bet there," Nick replied. He failed to elaborate on the fact that this measured bet was one of the few investments he had been able to get done in the last few months.

"How so?"

"The industry was moving this way before all this craziness. It's in the boutique, independent spaces. Nobody wants the big flags anymore. The best branding is about not being a brand. I dropped some mezz debt into one of the more interesting ones." Nick was referring to mezzanine financing, which sat in second position to the senior loan and thus warranted a higher interest rate. More risk, more reward.

"Mezz debt? You're not a lender. What the hell are you issuing debt for?"

"I'm sorry, Ron, would you like me to check in with you before I loan your money out at 15% with some potential for upside?" Nick's deftness with his clients was well practiced. Any time he produced a win, or even the potential for a large return, he would discuss it as if that particular client's money was the only money he invested. In truth, the paltry $2 million he placed in Launch Pad was less than 2% of the cash under his management. Ron's split of that return would be minuscule. But, for today, it was all Ron's money.

"Relax, Nick. Not bad. I know you've got instincts, but what's your play?"

"Right now, it's a simple rate grab. But I got a few ideas for a bigger move there, and I'm testing the waters. Think we might take a majority share in the whole brand. It's a female-owned company, and this lady is out there. She calls it Launch Pad. I like the story. I think it could grow, and if it does, we can place some real money with low risk." Nick, an ADHD poster child, began scrolling through his emails while still on the call. He'd made his point, and Ron's time was up—he was one of the smaller clients on Nick's list.

"How old is she?" Ron, a sixty-something and overweight Houstonite, asked.

Nick was reading an email from a colleague about the rise in private equity funding and missed the question. "What? Did you just ask how old she was?"

"Yes, how old is this hotel woman?"

"Why? You in the market?" Nick said facetiously.

"Does she know what she's doing?"

Nick was quiet.

"Nick?" Ron probed.

"I'm sorry, I was looking on my Outlook calendar for today's date. And sure enough, it's not nineteen-fucking-fifty, Ron. I can't believe you just asked me that, you misogynistic old bastard. Of course, she knows what she's doing, or I wouldn't have placed money with her. But maybe I'll consult Lee Iacocca before making any more high-level decisions. Would that make her owning the company more palatable?" Nick reveled in the chiding. He had enjoyed at least one night of steaks, wine, and after-dinner drinks with everyone on his client list. It was an old boys club, and at thirty-three years old, he was the young talent. Each of them respected his hubris in spite of the fact their finances heavily outweighed his; their egos could take the abuse—or at least most of them could.

"Isn't Iacocca dead?" Ron asked, as if the absurdity of the conversation warranted hard facts.

"Look, you gotta trust me here. I'm placing bets today. We'll move bigger in the near future. I know you get the idea, Ron. I think it was your idea to limp into a few positions on the tail end of this down market anyway, wasn't it?"

"Yes, it was. I remember telling you that."

Nick could envision Ron smiling on the other end; toying with these guys had become too easy. "Now, give me time to see this through. I'm out there placing bets right now. The real capital push comes next. I gotta go, Ron. I got a hundred calls to make today."

"Okay, keep it going, Nick," Ron said as Nick hit the speaker button on his phone, ending the call.

Nick Spencer leaned his head back and sighed deeply. "It's time to own Launch Pad, Nick," he said under his breath.

Chapter 14

*"Only when the tide goes out do you discover
who's been swimming naked."*
—Warren Buffett

35 DAYS TO RFP

"She needs cash, dude." Dexter sat down in one of the two large royal blue chairs in Will's repurposed dining room. He plopped the green file folder onto the side table between them and assumed a comfortable posture with his arm draped over the back so he faced Will directly.

"Char Teague? That's convenient," Will replied. "Shame I don't have any cash. How do you know she's short? Are her profit and loss reports bad?"

"No, her P&Ls aren't great, but they aren't the problem. The Launch Pad in Austin just opened a few months ago and these bad boys take about a year to hit stabilized numbers. When they do, her income's gonna be solid. The problem is she wasn't ready for Austin...at least, her bank account wasn't ready."

"You have her bank statements?" Will questioned, surprised that Dexter could have that level of information.

"I don't need them, man. I'm just looking at the capital stack on this Austin deal compared to her other two hotels."

Dexter referred to the "capital stack" as the various equity sources Char Teague used to purchase hotels. Before the 2008 recession, banks typically loaned up to 80% of a property's value—known as the loan-to-value ratio—but afterward, they shifted to a more conservative loan-to-cost approach, reducing their exposure by basing loans on a project's total cost rather than its projected value. Additionally, banks lowered the loan-to-cost ratio to around 65%, forcing cash-starved developers to rely more on two dubious sources: mezzanine financing and private equity, both of which carried higher interest rates. As the deals grew, so did the sources of capital.

Scrutinizing these sources could be an art. A bank underwriter could look at the capital stack and deduce the quantity of the total capital supplied. A talented investor, on the other hand, could look at the capital stack and determine the quality of the developer. Big difference.

"Okay, and what does the capital stack on Austin tell you?" Will quizzed.

"Let's back up. On her first hotel in Raleigh, it was as simple as they get. Char borrowed everything she could from the bank and put up the rest of the cash herself...about $500,000. The whole project was a little under $3.5 million, probably worth $6 million today. The hotel in Charlotte was second. It opened about three years later. She borrowed the money from the First Federal Bank of Charlotte and these guys actually made her a small mezzanine loan, too. Brought the loan-to-cost up to 75%. The rest was her cash again."

"And Austin?" Will, well-versed in banking, was following the line of reasoning. "I'm guessing she was tapped out of cash after the Charlotte deal."

"Austin is a friggin' mess. It's bigger than her others, I think fifty-five rooms. And she started renovating the building four months after she opened Charlotte...four months, man. You think she was cash flowing yet? Judging from these P&Ls, she's dumping money into the Charlotte deal." Dexter sat up in his chair and leaned in toward Will.

"And that's where the wheels come off. It gets weird. She formed a company to get the Austin loan, Austin Launch Pad Partners LLC, with a pretty complex operating agreement. Her agreements on the first two hotels are super simple, I mean really simple. Looks like the kind of fill-in-the-blank crap you get online."

"Alright, so if these operating agreement documents are complicated, that means she has partners in Austin," Will deduced. "Maybe one of them offered to use their own attorney to draft the documents. You know how that goes, some partner showing off their high-priced attorney. I bet she even paid the bill."

"Yeah, that would make sense. But there's more at play here, man. She got my least favorite type of capital, the mezzanine lender who wants control," Dexter said with disgust while uncrossing his legs. He bent forward, resting his elbows on his knees and placing the points of his fingers together from opposite hands, now fully engaged. "These guys are a special breed. Their operating agreement even goes back and ties into her two original operating agreements on the Raleigh and Charlotte deals."

"Why?" Will asked.

"Because if she defaults on this loan, they'll control her entire portfolio. Like I said, man, a special breed. I'm gonna be honest, I've never seen someone with the balls to ask for that kind of power before." Dexter reached for the green folder and thumbed through the pages until he found what he needed. "Here's the part I really don't like. Check out this math. Austin is a $16 million deal. There's a major lender, Chase Bank, placing $10.8 million. Chase also has a second note for $3 million at a higher interest rate. Then there's $2.55 million from a third source, a mezz loan from a group called Austin RE Fund III, which tells me they have other deals in Austin. I bet you anything they brought Chase Bank to the table."

"Wait! Hold on," Will said, placing his hand in the air to stop. Dexter paused as Will did the mental math. Will, possessing a banker's logic, was following the tranches of money as Dexter described them. After a short session of Will looking confusedly into the air for answers, his face scrunched up at the final tabulation. "You said $10.8 million, $3 million, and $2.55 million. That's $16.35 million. You said the deal was $16 million," Will blasted.

"Yep, these dudes made her over-borrow so they could make sure their first year's interest payments got paid. She has less than no money in this deal, and they control those first interest payments."

"That's not so bad. I'd love to have no money in a deal," Will said, half-jokingly, though he knew the strain debt could place on a project.

Dexter shook his head. "I rarely ever see a deal work out in the long term when the owner has negative cash in it. And these guys have the best of both worlds. They get 15% on their money and they own a big chunk of her company if she can't pay her interest. Using my old-school calculator, Char isn't getting paid a dime until this hotel is probably in its second or third year of operations."

"Damn, that's pretty heinous," Will realized.

"It doesn't stop there, man. You gotta remember, they've got uber aggressive rights in the operating agreement. I'm not sure she even redlined that thing before she signed it. There are all kinds of issues with it. Like I said, man, if she gets in financial trouble, they can take over all the hotels. They would even own the name Launch Pad. I can't stand vultures like that. This girl probably worked her ass off building this company and doesn't realize this group could take it all. I see this kind of thing all the time with software developers. They're totally focused on the product, dude. Don't even think enough about the deal structures. It's why I have a job."

"Do the P&L pro formas show that the deal will work? Should she be able to cover all the interest?" Will asked.

"Not sure," Dexter replied. "They barely covered the debt before the market softened. Her projections are pretty aggressive based on her other properties, and the world is just different right now, man. If her book of business doesn't skyrocket by year-end, she's in trouble."

"So I'm thinking she might not be the best tenant for the building in Golden I'm trying to do," Will said sullenly.

Dexter bit his lip. "Let me think about this for a few days. Where there's this much desperation, there's always a deal. And this lady might need some help."

Dexter had a contemplative look about him. Will had seen that look before.

The back door by the kitchen opened, and Will could hear Kirsty fumbling with her keys. Her heeled footsteps over the kitchen tile floor revealed her exact distance from the two men in the sitting room.

"How was work?" Will said without looking back into the kitchen, as if he was speaking to the space directly above Dexter's head.

"IT SUCKED," she hollered from the kitchen. "PS, NOT DOING DINNER TONIGHT. SELA HAS PRACTICE 'TIL SEVEN. GONNA SQUEEZE IN A YOGA CLASS. GRABBING MY BAG." Her tone was snappish. Will, sensing the unease, was content to leave her alone. Within a few seconds Kirsty had commandeered the bag and was out the door.

Dexter, changing his focus back to the conversation, turned to Will. "Your friend, Julian, you think he's up to meeting in person with me?"

"I don't know. He's pretty skittish. But, hey, he's the one that wanted you to look at these docs. Just come to our next meeting," Will offered.

"When is that?"

"No telling, but I'm sure it'll be soon."

"If you're cool with it, I'm in. Like I said, give me a day or two to think about this. There's an angle here." Dexter stood up, which prompted Will to stand. "I'm gonna hit the road." He reached over and gave Will a right-handed grip coupled with a left arm hug, and then headed out.

Finding himself alone, Will instinctively reached for his phone. He scrolled down the list of emails he'd skipped that morning. These rarely generated a return message unless he found himself with little to do. Will was about to respond to the first one when his phone switched to the incoming call screen and began ringing.

It was Kirsty calling already—not good.

"Is Dexter still there?" she said. Her tone had changed from snappish to concerned.

"No, he just left. What's got you bothered?" Will asked. "I could hear it in your voice earlier."

"I dug into him, Will," Kirsty said.

"You mean Julian?"

"Yeah."

"And?"

"He's for real," she responded.

"What does that mean?" Will asked. "Get specific."

"Julian Darrow is a minority partner on at least four high-rises in downtown Denver. He's the main guarantor on the loan for three of them. You know what that means."

"Yeah, my new friend isn't poor," Will said. "I'm guessing that's not all you found?"

"Not even close," Kirsty responded. "He has office holdings, land leases, industrial buildings. Apparently, the guy even master-leased an entire warehouse block and then subleased it to pot growers when that whole scene took off. Most of those are partnerships, and all of it is under separate company names. He's all over the place, Will."

"That's not surprising. Julian's an odd duck."

"Yeah, he is," Kirsty said. "He also used to work as a consultant on public projects on behalf of cities."

"What kind of consulting?" Will prodded.

"Negotiating with private developers," Kirsty informed him.

"Now that's the fox guarding the henhouse."

Kirsty sighed. "There's one more thing. Julian basically disappeared from consulting about a year ago. This guy's like a ghost."

"What the hell does that mean? How do you just disappear in your own town?"

"It's like he was blacklisted or..."

"Or what?"

"Or he's up to something dirty."

"Really? Those are the only two options?" Will said. "What about retirement? You think of that one? He's obviously wealthy."

"You're defending him?" Kirsty asked.

"Do I have to?"

"Not a single word of retirement. And not a single one of the cities he's worked with has mentioned him in over a year."

"Okay. But who cares, unless" Will paused. His voice softened as he said, "Let me guess, one of the cities was Golden, wasn't it?"

"Bingo," Kirsty answered.

"Hmmm." Will mused, considering the correlation. "Damn, how did you find all this stuff? I googled this guy and didn't come up with anything, literally nothing. And if it's all in separate companies, how did you piece all this together so fast? That's impressive, Boo."

Kirsty was silent.

"Kirsty?"

"You're going to be mad at me," she said.

"You earned some diamonds?" Will asked, humor being his only weapon against the tension.

Kirsty was silent again.

"What is it?"

"I called Brian," she said in an apologetic tone.

"WHAT!?" Will said emphatically. "You called Brian? What the hell, Kirsty? Now I know why you were pouting earlier at the house."

"That's not fair. I called him for you. He was my best option."

"I wouldn't have asked you if I knew this was your plan...calling that jackass."

"Well, you did. And he had info, didn't he?" she defended herself.

Brian Cole was a mortgage broker in Colorado Springs, and more importantly, Kirsty's ex-husband and father to Sela. Even more upsetting was the fact that Brian Cole was by all accounts—and his personal bank account—an extremely talented mortgage broker. His connections found him entangled in the networks of highly successful entrepreneurs.

Will attempted to gain his composure. "Kirsty," he said slowly into the phone as he rolled his head back and looked up at the ceiling. "I wish you hadn't done that."

"I know," she said. "But Brian has contacts I don't. He runs in those circles. He didn't know him, but someone in his office is friends with one of Julian's partners. He got the info from him."

"Did you tell him I was working with Julian?"

"No, of course not," she said.

"Good. I don't know why Julian has me fronting for him, but I can't have other people in the middle here. Especially not that asshole."

Kirsty was quiet for a few seconds. "Here's the thing. They don't know why he vanished either. Are you getting in over your head, Will?"

"What are you talking about?"

"You know what I'm talking about...with Julian," Kirsty said plainly.

"Julian? You think I'm getting in over my head with Julian? I guess that's good then," he said defensively.

"How could that be good?"

"Because here I was, worried about him being phony, but you're telling me he's so legit that I'm in over my head, which by the way is a pretty screwed-up thing to say."

"Me worrying about you is never a screwed up thing," Kirsty said boldly. The words landed heavy.

"Alright. Look. You don't have to worry about me. I'm not a kid out here. As a matter of fact, you of all people should know that. Julian's probably got some skeletons in his closet, I'll give you that, but this guy's not a hardened criminal. He's not built like that. Trust me."

"I always trust you, Will. You know that. I'm just telling you to be careful." She paused and drew a slow, audible breath. "This guy scares me a little."

"I hear you. Like I said, just trust me."

"I love you," she said before hanging up.

"You, too," he replied. "I'll be fine."

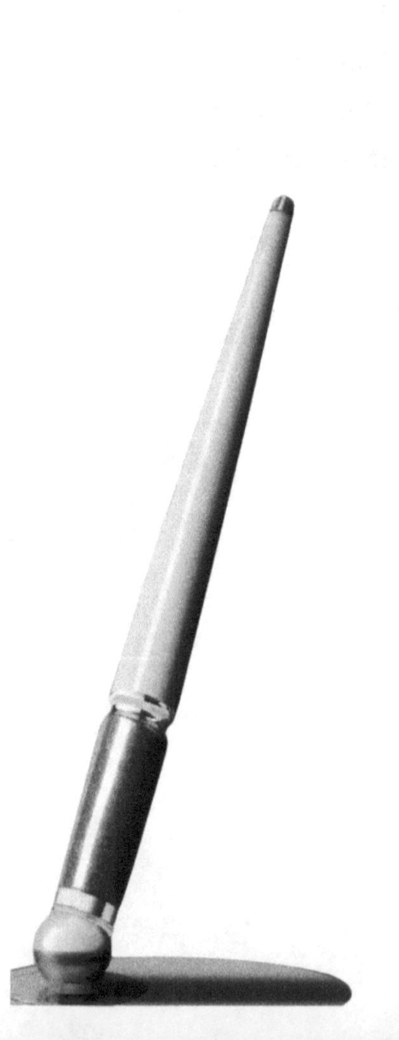

Chapter 15

"There is no such thing as a new idea."

—Mark Twain

34 DAYS TO RFP

To: Will Powell
From: Julian Darrow
Date: Tuesday, September 17, 2025, 11:10:22 MDT

Subject: My place. 6:45 p.m. Hippie invited if docs are reviewed.

Cheers,
Julian

Will found himself barreling down I-70 West toward Evergreen again. This time the black 4Runner held Dexter riding shotgun with the window down. Dexter was holding his right arm out the window and letting his hand lead a rhythmic, snake-like motion through the wind as he mouthed the words to the music he pushed to the SUV's sound system through his phone. Dexter did not leave the soundtrack of their trip to chance; it was pure '80s, guitar intros and solos aplenty.

"Hey, Dex, appreciate you going with me. Very cool of you."

"No problem, man. This sounds interesting."

Will allowed a moment of silence in deference to a guitar solo reaching crescendo. "But I gotta ask, why are you going?"

"Don't have to be anywhere else," Dexter replied as he returned to mouthing the words to the song.

"No, I mean it. Why are you heading to Evergreen to meet this crazy old bastard with me? You don't have to do this. I know you read the financials. You think there's an angle in here, don't you?"

"I know there's an angle here," Dexter offered.

"How can you be so sure?"

"'Cause everybody in the conversation has a problem to solve, man...including you."

Will paused and looked at Dexter briefly before returning his gaze to the road. He squinted in the sunset, and while nodding his head slowly, bit the side of his cheek—signaling the gravity of the conversation. "Don't pretend you're doing this for me. I didn't ask for backup, and I definitely didn't invite you into this mess. Julian's not sniffing around for friendship—he's circling for leverage. That's not someone I need in my corner."

Dexter didn't flinch. "I'm not here to hold your hand, man. I'm here because this thing needs someone who can close."

"I don't need looking after," Will snapped. "We're good, okay? I've said that. You know we're tight. And I love you, man. What happened with my sister—don't think you've got to earn points with me."

"Come on, Will. You know that's not me. We're friends." Dexter paused. "Look, there's something in it for me, too."

Will gave a bitter laugh. "Of course there is. You're not the guy who shows up without an angle. We'll walk out of here, and somehow you'll have brokered a deal that no one else saw coming. That's what you do, right? I'm just curious, what rulebook are you playing by? I want to know it."

Dexter smirked and put his left hand on Will's shoulder. "I wish I had it all figured out, man. But thanks. I'll take that as a compliment either way. One thing I'll say is I spend more time thinking about my approach to people than I do the numbers and figures. And I know I'm different that way. It pays to be different."

"Well, we got twenty minutes, so give me something for starters. Give me Rule Number One from Dexter Mathis's playbook."

"I don't have rules, dude."

"We got twenty minutes, and I'll turn this music off if you don't start talking."

Dexter looked out the window, his arm returning to the serpentine, wind-aided motion. Turning his head forward enough so the sound would carry in the SUV, but not looking at Will, he said, "Alright, for starters, we're much more like kids than we think."

Will's head instinctively shot back and cocked to the side. "That's your opening line? Unimpressed."

"You asked me, and I'm telling you. We like to think we're analytical, educated, disciplined, but really man, we're just kids running around acting like grownups. We're irrational, emotional, and stupid. We think we make decisions with logic, but we don't, at least not most of the time. That's a thought that runs through my head every day. Structures and numbers don't get deals done...it's understanding people. And I'll tell you, I'm just a kid, too. I make decisions at fifty just like I did when I was ten. Believe that with my whole soul. I swear that's what works for me, man."

"Okay, but what does that actually mean, though?" Will asked, now staring out through traffic as Dexter continued to watch his hand waving rhythmically from the tips of his fingers to his wrist out the window.

"Depends on your angle, I guess. What are you trying to accomplish?"

"Honestly, I want to negotiate better. Julian didn't show me that. I knew it. I've known it for a while now. He just gave me this crazy-ass opportunity to try it."

Dexter sat quietly, staring past his wind-aided hand. "Be nice to people. Make them feel good about themselves."

"Damn. You are a kid."

"Okay, fine," Dexter said. "Don't do that. Criticize their mistakes instead. Play devil's advocate instead. And when you do, see if they invite you to ride to some creepy old dude's house in Evergreen to do a deal with them."

Will smirked silently.

"It's hard to make deals if nobody wants you in the room."

"Are you saying it's that simple?" Will asked.

"Nope," Dexter replied. "Once you're in the room you gotta know how to play with the other kids."

Will turned to Dexter. "I think you're going to like Julian."

Twenty minutes (and four '80s anthems on the audio system) later, Will's 4Runner's tires made the unmistakable sound of transitioning from asphalt to the crushed limestone drive. It was a dry September afternoon, evidenced by the wake of dust left by the SUV as it climbed the series of switchbacks, causing Dexter to roll up his window.

"Nice place," Dexter said as he stepped out of the vehicle. He stretched his arms high in the air and yawned as he arched his back. The black Henley T-shirt hung open at the collar, and his dark jeans pulled tight over his snakeskin boots. "I like Julian's vibe. I could live out here."

"No, you couldn't," Will said, exiting the SUV as well.

"Sure I could," Dexter replied. "It's wickedly peaceful."

"Any man wearing those boots can't live out here. And 'wickedly peaceful' isn't a saying."

"I'll get you a pair, dude," Dexter responded.

There was a certain anxiety between them in the moment. It was a quiet that precedes a more meaningful moment on the horizon. Will was not willing to attribute it entirely to the fact they were at Julian's house, although Julian Darrow did elevate his senses. No, Dexter seemed to have an idea in mind, pre-baked before their talk, of course; vibrations just below the surface that only good friends or family could feel, and Will was getting that feeling. He was still ruminating on the idea that Julian and Dexter had more in common than he originally thought.

The RFP was due in five weeks and the fragility of this latest addition, Launch Pad Hotel, was beginning to weigh on him. It was no sure thing to say the least, a half-baked notion, but hopefully Julian had cultivated a grander plan for attracting Char Teague to the deal. At least, Will prayed that was the case.

They walked up the short run of steps, and Will rang the doorbell. The deep melodic chimes sounded, echoing through the sparseness of furniture and reverberating off the concrete floors and glass surfaces. Moments later the pair heard footsteps from a well-heeled Julian Darrow making his way to the front door.

"Good afternoon. I see you've enlisted the cavalry," Julian said with a smile. "You must be Dexter Mathis." He stretched out his hand. Dexter confidently offered a fist bump in lieu of the formal shake and the two shared a mildly awkward salutation.

"Not sure whether to bump or shake," Dexter said with a grin. "COVID ruined me."

"It ruined many people," Julian responded. "Hello, Will. Please, both of you come in."

Julian led the group across the living room and into his home office. He rolled his desk chair out from behind the soapstone-topped desk, which was organized just as before. Will again saw the large-format calendar and copious notes that filled each day—Julian's attention to detail was marvelous. And the other items were in perfect order too, including the single picture still facing away from the deep cognac leather chairs.

He offered the desk chair to Dexter and proceeded to usher Will and himself toward same cognac leather chairs as before. Then Julian leaned over, grabbed the pen and legal pad from atop the coffee table and rested them on the same bookshelf he had when Will visited the first time. Will noticed the rigidity of Julian's habits. It was as if Julian had to set the stage correctly for each performance. And in doing so, he commanded the room.

"So, Dexter, thank you for taking the time to accompany Will. I trust he has filled you in on the nuances of our agreement?" Julian queried.

"He did. And you found the right guy, Julian. Will knows more about the nuts and bolts of real estate development than anyone I know."

"Unfortunate," Julian responded dryly. "I can help you with networking," he said while looking at Dexter. He then looked briefly at Will and returned his gaze to Dexter. Neither of the younger men completely eschewed the notion that Julian might have been serious. "Assuming you reviewed the documents I sent with Will, perhaps you could give me your feedback."

Dexter opened the green file folder, licked his pointer finger, and began rifling through the pages until he found the ones he wanted. He picked them from the stack and began to hand them to Julian. "Launch Pad needs more fuel to launch," Dexter said.

Each property's entire profit and loss statement was reduced to three pages. All the hard work from the various employees milling about the properties could be summed up and judged objectively in a single report. The revenue categories were uncomplicated: rooms revenue, food & beverage, and other income. Char Teague kept it simple. However, the expense categories were a much more nuanced labyrinth of terms and concepts. Items like administrative & general and IT were loaded with hotel-specific jargon. But in the end, the bottom line was always the bottom line, and that was the figure any astute businessperson could understand.

Julian took the papers and studied them slowly. He was expressionless, his chin sinking slowly toward his chest as he followed the financial story on each sheet from top to bottom. "I presume you see something deeper in these figures. Enlighten me, Dexter."

"Okay, take a look at the three properties and add their bottom-line profits before loan payments."

Julian took a few seconds to flip through the stack and tabulate the three profit lines before the principal and interest payments. "It looks like roughly $1.5 million before the debt."

"Right," Dexter affirmed. "Here's the problem. The total debt payment between these three properties is almost $1.4 million a year. But it's just a little over a million if you subtract the Austin partner's payment."

Julian stood up, retrieved his legal pad and pen from the bookshelf, and began to pace the room while scratching notes on the pad. The room fell awkwardly quiet as he memorialized the current conversation in writing. Then, as if he were perturbed at the silence, he sat back down in the cognac leather chair. "I'm following," Julian said. "She has a dastardly payment to the Austin partner that is stifling her profitability. Proceed."

Dexter picked back up. "That's an understatement, man. Char Teague didn't have the cash she needed to do the Austin deal. Instead, she got the worst loan I've seen with even worse terms. She's paying a minimum of 15% on that last $2.55 million."

"And, again, that is crippling her profits," Julian stated.

"I'll put it this way, her payment to the Austin partner is more than her mortgage on the entire Raleigh hotel. It cuts her total profitability for the three hotels in half. If her projections are correct, she'll clear around $150,000 instead of the $400,000 she should be making."

"Should be making?" Julian asked.

"Yes, should be making, if that payment to the Austin partner was at standard interest rates."

"Troubling," Julian said.

Will, who had sat silently through Dexter's financial recap, chimed in. "She obviously has to restructure her debt. More importantly, it sounds like Launch Pad makes for a sketchy tenant. I'd be worried about her making the payments even if this lady did decide to come to Golden. Julian, this doesn't look good. What's plan B?"

"That is a poignant question, Will. What is Plan B? Suppose we go in a different direction. Do you have any thoughts on the matter?" Julian was doing it again: leading without leading. Will noticed it but did not want to stifle the momentum.

Will squinted slightly and pressed his lips together in thought. He then sat back and placed his hands on the arms of the leather chair. "Feels like a trap. Launch Pad is the exact type of product the city will salivate over. Downside is this woman's not in a position to expand. If she does, she'll end up with another equity partner like her Austin group and be in an even tighter cash flow position. To be honest, we'd be doing her a disservice to bring her in on this deal."

"And what about you, Dexter? Any thoughts?" Julian questioned.

"Yeah, I got one," Dexter said with reservation. "But it's a little more involved than just bringing Launch Pad on as a tenant."

"Let's hear it," Will encouraged.

"Okay, Launch Pad has a problem," Dexter began. "But it also has opportunities, man. Char is my kind of girl. She has a unique product, she understands her business, but she doesn't know how to finance and scale."

"Please tell me you're not talking about investing in this deal. You're talking about some major capital," Will interjected.

"Maybe not. It's like you said, this is a debt restructuring case all the way. I don't think there's much money I would need to inject, maybe none at all. Remember the software partner I mentioned when you brought up this hotel idea?"

"Yeah, but we didn't get into any detail. You just asked me to keep you in mind," Will said.

"Well, I own a minority share in a startup revenue management software company. It's called RevMax. I need a legitimate company to start using the software to prove its marketability. After I read the financials you gave me, I gave that partner a call. I hope you don't mind, Julian, but I showed him the numbers." Dexter looked to Julian for approval.

Julian shook his head and smiled. "Not at all."

"I asked him to review them overnight and give me a call the next morning. Turns out Char, even though her brand is fresh and cool, is operating in a very old-school way. She has two sales employees, and one of these dudes does almost nothing but revenue management. This isn't my expertise, but my partner, Preston, lives in this world. He can see in their expense structure that Launch Pad isn't optimizing their potential sales at all. She has this super unique product, but she could be doing soooo much more revenue. Preston thinks RevMax can cut their expenses by fifty grand a year. But more importantly, he's confident he can increase their revenue by a minimum of two-hundred-fifty-grand. He says that's conservative."

"But you can't get the bank in Austin to refinance that deal. The hotel just opened." Will, well versed in financing structures, knew the property values could not have appreciated enough to allow a refinance in such a short period of time.

"Right, actually none of her properties are ready to refinance yet. She's about a year away from that. But I was going down a different road. If they all three start to use RevMax software, then I have a different asset with an obvious growth story."

Will sat up quickly in his chair. "You're gonna borrow it against the software company's new income stream. That's brilliant, Dex." The conversation had shifted into lending territory, a comfort zone for Will.

"Not sure about brilliant," Dexter replied. "I'll borrow against my ownership. Launch Pad will be the first real client for RevMax. We'll use it as a proof-of-concept story. And if it all comes together, Preston will be trying to figure out where to spend all his new income."

"Interesting," Julian said.

Dexter leaned back in the rolling desk chair and stretched his arms out to the sides.

"I like the Launch Pad angle by itself. But if I can help grow two companies at once, and not put up much cash, this is a deal I could get excited about." He turned and looked at Will. "It would be pretty special, man."

"First things first, we'd need to get Char on board," Will added. "I know I'm Captain Obvious here, but we have four weeks to win an RFP and our main attraction has no idea she is part of the show."

"Gentlemen." Julian stood up. "I believe we have our marching orders. Welcome to the team, Mr. Mathis." He escorted Will and Dexter down the hall and through the living room to the front door. As the two men exited, Julian placed his hand on Will's shoulder from behind, slowing him down and separating him from Dexter. In barely more than a whisper, he said, "Did you learn something today, Will?"

"Dexter's got a hell of an idea."

"Indeed," Julian said. "A hell of an idea," he added with a smirk. "There's a rule to absorb here today, son."

"And what is that?" Will asked.

"We shall see."

Chapter 16

"The power of a relationship lies with whoever cares less."

—Uncle Wayne, Ghosts of Girlfriends Past

32 DAYS TO RFP

There were people running outside the window. It looked like that every day—people running. They weren't headed anywhere. Some were fast, others ambled painfully up and down the sidewalks. The bulk of them were young and driven, earbuds filling their heads with motivational music or TED talks. The streets teemed with them. They were bees buzzing about in an urban garden. On any given day, rain or shine, they passed below her second-floor window, which served as the backdrop to the large computer screen in her Glenwood Avenue office space, a single room inside the Launch Pad Hotel on the west side of Raleigh, NC.

Her menagerie of runners (the regulars receiving quirky names like Pinky, Jazz Dance, and Smurfette) were constant inspiration for her daydreaming. Admittedly, they did not know she existed as their perilous pace set about the sidewalks outside her window. The runners pushed themselves to whatever physical extreme they felt comfortable. Her thoughts drifted between them in an imaginative haze. It wasn't unproductive; daydreaming was a necessary part of Char Teague's creativity. Though she never met any of them, they were the closest things to friends she had—or wanted.

The urban garden produced new runners daily. She would never admit it, but dopamine surged each time she caught a glimpse of one of her own, especially Pinky. Pinky caused a taste of sweet caramel to form in her mouth. The taste of caramel, she had come to observe, was the taste of contentment. Char tasted things she shouldn't, or at least that others couldn't. She knew it made her different, strange even. The phenomenon started when she was nine. She didn't like to think about why it started; those were tough memories. But, for sure, nine years old was the first time she remembered tasting emotions. Of course, at nine, she did not understand the absurdity of that fact. Her predilection to the sense of taste was innocent and unnamed. She simply tasted things she shouldn't. The runners, however, didn't know that detail; they were the distant friends to whom she occasionally whispered personal, sometimes lonely, thoughts.

"Drones," she mumbled to herself as she set back to rifling through the emails, viewing her screen through vintage thick black glasses. Her fingers moved at lightning speed. Click. Respond. Click. Respond. Char Teague was in a hurry. That was the norm now. Before, she used to walk her dog or sit in the park and pound out notes on her laptop. She remembered making calls when she wanted, even though she found conversation exhausting when she did. And she missed the luxury of having time to read at night. Not that it was easier when she only had the nightly-rental houses, just simpler. It was convenient to forget the challenges she faced before Launch Pad: late-night messages from disgruntled guests or the plumbing leaks that seemed to pop up at the most inopportune times. It was easier to remember things like having the time to read alone at night without fear of constant notifications dinging on her phone.

It was 12:15 p.m. and Char was on her second black coffee, sipping from a silver insulated mug. She did not enjoy drinking it like she used to; she now used it as a means of fuel. There was a small, scuffed section on top of her black wooden desk where Char, without looking away from her computer screen, would instinctively grab the mug and then bang it back down quickly when she needed her heavily tattooed right arm to return to the trackpad or keyboard. The rest of her desk was covered in sticky notes, printed spreadsheets, two iPhones, and a protein bar wrapper. Her diet was balanced: equal parts coffee and refrigerated peanut butter protein bars.

One of the iPhones began to ring. Business phone. It rang a lot. No time to think, no time to plan, just reacting. She had to admit, it was definitely time to upgrade the system, but Char needed time to do that, or maybe she just didn't want to let that part go.

"Launch Pad," Char answered with her customary few words.

"Hello?"

"Launch Pad. Can I help you?" Char asked.

"Yes, is this Char...Char Teague?" The voice quivered slightly, not standing up to the brazenness of the call.

"She expecting you?" she said with a tinge of annoyance. Char resorted to that line from her days in rental houses. She never knew if it was a prospective guest or a vendor looking to get paid.

"No, she's not," Will replied. "But I'd like to speak with her."

"May I tell her what it's about?" Char said. Though annoyed, her years in hospitality afforded her a certain level of decorum.

"I have a property I'd like her to look at for the next Launch Pad."

Char sat quietly for just a moment. It was awkward. She enjoyed silence, but silence in the presence of another person made her uncomfortable.

"Hello?"

"Interesting." Her voice changed as she got out of character. "This how you go after business? Cold calling hotels?"

"No. I'm cold calling your hotel, because I'd like you to consider bringing your hotel to Colorado." He had blown Char's cover.

"I don't give a shit about opening another Launch Pad," Char said, completely ignoring the fact that he addressed her directly.

"Nice." Will was unfazed. "You're definitely the Char Teague I've read about."

"You must read some obscure articles. Can I help you...?" Her voice trailed off. She realized she had not gotten his name, or didn't remember it.

"Will Powell," he said. "I'm working on a project in downtown Golden, Colorado, right outside Denver. I read an article about Launch Pad, the product and the markets they're in. You have a really interesting concept."

"Uh huh," Char replied dismissively. "Kind of far away to be reading up on me, isn't it?"

"I'm resourceful," Will said. "Anyway, Char, I would like to discuss bringing your concept to the Denver area. It's exactly the type of hotel we need in the market."

"Not interested. I hate the Denver area."

"Okay," Will pressed on. "What if I wanted to talk about not just bringing the hotel to Golden, but also giving you a million dollars for a part of your company?"

The thought of selling a piece of her company was tangy, like licking batteries. It was metallic and acidic, a familiar taste. She swallowed hard. "I'd say, 'Will'...it's Will, right?"

"Yes. Will Powell," he said confidently.

"Gotcha. I'd say, 'I'm fucking busy, Will. Stop calling me.'"

Chapter 17

"I never learn anything talking.
I only learn things when I ask questions."
—Lou Holtz

31 DAYS TO RFP

"Will Powell," Don Andino exclaimed as he stood up and walked out from behind his desk. He was an elfish man of no more than five feet four inches, which gave him a certain level of approachability when he smiled. He had a dark, Middle Eastern complexion and spoke with a faint accent, though Will could not pinpoint the origin.

Don volunteered his hand for a shake. The warm greeting was much appreciated following Will's recent exchange with Char Teague; that wound was still fresh. "It's a pleasure to meet you, Mr. Andino."

"Mr. Andino?" Don said with indignation. His leathery palm suggested there were many days of hard work in his past, but the strong scent of cologne reminded him were many years behind him. "Don't give me that bullshit, it's Don. Only bankers and lawyers call me Mr. Andino. Have a seat over here, friend. I'm glad you reached out." He ushered Will over to one of the two chairs fronting his massive mahogany desk.

"Now remind me, where have we met?" Don said with the mysterious Middle Eastern accent.

"The last place I saw you was the RFP meeting at the City of Golden."

"Ah yes, that's right. That's a pretty large building. Tell me, what's your interest in it?" Don asked.

"I would ask you the same thing."

Don grinned. "I like that. No nonsense. Okay, I'll tell you my interest. It's to protect the building. Very simple."

"To protect the building?" Will quizzed. "Come on."

"To protect the building for a fee," Don said more precisely. "And to hopefully do the construction project after." He had a jovial demeanor that made light of the conversation.

"So why go through the gymnastics of the RFP process?" Will quizzed. "They're looking for a total development. They're not looking for construction bids."

"Because I have to."

"I don't understand."

Don rocked back in his chair. "I love RFP's. They're childish. The whole damn thing is silly. Instead of letting the free market work, they issue a blanket request to the public and give them a bullshit timeline to submit a proposal." Don paused. "It's a circus."

"So why do they do it?" Will asked.

"It's not the city officials' fault. They hate the system, too. It's a liability issue. They'd rather work directly with a developer to put a deal together, and a lot of times they do. They'll work a deal behind the scenes for months and then put out an RFP without much press. I swear that's where these ridiculous timelines started. They know damn well you can't put real deals together that quickly. You can have the idea in that timeline, but you can't put the whole deal together."

Will interjected. "So why are you interested in this RFP?"

"I'm not," Don replied. "Like I said, I'm interested in protecting the building, and the construction afterward. The important part is to get them focused on the right thing. Look around this office. It's what I do."

Will had canvased the office upon entering. The dark wood-paneled walls were covered in impressive buildings. He recognized several of the taller ones that dotted the Denver skyline. Will could imagine the comfort Don would have speaking to a developer in this office. It was a basic storyboard. Behind Don's head were photographs of varying sizes in myriad different frames, many of them gold, but they all had a cohesive theme: Don hobnobbing with the elite. There were past governors, city officials, developers and, curiously, photos with past presidents: Bill Clinton and George W. Bush. Don's political allegiance was wavering, and quite possibly for sale. One pass through Don's office would be enough to convince almost anyone to sign a contract without speaking with him directly.

"The Telemark Building is a great example of this...this damn stupidity," Don continued. "Nothing will come of it. You've got a fifty-thousand-square-foot building that looks like shit in downtown Golden and six weeks to put together the perfect plan. So my job is to get the city refocused. They left the RFP open-ended, no guideline. My proposal will be to demolish the interior, clean the exterior, and winterize the building. I'll get the building looking its best. After the RFP falls through, they'll be holding on to this empty asset. Telemark is moving out and winter is coming. If that plumbing freezes, they'll have bigger problems."

"That's brilliant," Will jumped in. He chuckled and repeated, "Winter is coming." He was truly impressed by the thoughtfulness of Don's approach. He had underestimated him.

"It is coming." Don smiled. "They'll collect these proposals in October. Any proposal will have some lengthy due diligence request in it. That building will require all kinds of consultants and engineers to walk through it before any reputable developer will purchase it. I don't need to win the RFP. I'll leave that to someone else who wants the headache."

The door behind Will opened and a voice interrupted. "You have a call on Line 1."

Will did not need to turn around; he could smell the perfume and hear the immaturity in the voice. Judging from Don's overall vibe, Will assumed the young woman was a knockout.

"Who is it?" Don questioned.

The young knockout, still behind Will, attempted to mouth the words so that Will would not hear, yet couldn't help but whisper "Sharon Peyton" very quietly—just not quietly enough.

Don wrinkled his nose and shook his head once. "I'll call back," he said, quietly mouthing the words back to her. Will felt invisible. Obviously they knew he could hear them, but both pretended that the quiet whisper would somehow dance around him. And he, in turn, pretended not to hear.

"It's about focus." Don picked up where he left off. "When I submit the RFP, the city will realize that winterization is important. It will become a focus, and their timeline will be too tight to take it back out to market. I will have it all put together for them, the winterization plan, the cost breakdown, a narrative about why it's necessary to protect their investment, an investment they paid for with the citizens' tax dollars."

"That makes a ton of sense," Will said. "But what if they actually choose someone from the proposals? There's a chance this gets put together. I'm planning on taking a real run at this. I believe it could be a viable hotel site, and I think I have an operator." Will said, knowing the last part was a stretch.

Don leaned in and placed his elbows on the desk. "I hope you do, and I hope you get it, friend. I'll have just submitted the winterization plan. I'll have just told them about the risk they hadn't contemplated yet, and I'll ask them to share the proposal if they do award the project to someone else. What do you think will be part of their first conversation with you? And who do you think they'll suggest?"

Will nodded. He didn't need to respond. Don's plan was solid. Having surveyed the pictures of completed projects, though, another question came to mind. The walls in Don's office were peppered with projects that were all north of $25 million, and he assumed a few were nearing the $100 million range. There had to be another angle to this effort. Something he wasn't sharing.

"I get everything you just said, Don. But this winterization contract can't be very large. I'm looking at these buildings you've built. Your overhead has to be pretty big to run a company like this. Surely you can't make that amount of money doing building winterization projects."

Don was shaking his head before Will finished. His excitement in imparting knowledge to Will was evident as his gestures became larger and his face more animated. Will noticed the same look when speaking to Dexter about his approach to investing. There was an air of accomplishment in their voices when dumping their knowledge on him. At the moment, Don, a tough guy by reputation in a tough industry, was almost giddy.

"No, no that's not right. You can't compare one of those buildings on the wall to this. It's two different worlds. It's about margins. And again, it has to deal with focus."

"How so?" Will asked.

"Let me tell you a story," Don said. "My father immigrated to Brooklyn as a child from Iraq in 1951." Don motioned to a small black-and-white photograph lost within the montage of elitism. It was of a man and a small boy behind the counter of what appeared to be a general store. Will had missed that picture originally. "He was ten years old when he got here. His father, my grandfather, had nothing in his pockets when he got to the states, so my father started working in the local hardware store owned by an Irishman with no family. There was a shitload of Irish in Brooklyn back then. Anyway, my father dropped out of school around eighth grade to start working in the hardware store full-time. That's him in the picture." Don turned and pointed to the boy in the photograph. "Twenty years later he bought the store from the Irishman. He had saved every nickel he could, and in truth, I think the old guy loved my father enough to take way less than the store was worth.

"And when I was around ten, he took me aside one day and explained what the Irishman had taught him. You see, every asshole knew what a lightbulb, a box of screws, or a roll of duct tape costs. That was the stuff they bought all the time, and they all knew what to do with it. They were focused on the price. He had to keep the margins low. The real profit margin was all on the specialty items, especially if they had to order it. On the specialty items, they were focused on service. They needed someone who could coach them to purchase the right item." Don paused and leaned over his desk toward Will. "You see, a man doesn't come into a hardware store to buy a drill, Will. He's buying a hole in the wall. That's what he's really buying. He just doesn't know how the hell to get it there. And when a man's trying to get help with something he doesn't understand, price is secondary."

Don glanced at the buildings behind Will. "Do you know the margins on commercial construction contracts these days, Will?" He paused briefly before answering, "4 or 5%. That's it. The margin is so low because owners are focused on the fee and making sure they don't get screwed. My construction fee for private deals is always 4%, especially with new clients. It builds trust because they know it's a fair, competitive rate. Owners typically care about two things: the total project cost and the contractor's fee. We focus on keeping our fee low and our professionalism high—that's how we get in the door. If a project is over budget, we work with designers to bring costs down."

Will thought for a moment, then asked, "Okay, so it's all about your fee...but what about the Golden project? The winterization bid can't be more than a million and a half. At 4%, that's…" Will trailed off, doing the math.

Don interrupted. "My fee won't be 4% there. I keep it at four with private developers, but cities are different. With them, it's not about price—it's about completing the project without issues. That's how they keep their jobs. You won't see my fee outlined in the proposal. Instead, there'll be detailed pages on the scope of services and why they're critical. At the end, there'll be a lump-sum price, and my margin will be reasonable, but it won't be 4%."

Don said the word "reasonable" with emphasis—too much emphasis.

"Look, friend, I need to jump on a conference call here in a few. You tell me if you need any help putting together your proposal. I have an estimating department that can help with your cost estimates on the front end. And I have connections in Golden, at the city, that can help you get this project through council. I'd love to build this project if you get the proposal." Don eased forward in his oversized chair and stood, the action barely changing his height.

"Thank you very much for offering," Will said as he stood. The question of why Don was being so candid was burning in his brain. "I'll take you up on the pricing estimates. It would be helpful to see numbers. But with this tight timeline, all I'll have is a basic concept, nothing too detailed."

Don walked around the desk to shake Will's hand. "I've been doing this a while. Nobody has more than a concept in an RFP. Once I have your concept, I can put something together in a week. No problem. If you would do me one favor."

"Sure," Will said. "What is that?"

"Maybe hint somewhere along the line that the city needs to winterize the building. They can sometimes use a little prodding."

Will smirked as he shook Don's hand and exited the office. Don was a pro. He had obviously orchestrated similar meetings hundreds of times in his career. Before Julian entered his life, Will would have dismissed Don Andino as a hard-charging, aggressive guy who bullied his way to the top; not the guy with whom he just spoke, the guy that aimed to understand focus and its causality. Don Andino built his entire approach around understanding the basic principles of positions versus interests. He tweaked the rule to suit his business, but it was Julian's rule nonetheless. At every turn, it seemed Will was running into the same reality. He needed to step up his game.

Chapter 18

"There is no force so potent as a promise that turns into pressure."

—Robert Greene

30 DAYS TO RFP

"Repeat after me, Warren," Nick Spencer offered with a grunt, raising his black loafers high enough to plop them on his desk. Warren was one of the investors Nick felt needed a double dose of bravado.

"I..." He waited for a brief moment. "Come on. Repeat it. I, Warren, will never..."

"Piss off, Nick," Warren, a trust fund warrior in his early forties retorted. Warren's father was also an investor and close personal friend of Nick's uncle.

Nick, seeing that Warren would not participate, continued anyway. "...will never...ever...bring Nick another shitty investment idea that involves my family."

"It's in a great area for condos. The demographics are some of the best in the state. We could own 50% of the deal for $4 million bucks." Warren's pleading sounded desperate.

"You're not listening. There's a zero percent chance that deal grows legs. I can't put money into something that never gets off the ground. It's a waste of time and effort. It's like packing your golf clubs in the trunk while it's raining...what's the point?"

"Just look at the demographics," Warren continued.

"Demographics? Your fucking family's in it. That's a

demographic."

"Maybe I should pull the funds and do it myself?" Warren proposed. He manufactured a forceful delivery, but failed to produce a proper punch.

"By all means, please do. Tell you what, I'll go to the bank today and ask them to hand me $4 million in cash...real cash. That way you can literally light it on fucking fire in the parking lot and save yourself some time."

"You can't talk to me like that, Nick."

"Warren, somebody needs to be honest with you. I take this shit seriously. Your money is my money. If I can't be real with you, there's no reason for you to use me."

Nick's investors rarely called when everything was simple, when the universe produced 10 and 12% returns just for showing up in the morning. When returns were plentiful, they found it more appropriate to forward a comical email chain or text a pic of a fish they caught in the Keys. Those were simple times. His relationship could be splendidly topical, even distant. Nick's monthly newsletter, delivered in the form of an email blast, offered solace to the group. The last newsletter stopped just short of an all-out endorsement of the hotel industry's potential. But he had to be careful. The Warrens of the world were the minority; most of the group were wealthy businesspeople with finely tuned olfactory for sniffing out half-baked motives. They were open to the wise musings from their secret sage, yet the fundamentals had to be sound. His recommendations would be whispered at dinner parties, or offered as advice to those less fortunate who didn't have a Nick Spencer to alchemize their holdings into gold. At present, Nick needed to convince the entire group of one common objective: a major investment in Launch Pad Hotels.

Michael, the CIO/assistant, walked in and dropped a note on

Nick's desk while Nick was still lecturing Warren on his condo idea. It read: "Your uncle on Line 2."

Nick craned his neck forward, feet still propped up on his desk, and squinted a bit as he read it. His eyes widened slightly in recognition. "Look, Warren, bottom line, we'll find better deals. Stay away from your backwoods, roughneck in-laws. They can't spell 'condominium' and now that you're disgustingly rich, they're going to have all kinds of shitty ideas...dangerously shitty ideas. Let's talk in a month. There are deals coming down the pipeline. Just leave the investments to me. I'll bring the interesting ones to you, the ones that take some brainpower. That's what you pay me to do. I gotta go." He hung up hastily before Warren said anything, which might have happened either way, but calls from Nick's uncle took special precedence. And, besides, he had successfully both berated and cajoled Warren, a standard tactic to put off further communication for weeks. Nick motioned to Michael to close the door. He instinctively slung his feet down to the floor and sat erect in his chair. As his finger hit the button for Line 2, he took a deep breath. "How's it going, Uncle Joe?"

Joe Spencer was the epitome of an oil tycoon—down-to-earth, approachable, and always the life of the party. With a deep, jolly laugh, he made his mark as a chemical engineer in a large, privately held oil company, quickly gaining a reputation for identifying underperforming wells and boosting their output with simple tweaks. As his career progressed, Joe seized opportunities to acquire wells, eventually building a successful business. By the late nineties, with $200 million in cash, he sold his company and retired, planning to travel with his family.

At the time, Joe's nephew, Nick Spencer, was a promising twenty-eight-year-old VP at Goldman Sachs. Joe, fond of Nick and eager to pass on his legacy, offered him a life-changing opportunity: an operating agreement for Boanerges Investments LLC. Nick would run the company and keep 100% of the fees while Joe retained profits from his own investment. To seal the deal, Joe handed Nick a deposit slip for $50 million. That evening, over scotch, Nick clutched the slip, overwhelmed by the responsibility.

"Hey, Nicky, what are you seeing in the market?"

Joe's regular check-ins were familiar and comforting to Nick, despite his reluctance to accept the help.

"It's dicey, Uncle Joe. The markets are fat, but real estate's gone to hell with these rates. The stuff that was overpriced in the low interest rate era is still inflated, maybe down 10% from the peak."

"They're coming, Nicky. What moves have you made?" Joe asked.

"Not much. Issued some debt at 14 to 15%, but it's boring stuff."

"Boring trades generate returns. People don't jump off buildings because of boring trades," Joe replied. "But why debt?"

"I'm setting up for a big move. I've got my eye on some hotels. It's risky, but I think it could be a homerun."

"Sounds risky."

"Investing is risky, Uncle Joe," Nick countered.

"The blood's in the water, Nicky. Now's the time to take positions with little downside," Joe advised.

Nick, eager to prove himself, responded, "Debt's easy, but these people are scared. I can grab some major assets in this mess."

"If they're scared, there's a reason. Don't make foolish bets, Nicky. Remember, these guys are watching the size of their prostates, not their holdings. There's no rebellion left in them. Nothing wrong with us managing some assets in this portfolio if they make a ton of sense. Send me over some info on the hotels and I'll take a look. Take care, and tell your dad hello." And with that Joe Spencer hung up before "Nicky" could say goodbye.

A sour feeling crept into Nick's belly. He admired his uncle to no end, but there was always one festering memory conjured up after a call with his Uncle Joe. On the night Joe Spencer handed Nick the check for $50 million, he did not ask Nick if he wanted to manage the fund—not even a thought as to whether Nick might have different ideas for their working relationship. He simply set up the company and handed him a check. And from that point on any time Joe Spencer insinuated they managed the fund together, it drove Nick up the wall. Maybe it shouldn't have, but it did. Joe Spencer seeded the fund, and without question influenced several of the other investors to trust Boanerges Investments with their hard-earned oil money. Nick would have to grant him that. In fact, Nick would have to admit there was no Nick Spencer, the fund manager, without the initial efforts of Uncle Joe. And possibly that also irked him over time, especially since Joe Spencer never made a single move within the fund. Nick was the guy; he was the one that dealt with the investors, did the research, and made the calls. The seed money was Joe Spencer's final effort as far as Nick was concerned. Nick had grown it from there. Nick was going to hold off a few days before sending him the hotel info. He didn't need Uncle Joe guiding his hand on what assets were prime for the picking. Nick managed the fund, and Nick alone.

Chapter 19

"Not adding value is the same as taking it away."

—Seth Godin

27 DAYS TO RFP

To: Will Powell
From: Julian Darrow
Date: Tuesday, September 24, 2025, 15:41:33 MDT

Subject: 6:45 p.m. tomorrow. Tell the hippie he can join. More the merrier.

Cheers,
Julian

Will stepped outside his home at exactly 6:45 p.m., his punctuality now second nature. Within seconds, the black Town Car appeared, as reliable as ever. He lingered, still stung by Char Teague's rejection of his $1 million offer for an undefined stake in her company. Julian didn't know about the failed attempt, and for now, Will thought it best to keep it that way. He would take the ride in silence, hoping to absorb more of the silver-haired gentleman's wisdom.

The Town Car came to a precise stop, its glossy hood reflecting the amber glow of the streetlight. Vince stepped out to open the rear passenger door, and Will, now accustomed to such gestures, waited like a dignitary. As the door swung open, the familiar scent of Julian's cigar drifted out, a warm contrast to the crisp evening air.

"Doctor's orders?" Will joked, sliding into the vehicle.

Julian pulled the cigar from his mouth with his thumb and two fingers, seemingly admiring it for its moist leaves and girth. "One never knows anymore. Today it's good for you, tomorrow it isn't." He returned the stogie to his mouth and enjoyed a long pull.

"Pretty sure it never was."

"For the soul." Biting down on the cigar, Julian peered into his lap. "Vince, I need a five-letter word for COURAGE. Starts with a B."

Will, now used to the random crossword outbursts, was more preoccupied by Julian's trivial schedule. "Why is it six forty-five every time? Day or night, it's always six forty-five."

Julian looked up from his notebook. Squinting through the smoke and brushing Will's query aside, he said, "How was your meeting with Don Andino? He's the man of the hour, is he not?"

"How'd you know about…" Will stopped short, his forehead creasing with contempt. "You're something else. I'll give you the short version."

"Was it fruitful?"

"He's not a challenger. He spent most of the time talking about putting in a proposal to winterize the building. Don doesn't want any part of the full development. I think we're down to Sharon Peyton on this one."

"Perhaps Don was just posturing," Julian offered.

"I don't think so. I believe him. Think he wants to be the contractor if I get the project."

"Of course he does," Julian said. "But it's smart to be wary of Don. He is everyone's friend and no one's ally."

"Well, he definitely wasn't who I thought he was. The guy's pretty sharp. Went on and on about his method. Gotta admit, it was impressive, Julian."

"You expected him to be a buffoon?" the silver-haired gentleman said harshly. "A man of his stature?" He paused for a minute.

"Financial stature," Julian clarified with a smirk.

"No, but honestly I didn't see him being as precise as he was...as calculated."

"You assumed luck was his weapon?"

"Easy," Will said as he put both palms up in the air in the universal motion to slow down. "Look, he obviously has a sizable business."

Julian took another pull from his cigar and asked, "So tell me, what was this method Don employed?"

"He said his key was focus. Claimed he could control the focus of the conversation."

"To what end?" Julian pushed.

"Well, he went in depth about changing the city's focus from getting the project done to just making sure the building was protected for the winter."

"Interesting," Julian said. "And why do you think that message will resonate with the city? Why will they focus on it?"

"Because they haven't considered it yet, and it's in their best interest. They can't have the plumbing burst or the roof leak while they own it. They would look like fools."

Julian excitedly raised his hands, palms up with the stogie dangling in his right, and nodded enthusiastically in a gesture of acceptance. "Precisely. That's precisely it. You said it. It's in their best interest."

"Right. That's what I said."

"But you must fully grasp the concept," Julian offered.

"I do. I said it, remember," Will scoffed.

Julian leaned in, peering down his nose, as if staring over glasses that were not there. "Don obviously has some understanding of the importance of interests along with his individual value in the deal. His ploy is simple. He implores them to focus on their interests, their interests that suit his needs."

"Wait. We're back to Rules Number Two and Three?" Will asked.

"Perhaps we are. A thrilling plot twist, I know. Let me explain: the city has almost certainly not spent its sleepless nights pondering the winterization of this building. Don, however, will graciously inform them of a problem they didn't even know they had. That's a rare gift. It's like handing someone both the headache and the aspirin at the same time. No friction there. He offered the solution, but more importantly, he introduced the problem to begin with. In doing so, he asserted a level of expertise...of authority."

"That makes sense. I can get on board with that logic," Will said, grasping the pervasiveness of the concept in his dealings.

"Excellent, because there is one other major point to glean from Don's meeting."

"And what is that?"

"In this entire exchange, I did not hear anything about price," Julian said.

"Yeah, he didn't think that was the important part."

Julian sniggered. "I'm going to assume Don's offer will not focus on price for good reason. A fine posture to strike when you're quietly hoping no one asks."

"I feel like you're leading me to another rule."

"Right you are," the silver-haired gentleman relented. "We shall pretend you have absorbed enough in the realm of interests. Now after you have established interests and communicated your value, it's time to make the offer."

"RULE NUMBER FOUR: GUIDE THE OFFER BY UNDERSTANDING THE ROLE OF PRICE."

Julian, leaning forward in his seat, continued, "And remember, price alone is not an offer. An offer is not a single event, it is an ongoing game. And only one party picks the pieces for that game."

Damn, Will thought. If Julian only knew Will had already broken it. His overture to Char Teague was a sloppy deviation from this new rule in every sense, not the least of which was his blind attempt at throwing a price of $1 million at Char Teague and hoping for some positive reaction. Needless to say, that did not happen.

"How are you supposed to know who's in control?" Will said, attempting to approach the rule from a different angle.

"If you don't know who's in control, it is most certainly not you." Julian stopped, looking down at his lap. "BRAVE?" He queried the air with an unusual lack of confidence.

"What?"

"No, BRAVE doesn't work. The second letter has to be an A. COURAGE is the clue. It should be BRAVE. Perhaps I've erred elsewhere." He frowned down at the newspaper in his lap, frustration etched on his face. "Take your time, Vince. If I'm struggling, I can't expect you to get there promptly." Vince glanced up at the rearview mirror, his expression unchanging, then returned his focus to the road without a word. Will shook his head, bemused. Julian's detours into crossword puzzles were as inexplicable as they were oddly endearing.

Will, acknowledging the mental departure, said, "You realize there's no prize money for solving it, right? Nobody's gonna know if you throw that paper away."

"I would know, and I dare not know defeat at the hands of the *Times*."

"Can we get back on point here? I'm actually interested in this rule."

"Of course. It's critically important," Julian said, easing back into the lesson. "I'd say 'control,' but that word tends to rub your generation the wrong way—raised on participation trophies and carefully scheduled playdates." He let the jab settle, then added, "But don't confuse control with taking advantage. It's not about dominance—it's about steering the process. You're not forcing the outcome, you're shaping it. Without guidance, both parties hold the door open for each other until there's nowhere left to go."

"Okay, but what do you actually mean? The rule's too generic. Everyone wants to control the offer."

"Do they?" Julian took another slow pull from his cigar, the embers glowing against the car's dark interior. He rolled the cigar slowly between his thumb and two fingers, inspecting the evenness of the lit end as he said, "I would not be so sure. Tell me, Will. Who makes the first offer?"

Will looked quizzically at Julian, understanding full well the question was a trap. "What kind of deal are we talking about?"

"Any deal you're trying to do," Julian said tersely.

"Am I the buyer or the seller?"

"Never mind, son. I'll answer it for you. The party in control. That's the one that makes the offer, the one who sends the contract draft, who sets the timelines, who communicates the vision, who suggests the terms."

"What if the other party undervalues their asset? What if they offer it to you for less than you would've paid?"

"Again, price is not an offer. Your thinking is horribly one dimensional. In my dealings, I'm not overly concerned with who tosses out the first price. I am concerned with communicating the first full offer."

Will leaned over the center console. "Explain the difference to me. Doesn't the first price kind of set the starting point, no matter who throws it out there?"

"If you don't understand offers, then yes, that would seem correct," Julian replied dryly.

"I'm listening," Will said.

"Price is not an offer. Let that sink in—it will save you from ruin. Take the RFP, for instance; it won't be won or lost solely on price. Even Don Andino, who you say isn't in the hunt, understands this. If you let the other side fixate on price alone, you'll end up in a hopeless tug-of-war. The key is starting correctly—the order, the movement of the pieces. The bigger the deal, the less power price has." Julian leveled a stern look at Will. "Soak it up, son. We're not moving on until you grasp this rule."

Will, accustomed to Julian's patronizing tone, was starting to think the silver-haired gentleman had earned it. He could feel himself being drawn into Rule Number Four, intrigued—because, as far as he knew, price had always been king. Especially with someone like Char Teague. "I get where you're coming from, Julian. I know it's not all about price, but you're making it seem unimportant. It's not unimportant in my deals."

"And it will always be important. But it will not be the fulcrum. That is, unless you intend on overpaying for your deals," Julian responded. "Ask yourself this, Will...at my house, what was my offer to you?"

"What do you mean?"

"Was it $20,000 per month, or a vision of what your life could be?" Julian pressed.

"Both."

"And what persuaded you take my offer?"

Will briefly examined his thoughts and said, "Both."

Julian smiled.

Will relaxed his posture and stared out the window for a brief moment, distilling the precious answers in the silver-haired gentleman's teaching. He now had little doubt Julian would accomplish his goal in the RFP, but the ultimate reward passed down to Will was becoming much clearer. He would inhale forty years of cunning and guile in a few short months, and he would own it forever. After his quick internal examination, Will turned his focus back to Julian in the other seat. "So how do I get my price then?"

"Indeed, an appropriate question." Julian pressed on. "Yet, again, you assume establishing price is by default the paramount piece of an offer. Nothing could be further from the truth. If the value you bring is strictly money, you are a commodity. You've brought no value to the deal. Remember, Rule Number Three." Julian was becoming more animated; the subject matter jolting his senses and causing his cigar hand to dance about to the point that Will was worried the embers would fall to the aged leather seats and inflict their first blemishes. But he dared not stop Julian's train of thought. "If we should find ourselves on opposite ends of a negotiation, and you carelessly utter a price with no other terms, you have ceded control to me."

"You would expect me to throw out a price without any terms?"

"Precisely."

"What makes you think I'd do that?" Will asked indignantly. "I've been at this a while."

"Ask yourself this question, and answer it honestly." Julian narrowed his eyes as he peered at Will. "Haven't you always done that?"

Will bit his bottom lip, his smirk melting into a sheepish smile. "How hard is it to regain control?"

"I detect a motive for the question," Julian prodded.

"I guess I should mention," Will said, "I went out on a limb and called Char."

"Unbridled action...a strength and a weakness. And who is now guiding the conversation?"

"Ummm," Will said in a high-pitched voice that trailed off into silence.

"I gather your machismo wasn't well received?" Julian observed.

"Char told me not to call her again. Technically, she said to 'stop fucking calling her'."

"Unfortunate," Julian added. "What elicited that response?"

"Don't know. I said we might be interested in investing in her business and then—"

"You said what?" Julian's tone sharpened. "Have you learned nothing from our conversations? There is no 'we' in this deal. I thought I made that painfully clear."

"Hold on," Will shot back. "I don't know if I said 'we' or 'I', but either way, I didn't mention you."

Julian's eyes narrowed. "Irrelevant. What is relevant is that my name stays far away from this Launch Pad project. Vince," he said with a wry glance toward the rearview mirror, "it seems I've lost my ability to communicate with the youth."

Vince's stoic gaze flicked to the mirror and back to the road.

Julian turned his focus back to Will. "The real problem now is her reaction. Why did she cut the call short?"

"I had nothing," Will offered. "She gave me nothing when I mentioned the Golden property. The call was going to go nowhere, and I just mentioned that we might be interested. What was I supposed to do, just say goodbye and hang up?"

"It would have been preferable," Julian said coldly. "From the sound of it, you were defeated before the call even started."

"Come on, Julian. You can't be so sure. You weren't on the call. It's always a bit different when you're the guy on the call."

"I didn't need to be. You tell me, Will, what was the focus of your conversation?" he said with a warmer tone, a forced calm he had obviously practiced. "You and I just spoke about Don Andino's use of focus."

"I was focused on moving this along," Will said frustratedly. "I reached out to her so we could move things along. I'm running out of time here."

"Yes, you are. And isn't it a peculiar scenario that you've now delayed the timeline? You have no concept of her interests and therefore have commoditized yourself."

Will sat silent again, his mouth open, and his lower jaw now shifting to the left as if he wanted to shoot back hard at Julian but thought better of it.

"Take a breath, son. There's a process. You can move quickly, but you can't circumvent it. Guiding the offer process is nuanced; it relies on strategic movement. The first step is crafting an offer that demonstrates a deep understanding of all parties' interests. But remember, that's merely the beginning. The offer sets the stage—it defines the pieces and parameters of the game. The dynamism of the negotiation depends on the strength of that first offer. Fortunately, you're not off course yet. No formal offer has been made—just an uninspired price."

"Alright, fair enough. But what if the other party has the same objective? Let's say I understand all this, but we're both working to control the offer process. Then what?"

Julian's expression brightened. "That's the right question—a sharp insight. Negotiation becomes fascinating when both sides seek control. It's a test of skill, patience, and strategy." He glanced toward the rearview mirror. "Vince, the kid's got your touch—cerebral."

Vince's eyes flicked to the mirror, meeting Julian's gaze, but he said nothing.

Julian smirked, leaning back. "Perhaps we'll revisit this conundrum later. For now, I must conquer the riddle of COURAGE. Five letters, still eluding me."

"BALLS," Will said.

"Excuse me, son?"

"BALLS. That's your answer...the crossword puzzle...five letters for COURAGE. It's BALLS. I can help you with more answers if you need them." He continued to badger Julian.

Julian scrutinized the paper in his lap as if it were newly tainted by the discovery. He quietly mouthed the clue again to himself. "Dear God," he said. "BALLS. In the *Times*? What has come of us?" Julian said directly to the lifeless newspaper with disdain, as if standing over a senseless murder.

"Let's hope we never go head-to-head on crossword puzzles," Will quipped, his tone smug. Julian's irritation was evident as he glanced in the mirror and gave Vince a curt nod, signaling the ride was nearing its end.

Will leaned against the door, his head propped on a fist, watching cars pass in the left lane as the Town Car cruised methodically in the right, perfectly paced to Julian's rhythm. The silver-haired man briefly scanned the road ahead, swaying his head thoughtfully, then glanced behind them, as if checking for a tail. The moment unsettled Will—a stark reminder of how little he truly understood Julian Darrow or his motives.

Breaking the tense silence, Will finally spoke, his tone resolute. "I can put this deal back together, but I need to meet with Char in person. I need to go to Raleigh—and I know exactly who to take with me."

"The hippie?" Julian queried, now looking at the right-side window.

"Yep. Dex is always up for a trip, and he'll like to meet her. This girl's a piece of work."

"She certainly appears to be."

Chapter 20

"Every problem has in it the seeds of its own solution. If you don't have any problems, you don't get any seeds."

—Norman Vincent Peale

24 DAYS TO RFP

"I love you. Have a great flight," Kirsty said as Will grabbed his bag from the back seat of her car, just outside the sliding doors of Denver International Airport. He shouldered his laptop bag and pulled the small rolling suitcase toward the driver's side door to say goodbye. "Miss me," Kirsty said. "And I'll need a picture of this Char girl before I can approve."

Will leaned in and gave her an airport kiss: an obligatory smooch with a lingering hint of hope my plane doesn't crash. "I love you, Boo. See you tomorrow."

Will turned and walked toward the sliding doors at the upper concourse. He moved quickly across the polished terrazzo floor, glancing at the flight monitor as he passed. Though he had a conservative hour and a half before his flight, the setting made his heart rate climb. The stale smell—a mix of luggage, fast food, cleaning supplies, and escalator grease—didn't help.

The hard plastic wheels of Will's bag clacked across the terrazzo.

"Hey, man!" a voice called. Dexter was at the top of the escalator, wearing a black AC/DC T-shirt, black jeans, and his trademark snakeskin boots. He hooked the straps of a small backpack with each thumb.

"Damn, Dex," Will said. "Traveling light?"

"The staples. Underwear, book, T-shirt, toothbrush…" Dexter nodded at Will's bags. "Why do you have two? We're going to Raleigh for one night, right?"

"Yeah. And you pack like a kid, Dex."

"We're all kids, remember?"

"Let's get moving," Will said. "I skipped breakfast."

"Who's the kid now," Dexter said, stepping ahead toward the checkpoint and gate C-42.

"Good morning. Welcome to flight four seventy-three to Raleigh-Durham. We will begin the boarding process shortly. Please have your boarding passes ready when your group is called."

As they sat, Will gave a shameful smile. "Before we board, I gotta tell you something, Dex. This might be a tough meeting."

Dexter was now seated in the concourse, thumbing through a paperback book. From the looks of the cover, he was giving it a second read. "That's cool. But what do you mean?"

"Char didn't exactly invite us with open arms," Will explained. "My first call to her was a bust. Second call, I told her about you…described you a little. Told her she had to meet you. No strings. We'd be there fifteen minutes."

"No worries. I like a tough meeting. What'd she say to that?"

Will was quiet. His shameful smile morphed into a smirk.

"What?"

Will smirked. "She said, 'He sounds like a douche bag.'. "

Dexter grinned. "I like this woman already."

"Maybe you can get her to like me, too."

"Is Char kicking your ass?" Dexter asked, still reading.

"Maybe."

Dexter closed his book. "You and Char are after the same thing. A deal. She doesn't take this meeting otherwise."

Will rubbed his face. "I don't think she sees it that way."

"We forget the other side wants it, too. You haven't let her see that yet."

"Maybe so," Will half-heartedly conceded. "But without communicating your value and authority you don't control the focus or the offer process. That's how Julian sees it. Here's the problem, Dex, I can't just say, 'I have value and I have authority.'." Will said the words with his finger in the air. "She's not interested."

"Okay. I see where you're coming from, man. Forget Char for a second. Let me ask you this...are you and Julian on the same team?"

Will's lack of immediate answer revealed his insecurity. Were they on the same team? It appeared to be an innocent question, but he didn't dare share that Julian began paying his loans without asking, or that he was receiving a monthly stipend of $20,000.

"Are you?"

"Let's just say our interests are aligned."

Dexter dropped the line of questioning and moved on. Though Will couldn't be certain, he assumed Dexter gleaned more from his answer than Will had hoped. "Okay. Whatever your arrangement is, you must be comfortable with it. So, what did Julian do first? Did he walk past this imaginary line between parties you're talking about? Seems like he did. Seems like, whether you've figured it out or not, you and Julian are acting like teammates, at least for now...just trying to get a deal done. You respect his authority. So maybe it's easier to have authority when you're on the same team."

"Char Teague isn't on my team yet."

"That's the issue. Julian understands more than he explains. I bet he did something you missed."

"What?"

Dexter looked out across the terminal. "Problem solvers are everywhere. But the real value comes from people who see problems others don't. Those are the people we trust with authority."

"I'm following."

"Julian probably showed you a problem, then laid out how to solve it together. Right?"

"If you only knew," Will mumbled.

"What?"

"Nothing. Still following. So, what about Char?"

"Maybe she isn't a team player yet because you haven't shown her the problem she has. New problems create new interests."

"You're going to be a real pain in the ass in this meeting."

"If you explain the problem, you become the authority on it."

"And then we're on the same side?"

"Not yet. There's one more piece. You have to acknowledge their value, make them feel heard. That part has to be real, man."

"Now you want me to establish their authority?"

"Exactly. Acknowledge them, and they're cool with you having authority, too. That's how I connect with people. And is that how your boy, Julian, explains it?"

"Full disclosure, he hasn't given me his rule on authority yet. But it can't be that simple."

"It is. I deal with smart people. I acknowledge they know their stuff. I don't try to tell them how their software should work...that'd be silly. But I make sure they understand I bring something to the table too—investing. That's my authority."

"Of course it is, Dex. That's why they're talking to you."

"Exactly. So, we can both have authority. We don't have to dispute that. The trick is directing the focus afterward. I want to make sure the focus of the conversation is whatever problem they have that needs my input...that needs my authority. It's the problem they didn't know they had. Or at least, the problem they haven't given enough thought to yet. Maybe Julian calls this part control. I call it directing focus. Everything we talk about is pointing toward that common goal. Then my job gets easy. I just gotta figure out what problem they have and the value I bring to solve it...a value that gets their engines revving, gets them either wanting to do the deal with me, or afraid not to. Either way works for me."

"You invest money. Isn't that what gets them excited?"

"Dude, I never focus on the money. You're not listening. The next guy can always pay more money. I'll let them haggle over dollars. I'm there to solve a problem with them, and the best problem to solve is one they didn't know they had, man. Sure, I sit down to talk about how much I'm willing to invest for whatever percentage. And we talk about the typical problems anyone has scaling a company. But then you can bet your ass I'm gonna explain the supply chain problem they didn't know existed because their product doesn't integrate with another software, or the heartburn they're going to feel if they don't lock up the international patents."

"So you're the problem solver."

"No. Problem finder...not solver. That's the part you can't screw up. You can't solve the problem for them ahead of time. You gotta solve it together. They are part of the solution. That's the ultimate confluence, man. You can see it in their eyes. If I bring up a problem they didn't know they had, then my value is unquestionable...it's real. So, they're cool letting me be in control of my piece, and they're in control of theirs. We solve the rest together."

Will glanced at his phone again. "I feel like I got off on the wrong foot. I didn't do any of this upfront work. I'm basically begging her to do business. That's why I brought you, Dex. I've never begged for anything with a good result. I've gotta right this ship with Char."

"Amen to that. Look, half the people I deal with think their product is the next best thing. Their IQ scores are in the 140s and they'll tell you about it. They're already thinking about which house to buy in Boulder before they've made one dollar. At least Char has already built something that turned a profit."

"So how do we get her on board?"

"Group Three. Now Boarding Group Three."

Dexter, hearing their group called, stood and slung his backpack over his shoulders. He hooked his thumbs through each strap again and girded them toward the center of his chest. "Every business has problems. We happen to know her biggest one right now. That Austin loan is going to bite her. Now let's go get her in the right mindset. Let's acknowledge the badass company she started, focus on the problem she's neglecting, show our authority, and get this Launch Pad deal going."

Chapter 21

"There's nothing makes you admire people like seeing yourself in them."
—Eleanor Hibbert

24 DAYS TO RFP

"Nice shirt," Char Teague said to Dexter as he and Will took their seats. Dexter had switched from AC/DC to Metallica. His comfortable confidence made his T-shirt and jeans ensemble look fashionable, rather than unemployable.

"You, too," Dexter replied.

"Saw them in Philly. Pretty epic," she offered in her typical clipped speech. Char unwrapped a refrigerated peanut protein bar. Her hands were noticeably pale as she took what Will guessed was her first bite of food for the day. She exhibited no nerves; Char did not appear to react to people in general. Will and Dexter sat before her now in unmatched office chairs. "Sorry for the eating, fucking starving. Emily's out today, and our accounting software can't generate food cost reports," she said while staring at her computer screen to the side and chewing between declarations. "Been screwing with them all morning." She grabbed her mug from beside her computer and washed the protein bar down with coffee. The coffee did not help with the taste; she tasted batteries. At the top of the meeting, Char had uttered more words to Will and Dexter than anyone that week. She tried to suppress it, but she could feel the anxiety. "Need to hit the social media posts before lunch. People are vicious."

"So why mess with it?" Dexter said.

"Easy to be a troll. Easier than being real." She continued staring at her computer, avoiding eye contact. "Can't leave them unanswered."

"But you don't have to answer them," Dexter pressed.

Char turned and looked at him disappointingly. "My company. I have to do it."

"Do you?"

She cocked her head to the side deploringly and rolled her chair more to the center of the desk in better view of Will and Dexter. Her 1950s thrift-store button-down blouse set a semiformal tone that starkly contrasted with her torn blue jeans. She pushed up her thick, black-rimmed glasses, which were settling mid-bridge on her nose, complementing her jet-black hair; her tattooed arm provided the only real color to her outfit. "Fellas, I agreed to take the meeting. We're sitting here. I'm trying to keep my four-point-three rating on Tripadvisor. And I do need to respond to these." Char offered a dissenting smirk, which drew attention to her face. A thin but conspicuous scar trailed down the side of her cheek, adding to her unorthodox look. She had on little to no makeup; the dark, narrow scar famed her left cheekbone as if carved there by an artist.

She saw Will staring at the scar. He quickly looked away, caught red-handed.

"Why does that matter so much?" Dexter asked.

"Bad scores...less rooms sold. Simple as that. Launch Pad guests do their research."

"I'll take you at your word on that. I don't know anything about e-commerce with hotels."

Will jumped in. "Don't let him off too easy on that one. Dex invested in a revenue management software company recently. He's a nerd when it comes to research."

"Impressive," Char said, as she peeled back the wrapper and took a large bite of her peanut protein bar. "You want Launch Pad for your trophy case?"

"Launch Pad isn't a trophy. At least, not right now, dude," Dexter responded—successfully pulling off the word "dude" as a genderless noun.

Char looked at him harshly. That comment obviously struck a chord. The meeting had finally started.

"Excuse me," she said.

"It should be. It has all the parts of being a trophy. But it isn't today," Dexter continued.

"Bold fucking statement considering the circumstances," she said cynically. "Let me take a stab. You guys are savvier than me. Went to school for this. You can look at my company from thirty-thousand feet, twist a few levers and, BOOM, Launch Pad's ten times bigger." She made the "raising hands" gesture like the emoji.

Will, sensing Dexter had made the impact he intended, jumped in and said, "Char, first off, I have ridiculous respect for what you're building. It's innovative, it's clever, and it's deeply personal. You should be extremely proud of it. I read the articles. Pretty inspiring to do all this in the face of the autism."

Char looked quizzically at Will. "I don't have autism."

Will, taken aback by her response, said, "Oh, it said that in the article."

"Yeah. Still pissed about that. I told those idiots my doctor said I might be on the spectrum. What's a fucking spectrum anyway? You either do, or you don't. I don't...at least, I don't think I do," Char said playfully, toying with Will.

"Okay. Well, you picked an interesting business to be in either way.

But back to the point. We don't want to grow your company. Not yet."

"Why be partners then?"

"Because of you. Your ideas."

Char's chin lurched forward abruptly as she brought her hand to her face. "I think my autism's acting up. I just threw up in my mouth." She reached for her coffee. "I don't need you. And don't patronize me with a bullshit line like that. I've already got investment. It's how I got Austin off the ground. And those guys don't want to be partners. They don't want any say in my business."

"Is that why you leveraged the Austin deal up so high, to keep partners out?" Will asked. He glanced at Dexter, who discreetly granted a nod of approval.

Char's chin now recoiled in the opposite direction, toward her neck in retreat, and her eyes displayed disapproval. "How do you know so much about my company? That takes research. You really want a piece of Launch Pad, don't you?"

"It's my job to understand where the problems are," Will responded, paraphrasing a line that Julian and Dexter had both used on him. "Is that it?...to keep partners out of your business?"

"Yes," she relented.

Dexter jumped in, "What's important here isn't that we want to invest, it's how we want to invest in your company. That's totally different from your current situation. And, Char, it would put you in control of your company again. That's what you need to keep, right?"

"I'm in control now."

"You're in control now?" Dexter repeated. Will noticed his use of Julian's tactic.

"They don't care about the hotel."

"Right. They don't. But here's the problem: Your investor can change the control if they want to."

Char was silent for roughly fifteen contemplative seconds. Then she said, "So how would you be any different?"

Will shot Dexter a look, who returned a satisfied glance that seemed to say, *It's that easy, dude.* There it was, a simple focus shift. For a fleeting moment, in between the conversation, Dexter introduced the problem—the problem Char didn't know she had. Will, by his visible nod, was proud of recognizing the move. He couldn't play the game if he didn't recognize the moves.

Will jumped in. "We don't want to run your business. We don't know enough about your business to do that. But we want to offer you something these other groups won't. We want to offer you the time to work on your business. Launch Pad is creative, fresh, exciting, but it's none of those things if you aren't constantly touching it. Char, you're the passionate one. You need the time to be passionate. Time is what we can offer you."

"Amen, man. And if I'm being honest here, Char," Dexter added, "I don't think you obsess over those scores just because it brings business. If I believed that, we wouldn't be here. You obsess over those scores because you love your company and you're proud to run it. Low scores aren't tied to money, they just aren't acceptable. Those are the kind of people we want to invest in." He paused and leaned in, bringing his voice to a comical whisper. "And you're kinda right, it just so happens I think your product is where the world is headed, and it can scale exponentially," he said with a smile. "Just not yet."

"I appreciate it. Maybe that's dead fucking accurate, but my business isn't for sale." Char said. "So where does that leave us?"

"What concerns you about selling a piece of your business?" Dexter asked. The deftness and genuineness of Dexter's delivery elevated the statement. It caused immediate transparency.

"The soul of it," she shot back without hesitation.

"What's the soul of this company?" Dexter asked. Will again picked up the craft Dexter was using. His questions were simple, but beautifully open-ended. Even Char's brevity could not elude them.

Char reached over and took another sip of her coffee. She looked up and delivered the next lines without the slightest hint of emotion. "I started this as a single woman. Never doubted my ability, but I doubted the world's acceptance of me doing it. There were tough times, really tough times. But in the end, I built this company...me. Had no idea what I was doing. I did whatever I had to, cleaning rooms all afternoon, having events all night, running up credit card debt to buy furniture. A few times I just got on my knees and prayed that it would work. And it did. And I'm fucking proud of it. If you had any idea how much time I've spent thinking about this stupid company...about the stupid little shit that matters to me," she said rhetorically. "I'm sorry, but my vision isn't, and never will be, to sell out to two people, two men, so they can take the soul of what I built here and prepackage it. It would never work. The soul of this place, the simplicity of it, is what brings the people here. It's why they share it with their friends. And I've put in too much time, and too much effort, to watch this thing lose its soul."

"Good," Dexter said. He stood up, his seat making an irritating scraping noise across the old wood floor as it slid back against his legs. "So, that's it?"

Char looked up at him confusedly. "I...I guess so." She took off her glasses and wiped a smudge off one of the lenses with her blouse.

"You should be passionate about your company," he declared as Will took the hint and stood as well. "But, Char?"

"What?"

"You need to get ready to work with Will and me."

"Why?"

"Because if that is really your biggest concern, the soul of this company, then I think we can all work together. The last thing we want you to be is a sellout. If we kill the soul, we kill the value. And you need control to keep the soul."

"You're probably wasting your time," she said. "But I'll listen. You didn't fly all the way out here to listen to me bitch."

"Let us wrap our heads around today's conversation." Will inserted himself again, stretching his back instinctively to relieve the pressure of the meeting. "When we're back in Denver, one of us will reach out." Dexter volunteered his knuckles to Char for a fist bump. She returned the bump, their knuckles touching slightly longer than a customary gesture. As Dexter and Char exchanged appraising smiles, Char detected Will's gaze and quickly turned her attention to him, offering the obligatory bump. She made a funny exploding hand gesture when Will presented his fist. It was purposefully dramatic and a quirky reminder of her odd personality; it also helped to divert attention away from her awkward exchange with Dexter. But that exchange had done something. It produced a taste far different from the metallic tang of batteries. Char detected the very distinct flavor of purple popsicles; purple popsicles tasted like curiosity.

***

Will and Dexter stood in front of Launch Pad Hotel as Will looked for the rideshare app on his phone. It was a short car trip to the Raleigh-Durham International Airport, and Raleigh had no shortage of young, techy, entrepreneurial spirit, which manifested into throngs of rideshare drivers. They would not be on the sidewalk for long.

"Dex, you were impressive in there. Appreciate you coming."

"Absolutely, my man, I like that girl. She's got something I don't."

"What's that?"

"I don't know, but I like it. Something sexy about her whole vibe. Nothing she's into would surprise me."

"Is that why she opened up to you so quickly? Or whatever that was?" Will asked while looking at his phone. He was a tad uncomfortable with the idea of sourcing information so blatantly, but the pace of his learning had to be expedient. The RFP placed a clock within his brain to the point he could literally hear it ticking, if he was quiet and still long enough.

"What do you mean?"

Will continued, "She started talking to you immediately. It would've taken me three meetings to get her to open up like that. Granted, she's weird, and you're weird...so that helped. But, really, what did you do in there? I know you. It didn't just happen. You think too much for that. You got her to focus on the problem, like we discussed."

"Hey man, you actually said the bit about giving her time. That was great. She'll remember that. I couldn't have said it that simply. Time is definitely a problem for her."

Will's eyes darted up from his phone. "Yeah, but you got me somewhere with her. All of a sudden, she's open to our ideas...well, as open as she's gonna get. I want to know how."

"I listened to her, man," Dexter replied without any hesitation.

"It was more than that."

"Not really. It's just empathy, dude. I acknowledged her and made sure she felt heard. It's that easy."

"So that's all you told yourself before this meeting? Be empathetic and you can dupe this girl into opening up?" Will asked, without hiding the doubting look on his face.

"Dupe?" Dexter winced. "Man, I don't think so. If I've gotta dupe somebody then our relationship is doomed. I don't think you're hearing me. I don't tell myself to do it, Will. It's who I am." Dexter stood there crossing his arms across his Metallica shirt, his snakeskin boots teetering off the side of the curb as he balanced, the ever-present boyishness of his demeanor on full display. He was currently the most approachable looking fifty-year-old man with a ponytail on the streets of Raleigh.

"I'm listening. But if you're saying you're genuinely interested—"

"If I can't be interested," Dexter injected, "I don't need to be in the meeting. I'll go find somebody else, man." He began to rock back and forth using the curb as a support against the hard midsole of his boots, his hands partially tucked in his tight jeans pockets. "I guess, in the beginning, I started out only wanting to invest in companies that were cutting edge...whatever that means. That sounded like the coolest way to operate. That was how I'd be different. But really, man, that just kept me from investing in good deals. There's nothing cool about not doing good deals. I don't know exactly what it was, but somewhere along the line I changed my philosophy." Dexter paused. "Actually, the biggest thing I did differently was to read a ton of books."

"You've always read books, Dex."

"Yeah, but I got into a different subject. I read stuff like Carnegie, Cialdini, Kahneman. Learned what it means to understand people. I was looking at it wrong. I was focused on understanding companies. There's more money in understanding the people that control the companies, man."

"What made you change?" Will said, returning his attention to the small car icon on his phone app as it weaved through the cartoonish streets on the screen.

"If I'm being honest, it gave me people to be interested in," Dexter said solemnly. "And Char is nothing short of interesting."

"Yeah, I saw you look at her," Will said. Dexter said nothing. "Steer clear of this one, even if you're interested. She's a ballbuster, Dex."

Chapter 22

"A wise owl sat on an oak, the more he saw the less he spoke, the less he spoke the more he heard. Why aren't we like that wise old bird?"

—Anonymous

14 DAYS TO RFP

After the trip to Raleigh, Will was determined to put his new training to the test. The RFP was two weeks away, and Will could feel the clock ticking. Julian and Dexter had both exhibited a fondness for understanding the interests of the parties involved. Will realized there was one important person whose interest he had neglected.

"Ms. Peyton?" Will said in the form of a question, although he had dialed her mobile number. It was Monday at 6:30 a.m., an odd time for a scheduled call with anyone except Julian, but Sharon's assistant had given him that time in an email exchange the day prior as "the only time she can fit it in."

"This is Sharon," she replied. An audible hum in the background was interrupted synchronously by a metronome-like clicking sound. Sharon's breathing was heavy.

"Did I catch you at a bad time? This is Will Powell."

"Nope, I see you here in my calendar. Sorry for the early slot," she said between heavy breaths. "But I've got scheduled calls and meetings all day, so you're going to have to deal with me on my bike."

"You're riding a bike?"

"Don't worry, I'm in the gym. And I've been here since five thirty. My Pilates class ended ten minutes ago."

"Early riser, huh?" Will asked.

"I'm fifty-two, Will. Things are starting to settle in the wrong places. I got forty-five minutes left on this sucker. I'm glad you called. Don Andino is an acquaintance of mine. He told me you had an interest in the Teleprime RFP."

"Small world. Yes, I do."

"You do realize I'm going to get that project, right?"

Will was not surprised by her confidence; a little thrown off by her conference call/workout double-booking, but not her confidence. Sharon Peyton was the biggest residential real estate broker on the front range, dabbling in commercial ventures as a result of the connections with wealthy homeowners.

Sharon Peyton dominated Denver's high-end real estate market through sheer effort and strategic finesse. While other agents envied her success, they never missed an invite to her exclusive wine and cheese events—unless they were unfortunate enough to be left off the list, a slight that no self-talk could mend. Unlike her peers, she eschewed the flashy trappings of luxury, opting instead for a red Jeep Wrangler and her signature cowboy boots. Yet despite defying the typical high-powered agent aesthetic, she embodied the most important trait of all: an unmatched work ethic. Years of relentless effort had honed her ability to steer any conversation toward a sale, making her the undisputed center of Denver's residential scene.

"I'm sure you have a very good shot at the building if you want it," Will said. "You know, we haven't met, but I've spoken to your office before."

"Really? How did we not meet then?"

"I needed a broker for my condo project in Jefferson Park. Honestly, after the lady in your office heard the price range, she tried to pawn me off on some first-year agent in your group."

"That's a shame. I would've surely loved to represent your project, Will," Sharon said. Will knew she was posturing, and so did Sharon. "But I can assure you, I don't have junior agents on my team."

"Doesn't matter, Sharon. That deal's sold out." The information wasn't 100% accurate, but close enough. And he was still a little bitter that his project was rejected. "What draws you to the Teleprime Building? I guess you're looking to put residential there?"

The pedaled metronome sounded in the background: Click...whir...click.

"Hell no. Even if I wanted to, the city would never let me do apartments, and the state's condo laws are too tough for me. I did look at the old boarding room ordinances, which would technically let me do three-month rental contracts, but I couldn't make that pencil out." She took a second to catch her breath between thoughts. "My interest in the Teleprime Building is really simple. I've got a client, a client with a lot of money. He was hand-delivered to me. I also just sold his house in Cherry Creek in two days...above asking price. He wants to get out of the city, move to Golden, so he can be closer to the mountains. I'm trying to find him a house." She caught her breath again. "I was just on the phone with him yesterday, talking about the RFP. He asked me if we had a shot at putting it together. I don't think he realizes I've never missed a shot." She paused again. Her breathing had intensified to catch up with the excessive talking. The longer pause allowed Will to process the information. Click...whir...click.

"I have a pretty nice project I'm putting together for the RFP," Will said, pretending to not be crushed by Sharon's enlightening tale.

"That's great. Tell me about it," she said, still panting a bit. It wasn't clear if she was interested or just simply couldn't keep the conversation going due to her workout intensity.

"It's a hotel project. The city wants to see more tourism downtown.

This building's in an awesome location to walk around. Perfect for a hotel."

"A hotel, huh?" Sharon said. "How solid is your deal?"

"Pretty solid," he feigned, knowing the Launch Pad deal was rocky at best.

"Are you dead set on Golden?" she asked.

"I'm committed to the Teleprime Building."

Click…whir…click…Will could hear the intermittent heavy muffling of sound. Sharon must have resorted to toweling off the sweat she was accumulating. "Tell you what, let's get together and talk about finding you a spot for that hotel."

"I appreciate that Sharon, but I'm going ahead with the RFP. I think I have a compelling project."

"Sounds like it. Probably more compelling than mine. But you have a problem, Will." Her tone changed. Out went the salesperson, and in came the bully.

"Let me guess," Will said plainly. "You're the problem?"

Sharon laughed through her panting, her tone demonstrating he was dead on the mark. "You're funny. I like that. I'm not your problem. Your problem is that nobody will be certain you can pull it off. The city doesn't want a false start. Look, I don't want to be over the top here, but Terry, the city manager, is a friend of mine. They reached out to me before the RFP release. And besides that, Will, I know things about this deal. Things you couldn't know. Things that make me confident it'll be mine. Let's not butt heads on this one."

Will was speechless. A defeated "hmmm" was all he could muster. Sharon, seemingly thankful for the pause, was now in full on breath-catching mode.

"You seem like a stand-up guy, Will. I'm sorry about Jefferson Park. I obviously missed the boat on that one. Just don't want you wasting your time on this. But I'd like to work with you, so let's get together and figure out a spot for that hotel."

***

After a rough morning with Sharon, Will spent the rest of his day buried in projects. By evening, he was reclining against the headboard, tapping away at his laptop. Late-night catch-ups with Kirsty had become their unspoken routine since Julian's offer. Meanwhile, Kirsty had slipped into the satin sheets in her flannel pajamas and was scrolling through her social media feed. When their eyes met in passing, Will offered a quiet wink that drew a playful, knowing smile from her.

Leaning in, Will pressed a gentle kiss to her forehead. "Before you start snoring," he murmured, "I've got something for you." He set aside his laptop with a clumsy stretch, then opened the nightstand drawer to reveal a small velvet box. "It's nothing huge—I was just thinking about you today."

Kirsty swooped in, snatching the box from his hands. "Really, Will? You shouldn't have. But I'm totally good with this new approach,"

"Wait, before you open—" Will started, but she cut him off with a soft laugh.

"I love it," she declared, lifting the white gold chain with its delicate solitaire diamond between her fingers. "But honestly, you didn't have to go all out."

Will grinned. "It's been too long. If I can't spoil you once in a while, what's the point?"

"Agreed," Kirsty quipped, wrapping him in a warm, teasing hug.

At that moment, the sudden glow of Will's phone drew his attention. A notification blinked on the screen. He knew better than to dismiss his offering to Kirsty so quickly. Kirsty, noticing the distraction, seized on the opportunity to begin clasping the necklace behind her neck. She glanced at him and nodded. "It's okay. Go ahead. You bought yourself some screen time."

He snatched the phone to find the message: "Substantial Snowfall in the Denver Area Tonight." Heavy snow in Denver wasn't exactly breaking news, yet the alert seemed oddly timed—and a bit unsettling—especially with the nagging email still at the top of his inbox.

> To: Will Powell
> From: Julian Darrow
> Date: Monday, October 7, 2025, 20:05:11 MDT
>
> Subject: Pick you up at 6:45 a.m. tomorrow.
>
> Cheers,
> Julian

With what seemed an almost involuntary movement, Will hit the reply icon in the mail client on his phone and copied an all too familiar link. Knowing his partner in crime, he thought it best to give some direction.

> To: Julian Darrow
> From: Will Powell
> Date: Monday, October 7, 2025, 22:11:28 MDT
>
> Subject: Re: Pick you up at 6:45 a.m. tomorrow.
>
> Julian,
> It will be snowing in the morning. You don't need to be out in that. Instead, at 6:45 a.m., click on the link below and sit in front of your computer. I'll walk you through the rest when we're on the Zoom call.
>
> Join Zoom Meeting:
> https://zoom.us/j/98350382061?pwd=LzhINjYrSFRqTkJDN0pyN2pkUUZrZz09
>
> Welcome to the 21st century,
> Will

Chapter 23

"Empathy is not about being nice or agreeing with the other side. It's about understanding them."

—Chris Voss

13 DAYS TO RFP

As promised, the snow had dumped all night. Roughly eight inches of pure powder dropped on Evergreen and five inches accumulated in Denver. It was early in the season for such a snowfall, the virgin ground quickly falling victim to larger, fresher flakes with each passing second.

"Julian?" Will asked to the black screen in his home office with near giddy amusement. The Zoom format felt more like his turf than the confines of the black Lincoln Town Car. Will took some greedy comfort in his counterpart's absence of technological savvy. The Town Car, the newspaper, and the anachronistic driver, Vince, were telltales that this online meeting was a foreign platform for the silver-haired sage. "Julian?"

No response.

It was 6:45 a.m. He should've been on. Possibly Julian was struggling to log in, and the mere thought of his grumblings at the keyboard added to Will's enthusiasm for the meeting. Then the thought occurred to Will that Julian could fall in line with the throngs of online meeting dissenters, cloaking their appearance in darkness as they opted to dial in instead, a generic initialed circle denoting their presence. He better not call in, Will thought. But the dial-in-only option now seemed the most likely scenario. Will rebuked himself for not thinking of it. Julian's proclivity for simple dialogue should have tipped him off. Will's foot started involuntarily tapping, and he scrunched his mouth to the side, annoyed at the unwavering black screen and the silence. "Julian, you there?"

Shards of lights shot through the semi-closed blinds of Will's home office. They grew against the wall like large blades and then contracted as the vehicle approached. Will stood up and walked to the window, forcing a section of the blinds far enough apart to see clearly.

Steam bellowed out the back of the Town Car. With two wheels perched atop the embankment of snow collecting at the curb, a warmly dressed driver traipsed through the slush to wait by the door. Will shook his head and smirked to himself. Of course this asshole drove here.

Will, by no means dressed for a wintery outing, quickly slipped into his sneakers, grabbed his coat and beanie, and headed toward the door. As he exited the house, the bite of the cold air nipped at his face and the snow-covered ground soaked his sneakered feet. He shot his hands deeply into his pockets and awkwardly shuffled toward the car with his head down against the wind. He offered the unflappable driver a nod and an eyebrow raise as Vince opened the door precisely in time for Will's entry and then slammed the door hurriedly behind him. The sound of the Town Car's heater reverberated through the back seat in a mighty display of American excess. Julian's overcoat and cap were lying across the front console as he sat comfortably in his trademark collared shirt and sweater, even rolling the cuffs of his shirt back to combat the massive warm airflow, which failed to have any impact on his perfectly combed hair.

"So you drove?"

"It snows in Denver. It will snow again." Julian said intrepidly, preoccupied with an apparent missing word in his lap. He shifted his torso to the right and looked across the crossword puzzle as if a new vantage point might gain him perspective.

"I guess the Zoom call was too easy?"

"Son, I don't conduct meetings in imaginary places," the silver-haired gentleman replied, adding, "It will be snowing in hell before I watch lapsing images of you on my computer while we talk over each other." He looked up at Will. "Now tell me about the mysterious Miss Char Teague."

"Dex's girlfriend is playing hard to get."

"Surely you jest," Julian offered sharply. His disapproval of Will's comment was palpable. He shuffled uncomfortably in his seat. His fastidious attention to detail materialized in the predictable placement of the items in his lap that he kept stacked neatly as he shifted. Julian leaned in more closely than needed, as usual. "She's half that man's age," he said with some disdain. "Perhaps he should cultivate a fondness for women outside the margins of this deal. There's no time for distraction here." Julian sat back quickly, annoyed at the subject matter. The RFP was fast approaching, and apparently Julian expected more that morning than schoolyard relationship banter.

"Relax. I didn't mean it like that." Will forced a smirk, brushing it off like a joke, though something about the moment lingered. He'd seen that little fist bump—too casual, too easy. Something had passed between Dexter and Char, and it wasn't nothing. "Yeah, Char came on a little cold at first," he said lightly. "But once Dex got her talking about her company, it was like I disappeared."

"Lauding her company is secondary to procuring a piece of her company," Julian refused to deviate from the task at hand. "What did she say?"

"She said she wouldn't sell her company," Will responded.

"That appears to be definitive," Julian remarked.

Will held his hand up, his forefinger and thumb coming together, appearing to hold an imaginary precision tool. "She actually said we were probably wasting our time." As he said the word "probably" he gingerly moved the imaginary scalpel, as if touching the word in the air as he said it.

"Ah, now that's a major detail. Adverbs are tricky...especially the '-ly' ones. They show softness in positions. What did it sound like to you?" Julian queried.

"It sounded like she left a door open. I think we've got a shot with her. Trust me."

Julian was now reading something in the notebook that formerly sat beneath the crossword puzzle. "Trust you?" he said plainly, still looking down. "The RFP is due on October eighteenth. That's thirteen days away." He paused and looked directly into Will's eyes, adding gravity to the situation. "I believe my trust is placed squarely on your shoulders. Now, knowing what you know, Will, what offer did you two make her? My curiosity is piqued."

"I didn't actually make her an offer. But I tell you what, she really opened up in the meeting. Bringing Dex was a major deal. They hit it off, and she just started talking."

"Progress." Julian levied with faint praise. "Did you glean anything of use from the conversation?"

"Possibly...and I think I learned something in the meeting. You're starting to rub off on me."

"Is that so?" Julian indulged in a smile.

"Yeah, I picked up on something Dex uses...it's empathy. He's good at it. And then it occurred to me, isn't that part of focusing on interests instead of positions? Aren't you just too much of a jaded old codger to use that word...empathy?"

Julian smiled, grabbed his half-empty coffee, and while raising it to his lips said, "That's why hippies don't own companies."

"Dex isn't a hippie, and Dex has enough money to own whatever company he wants."

"He's lucky," Julian challenged. He took a long sip of coffee, the kind that can only be achieved with lukewarm contents.

"Thought you taught me not to believe in luck."

"Perhaps. But if he believes empathy alone produces results, he simply doesn't understand the method he's employing."

"Doesn't make it any less impactful. If it works, it works," Will retorted. "And I didn't say empathy is all he uses. It's just at the core of his approach."

Julian turned and looked out the car window. The sun was not yet visible, but its glow illuminated the face of the Front Range. He took a deep, audible breath while staring into the distance, seemingly mesmerized as he collected his thoughts. "Empathy, as a rule, is good. I would even say necessary. It creates the space to feel...to listen. Keeps you from missing the sunrise, so to speak. But then what?" Will locked in as Julian continued to stare at the front range and said, "Some men see the sunrise and are moved to tears at its beauty. They connect with it. It stirs things inside them. Emotion is the output for them...the end game." The silver-haired gentleman paused. "Others see it rising and ponder how to harness its energy. Both sets are affected by it. One becomes emotional, temporarily. The other allows emotion to awaken thoughts within him...to reveal interests he didn't know were there. You connect with empathy, son. But it only produces a result if interests are revealed. Empathy is a wonderful quality for a dealmaker, but empathy that doesn't reveal interests." Julian stopped and looked at Will, narrowing his eyes. "Son, that's only good for crying."

Will nodded and smirked. "You just described Dex to a T. He

understands more than you think. It's settled, then. You use empathy, too. You're just too old and jaded to admit it."

"I most certainly am not. Perhaps you remember the first invitation to my home. We spoke freely, did we not?"

"Sure."

"And your interests became abundantly clear."

"Really? Mind telling me what they are?" Will quizzed.

"In the short term, to cover your debts."

"Not fair. You'd already taken care of that before we met...without my approval," Will scowled. "And the long term?"

"To understand the craft, so you may cover your debts in the future," Julian sneered.

"Cute," Will dismissed. "Anyway, Char connected with Dex either way, and he believes wholeheartedly in empathy. Believe it or not, some of her interests are now very obvious."

"Chief among them?" Julian asked, foregoing a continued debate.

"She wants to maintain control of her company. That's definitely a big one. Secondly, I think I hit on something. She wants more time to work on the company."

"Excellent. You see, that's the spoils of empathy...it reveals. Your second point is too general. It's more of a question. Define that better," Julian coached.

"She has an interest in working more on her company. Doing less of the day-to-day. She's stressed."

"So then, does she understand the value you bring?"

"Yes. I really think we moved the needle here."

"Then you are ready for an offer," Julian clarified. "These are awfully common interests. Can you fashion an offer that fits those interests and accomplishes your goals?"

"The valuation is tricky. In this market, deals are trading at a discount to last year's numbers. But the Austin Launch Pad is a new hotel, so last year's numbers are a very bad indication of stabilized revenues. The most accurate way to——"

"That's not what I asked," Julian interrupted. "The monetary valuation is subjective. That's for you to tabulate. I'm more concerned with your offer. The question remains, what are you going to offer that brings her value...that speaks to her interests? If your offer is simply a number, you've already lost."

Will raised his arms and laced his fingers behind his head. "That's the thing. This girl's tough to read. She's obviously not in sound financial shape, but she'd sooner die than give up control of her company."

"Ask yourself this, Will: Do you want control of her company?" Julian probed.

"No, she's solid on hotel operations. She needs someone to fix her finances and put organizational systems in place. That's Dex's specialty. She can't find the time to think right now. She's got too many balls in the air."

"Perhaps she's losing control with or without you." Julian smiled. "There's an offer lurking in there somewhere. You need to sit down and tease it out."

"I know it's time to put an offer together. I told Dex I'd think about it. I'm struggling a bit to find the right way to package it up."

Julian raised his eyebrows and pressed his lips together in a look that seemed to say I've been there. He crossed his arms and leaned forward, his back leaving the seat. "There are two vantage points from which to make an offer. One is an offer of vision. It's the promise of something better...a gift, that if accepted, excites and entices the other party. The other is the less chosen path, less enticing to consider, yet extremely effective."

"What is it?"

"Are you a religious man, Will?"

"Yes. And please don't try to dissuade me."

Julian continued, "Which affects you more...the promise of heaven or the prospect of hell?"

"I don't know. Both, I guess."

"Do you pray?"

"Can we stop?" Will asked, his face contorting into an uncomfortable scowl.

"I suspect your most earnest prayers have been to stave off loss, to protect what you hold dear...your family, your health. That puts you in the vast majority of people. The others, by contrast...well, they are saints. Fear of loss is the universal motivating factor for anyone who has something to lose. And therefore, an offer in a manner that assuages her fear of loss is intensely effective."

"Remind me not to ask you to speak at my daughter's school."

"Both are applicable. You can deliver the vision of something better, something that appeals to her passion, or you can deliver protection from loss. Both are targeted at interests once you have defined them. And on occasion, when the situation presents itself, you can use them simultaneously. But if she cannot be swayed by vision, you can likely find fear. If you control the offer process, it is your decision to make."

"Alright," Will said. "I'll figure out my offer."

Chapter 24

"Simple can be harder than complex: you have to work hard to get your thinking clean, to make it simple."

—Steve Jobs

13 DAYS TO RFP

"Hey, fellas. We drinking light or dark tonight?" The waitress wore a snug pullover and athletic pants, radiating that effortless "anything goes" Colorado vibe.

"Ummm, whatcha got that's light?" Will asked with a swagger saved for high school fights and pretty girls. It was later now, after Julian's car ride, and Will was seated across from Dexter, carnitas tacos in front of him, at New Terrain Brewing Company in Golden.

"I got Suntrip. Or if you're into IPAs, the Joshua Tree is awesome." She said the names like anyone worth knowing should know.

"I'll do the Joshua Tree."

She turned to Dexter, raising her eyebrows. "Back in my section? Good to see you again. Your friend made a good call. You thinkin' light, too?"

"I'll take your word on the Joshua Tree, Shelly. Bring us two. Appreciate it."

"Sweet. I'll get 'em coming." She turned to Will. "Like he said, I'm Shelly. Gonna take care of you boys tonight. Just holler."

Dexter waited until she walked off before speaking. "So, what's up with Char?"

"Honestly, it's kind of a mess."

"What's the problem?"

"Trying to figure out how to approach her. Before all this with Julian, I'd just call her. Now I'm overthinking. I'm supposed to lock in on her interests, then show my value, then guide the process. It's too stiff. Julian hasn't met her. She's not gonna be cool with me playing from a script. That's not me, Dex."

Dexter smirked. "Sure isn't, dude."

"It's getting too academic. Checklists don't close deals. This stuff might work for you. I'm not sure it works for me." His phone buzzed. A text from Kirsty:

> Was just thinking...I love you 😘

As Will smiled at the text, the waitress with the vibe showed back up at the picnic table brandishing two ice-cold Joshua Trees. She plopped them down, the condensation from the glasses dripping heavily. "Want me to come back and check on you or get two more coming now?"

"Go ahead and bring two more," Will said. "Gonna be a minute. I need some answers from Dex." Then, he turned to Dexter mid-bite of his carnitas taco. "By the way, great call. I was starving. Food truck was a nice touch."

"Glad you like it." Dexter leaned forward, rocking slightly, arms crossed, eyes scanning the patio.

Will caught the movement. "What is it, Dex?"

"You know what I think? I think Julian's exactly what you needed, but you just gotta get out of your own head and apply it."

"You saying I'm overthinking it?"

"Maybe. But that's what Julian's got you doing—thinking. That's what you wanted, right? A few weeks ago, Char wouldn't have taken your second call."

"Yeah, but this stuff just oozes from you, Dex. It comes naturally."

Dexter reached forward, took a sip of Joshua Tree. Staring at his glass, and rubbing his thumb over the condensation, he said, "I got a confession. When you called me about Char, I could tell you were struggling with all this, man. I thought about this place. Really, I thought about Shelly, our waitress."

"Shelly?" Will asked as if the concept were unfathomable. He turned over his shoulder and spotted her with a tray of beers half propped on her shoulder.

"Not cool. Turn around. I want her to keep serving us. You're staring at Shelly like a sex offender."

"She's our waitress."

"She's the best. I brought you here for a reason. When you see how this stuff works, you see it everywhere."

Dexter now held his glass on the table with two hands and looked past Will again at the other patrons. There were at least fifty people spaced out among the covered patio and fifty more at the tables strewn about the uncovered gravel area nearest the food truck. "I came here three or four times before I picked up on it. I love it...why people do what they do...how to spur them to action. I nerd out on it. And when someone does it right, it's still invisible to me. That's the beauty of it."

"Shelly? Our waitress?" Will repeated, unamused. He scanned the scene for her.

"Dude, don't turn and look at her again. She might call the authorities. She's coming now."

In timely fashion, Shelly approached their table and placed a hand on Will's shoulder. "I see Dexter's friend liked the Joshua Tree."

"It's Will."

"Okay, Will, I'm about to come back with that next one, or do you want to try the Suntrip? They're both great. I'm a fan of the light stuff, too." Her hand stayed on his shoulder the entire time. And for a married man, a good fifteen years older, it did not go unnoticed.

"We'll both take another," he said. "It's bitter, but I like it."

"Great, I'll be back as soon as they can pour it." Shelly sauntered off again toward another table. Dexter wore a thin-lipped smile and exhaled a barely audible chuckle through his nose, while shaking his head. "She's good, man."

"She's a flirty waitress."

"You wish. She's got you pegged. Julian would be proud. Shelly keeps it simple—like you said, she's just a waitress."

Dexter scanned the patio. "Look at the tables under the pavilion. What do you see?"

Will glanced around. "People drinking beer."

"Now look at our section."

Will scooted in his chair. "More beers?"

Dexter nodded. "A lot more."

"And you think that's 'cause of Shelly?"

"I know it is, man." Dexter reached up, either out of habit or persuaded by the current conversation, grabbed the sweating glass, and took a large swig of beer. He pressed his lips together after, seemingly refreshed. "I bet Shelly makes twice as much as any other server here tonight. And it's like that every time I come here."

"Dex, only you would think like that."

"Shelly runs a system. It's simple, but it checks all the boxes. She doesn't overthink it. And we, my man, are falling for it now."

"I'm having a beer. That's what I came here for."

"Sure. But odds are you'll have two, maybe three."

"Because she touched my shoulder?"

"That's part of it. But it started earlier. She gave you options:

Suntrip or Joshua Tree. She controlled the focus. She became the authority. And you didn't consider not ordering. She framed it. That's what I do with investment offers. Two good options. It's not manipulation. It's design."

"Because your waitress does it?"

"Nah," Dexter said dismissively. "I've always done it. Shelly and I just agree on that methodology. She listened to you, gave you options, and guided the offer process. That's what your boy, Julian, preaches, right?"

"Come on, man. She's selling beer. We're pitching a multi-million-dollar business deal. Don't put those things in the same folder. And letting me choose is not controlling a process."

"Guiding a process. And isn't it, dude? When your mom let you pick between two options for dinner, you made the decision, but who guided the process? Remember, we're a bunch of little kids running around." Dexter took another sip and stared up into nothingness— looking at memories. "A piece of you had to like the two dinner options, just like a piece of Char has to like what you propose. But the point is, what was your role? If your mom just said, 'I'm going to make meatloaf tonight,' you would probably start asking for something different...something more than she was willing to do. But when she offered you two reasonable options, your role changed. You weren't a negotiator; you were a decision-maker. You had some autonomy. And you were cool with it."

"Alright, then. What else does Shelly do? If that's her whole game...options...then I'm not impressed."

"She connects. Subtle, but real. She'll bring the bill, say your name, plant the idea of seeing each other again. You'll feel acknowledged. And then she's gonna invite you to try a different beer next time you come back. She'll reinforce the idea that you'll see each other again...that's she's gonna be in your future, and she'll hammer home that connection. Whether you admit it or not, she'll be one of the few people that makes you feel acknowledged today. And even though you're married—and you would never act on it in a million years because Kirsty would whip your ass—your caveman brain will tingle. You'll tip her more. You'll drink more. And you'll come back."

Will shook his head slowly, fighting a smile. "So, give Char some options?"

"Give her some options that speak to her interests, that let her know you've heard her. And if you communicate your authority in the process, she just might take you up on it."

They sipped their beers and tossed around ideas for Char's proposal. Eventually, Dexter caught Shelly's eye for the check, pantomiming his signature on his open palm. Shelly winked and was at their table in no time, a black folio in tow. Dexter pointed at Will, who raised his hand in acceptance.

"I enjoyed it, boys." She looked at Will. "Next time you're here, Will, you gotta try the Freestyle. It's light, but not as bitter." Will glared at Dexter, who smirked victoriously. As Shelly walked away, Will opened the folio. He scanned down to the bottom and, sure enough, a personal note appeared:

Come back and see me.
—Shelly.

Chapter 25

*"Trust is built on telling the truth,
not telling people what they want to hear."*
—Simon Sinek

11 DAYS TO RFP

The silver insulated mug sat in its indelibly scuffed spot on the desk next to the two iPhones and a half-eaten peanut butter protein bar. Char rubbed her face with both hands in exasperation as she stretched to relieve the vibrating sensation of sitting motionless in an office chair for too long. She was tired of looking at the computer screen and the misting rain through the window beyond it. She was bored; boredom tasted like crayon wax. The revenues and expenses from the night before reflected in her thick, black-rimmed glasses. Revenues were climbing, but slowly. Launch Pad Raleigh was enjoying steady growth. Her darling city, replete with highly educated young professionals who collectively decided to live and work near downtown, consistently drawing travelers to the city core and keeping occupancy rates up. Launch Pad Austin had enough leisure travel to create reasonable returns even though hotel rates were depressed. Launch Pad Charlotte, however, was an absolute bloodbath. Nearby office vacancy rates were approaching 24%, highlighting an over-exuberance of development when interest rates were low.

The myriad coworking spaces, once bastions of unkept hairdos, earbuds, and deadlines, were barely keeping the lights on, and some couldn't even do that. The major office tenants allowed many of their young constituents to utilize hybrid working schedules until the trend shifted—if that was ever going to happen. In doing so, the city shunned the throngs of business travelers that reliably descended on Charlotte throughout the week.

Her world was easier before. The economy had been hot, new hotel concepts popping up all over, and the proliferation of e-commerce-driven hotel businesses afforded smaller players, like Char, the opportunity to play with the big boys like Hilton and Marriott. For considerably less spent than one might think, she could buy her way to the top of web searches and various travel sites—she was good at appearing to be bigger than she was. When guests found Launch Pad, they were inundated with stunning imagery. Char had a passion, or possibly an obsession, for the way her properties were photographed. And Char alone selected which guest-generated pics would find their way onto Launch Pad's various platforms.

Recently, her late-night routine felt much different. It wasn't busy—busy would be good. It was vacant and answerless. The revenue simply wasn't there to support the expenses. In an effort to keep the monthly reporting looking solid for her lenders, Char had begun to age some payables. Now the vendors with delinquent payments were starting to call. Something had to give. Launch Pad was getting its fair share of the guests in its markets; there just weren't enough guests to go around. Char was understandably frustrated. Even in her frustration, she looked at the guests' social media feeds each night. They had become the solitary light amid the financial darkness that had settled in on the hotels.

One of the iPhones began to vibrate on her desk. It was the office line. Char reached over to grab the phone, shaking her head before she could even see the Caller ID. It was not a good time; it was rarely a good time.

"Launch Pad," she answered flatly.

"Char? That you?"

"Yes?"

"It's Will," he responded. "I was following up from our meeting. Got a second?"

She looked at her computer. It was fixed on the accounting software's dashboard screen, displaying the weekly profit and loss statements for each property—her entire business captured simply on a twenty-seven-inch monitor. "You know what...sure," she said with a surprisingly pleasant change in demeanor. At least Will wasn't looking for a payment.

"Great. How's the weather there?" he offered, breaking the ice.

"Shitty. It's raining, or misting, or something. Just gray outside."

"That's no good."

"Yeah, jogging is questionable today," she said.

"You're a runner?" Will couldn't hide his surprise. "I like to run myself. Helps with the stress."

"Me?" She sneered. "God, no. Watch 'em through my window. I'm addicted to them." She paused and grimaced at the absurdity. Char continued to look through the window as she spoke, dodging her head from side to side for a shot at recognizing any of the joggers. "Gets worse. I named each of them."

"Don't they already have names?"

"I only know my names."

"And what would those be?" he asked, continuing down the rabbit hole of aimless small talk.

"There's a bunch of them...Tight Shorts, Pinky, Serious Guy, Jazz Dance, Smurfette..." Her voice trailed, insinuating there were many more characters; the names rolled off with relative ease, giving credence to the fact that her fascination with these players was real.

"Who's your favorite?"

"Don't pick favorites." She reached down out of habit and tapped the trackpad on her computer. The screen had gone dark. Focusing on her monitor while playing voyeur to the street athletes was a skill honed with hours of practice. "Okay...it's Pinky."

"Wait. Let me guess. Does she have pink hair?"

"Nope. It's a guy. He's doughy and runs with his arms tucked in like a T-rex."

"So his name is Pinky?" Will asked, obviously not connecting the dots.

"Keeps his pinkies up." She shifted her head over, pressing the phone to her shoulder so she could downsize the budgets on her screen. "Like he's holding two glasses of tea. He's beautiful." She grabbed her insulated mug from its spot on the desk and slurped a sip, banging it back down out of routine. "You didn't call about my jogging friends, right?"

"No, guess not. I would like a video of Pinky if that's cool, though." Will chuckled. "So have you given any thought to our last meeting...with me, you, and Dex?"

"Nope," Char said bluntly in a disappointed tone. "We did this already, Will. Look, you and Dexter seem like nice guys, but this conversation...I just don't have time for it."

"Okay, that's fair enough. But what about the soul of your company? That's what you called it, right?"

Char scoffed, "What do you know about the soul of my company?"

"Nothing. That's the point, Char. That's not where I bring value here."

"You're not making sense."

"Look. Launch Pad is a great idea, and great ideas have a knack for growing. Sometimes they grow too fast. I used to see it at the bank every day, somebody borrowing money to catch up with their great idea. But then what happens? If the idea is good enough, it keeps growing. And the visionary—that's you, Char—becomes a business manager overnight. The creativity stops. The idea dilutes. And why? Because the great idea is bigger than the visionary. It has other needs."

"Still don't see your value."

"I'm getting there. Let me put my options on the table of what a deal might look like, then you tell me if I'm bringing value."

"Be my guest," Char responded. It was subtle, but something about the idea of options physically relaxed her. Though she had already shot the idea down, she sat back a bit in her chair and listened. She tasted caramel: the taste of curiosity.

"Option one. I give you a million dollars...well, technically Dex gives it to you...for 33% of your company. More importantly, I want to pay off your $2.55 million private equity loan on the Austin deal by refinancing your entire portfolio. Before you say no, please understand that move alone will create some bottom-line profit you don't currently have. After our share, you're still better off immediately based on the numbers."

Char interrupted him. "Interesting. But there's no way I can refinance the portfolio right now."

"You're right, me neither...and Char, I worked at a bank. But I do understand how it needs to be restructured, and Dex agreed to sign onto the note if I can get this deal done. His balance sheet is what you might call...stout."

"What's option two?"

"We refinance your portfolio, just like the other option, but we don't take an ownership role. You just make the same mortgage payments you're making now, and we keep the spread we created by refinancing your interest payments down on the hotels. And we'll have the same rights as your private equity partner in Austin." Will paused and let that concept sit for a minute.

"So you wouldn't technically be a partner?"

"That's right. As much as you may think otherwise, I listened to you, Char, and I'm trying to stitch together something that works for both of us."

"Why do it then?"

"Because, like I said, I don't want to control your company, Char. I want you to do that. But there are a few conditions in either scenario. One, Golden, Colorado, is Launch Pad's next stop. That's a big one for me. Two, we form a board to make important decisions about the company. If you and I disagree, then Dex breaks the tie."

"Your friend breaks the tie? That's more than a partnership. That's control. You're not hearing me. I don't want any partners. Get creative as you want, talking about restructuring and whatever other bullshit you can think of, but I still don't have control of my company. I didn't start this so someone else could tell me what to do."

"That's not what I offered you, Char. I don't want any creative control in your hotel operations...none. The day-to-day operations will never be a topic of conversation. I heard you the other day in your office. You're passionate. But here's the thing, every time we talk, you're working on numbers and expense reports. You can't work on your hotels if you're stuck working in them. We need to set up better systems. And we need to work on capturing every penny of profit we can and cutting every frivolous expense. But you...you need to be figuring out how to make sure the soul of the hotel is right. You're part of the product, Char." His lines were heartfelt, even if rehearsed. The idea of autonomy had been baked in by Dexter.

"So why try to get involved? If you don't want some control, what's the fucking point?"

Will answered, "Because I can't do what you do, Char. It's not my talent. That's the point here. Everything you're good at, I'm not. Every odd little nuance to your product that gets you going...none of that matters to me. God made me to do certain things, and none of them involves what you care about. But what I do care about is real estate and profits. You need that part now more than ever. Dex and I can help you there. You need two guys looking at a spreadsheet, not picking out which piece of art to use." He stopped as she chewed on the idea. "And, I guess, selfishly, I want to bring this project to my deal in Golden. I need something that'll make them move. For me, it's a no-lose proposition. For you, Char, either option accomplishes the most important thing first...it lets you sleep easier knowing you will have full control of your company no matter what."

"But if Dexter breaks a tie, I don't have control."

"Let's focus on what that means, Char. We can draft up an agreement that doesn't give us any say in the day-to-day operations. But it can give us some say in major business decisions. We'd have skin in the game, and we'd care deeply how that goes. You have a company that wants to scale. You need some people with aligned interests who can help you make solid decisions. That stuff doesn't have to keep you up at night."

Char sat gazing at her screen, her reports staring her in the face. The sea of red between the budget and actuals was daunting. She used to be almost giddy at the site of the daily numbers. It was the positive feedback loop with which she started each day. At one time Launch Pad Raleigh had soared past her budget estimates. Its success was the impetus for the entire idea of expanding Launch Pad to other cities. Now, the dog of the group, the Raleigh location was a reminder that the world was upside-down, and no answers seemed to be easy at the moment. The contemplative silence lasted long enough to warrant

Char snapping back to, and looking at the phone screen to make sure she hadn't let the call drop by mistake.

"What would keep me up at night right now..." Will continued without skipping a beat, "...is that shitty private equity deal you have in Austin."

"Why do you keep talking about that?" Char quizzed. "It's a high interest rate, I get it, but I can pay the note in Austin. That guy you're bashing helped me put the whole loan together."

Will sighed and said, "Dex dug into the math in your loan, Char. And then I calculated it myself. For starters, they're crippling your income. And nobody with an operating agreement that complicated is out to help you. That's for sure. The guy may be a private equity investor, but he's more like a loan shark, and you need to get him away from your business."

Char found herself defending Nick. "He supplied money, that's it. I needed it. We don't talk about Launch Pad. In fact, he reached out last week. First time in over a month. Wants to talk about the renewal. It's coming up. He wants to discuss—"

"Wait," Will interrupted. "I thought that was a five-year deal with the private equity group."

"Yeah, but it renews every year. Just kind of automatic."

"Oh man."

"What?"

"Char, I think you're about to find out what an asshole this guy really is."

"What do you mean?" Char replied with concern in her tone. She had unknowingly given Will a critical piece of information.

"What I mean is, I want you to consider the options on the table before that call. You don't have to answer me now, but think about them before you talk to Nick. Just trust me here," Will paused, seizing the moment. "And Char?"

"What?"

"If I'm right, maybe you'll see some value in me hanging around."

Char hung up the phone. She swallowed hard and pressed her tongue against the roof of her mouth. A far too familiar taste came back again: batteries. She got very little work done for the rest of the day.

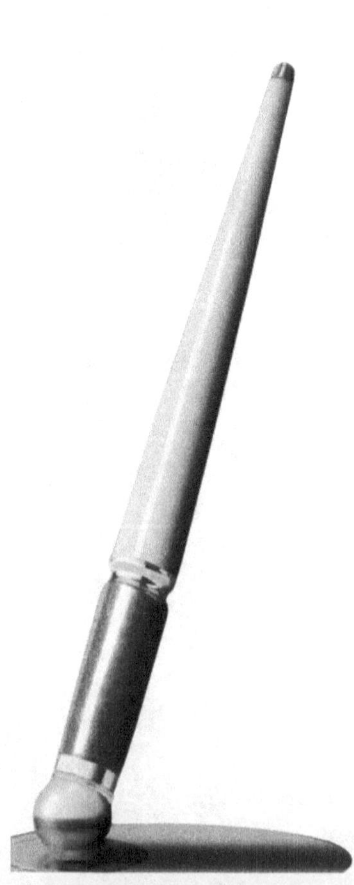

Chapter 26

"When someone shows you who they are, believe them the first time."

—Maya Angelou

10 DAYS TO RFP

The wheels of Nick's 911 Turbo S rolled to a stop at the intersection of South Congress and Mockingbird. A confident brunette stood at the corner waiting to cross. Her pure white blouse—an extra free button away from formal—gave way to long tight slacks above stunning gold stiletto heels. She represented the newer sect of South Congress inhabitants: young, beautiful, and confident, a far cry from the unabashedly weird that first made the area enticing. She started to cross, business tote in hand, and noticed Nick rolling his window down to ogle her. A coy smirk came across her face as her eyebrows lifted above her designer sunglasses. Nick nodded his head slowly in approval, shifted into neutral, and tapped the gas pedal. The engine revved, the equivalent of an audible catcall from his sports car. His phone began to ring. He glanced down quickly to see if he could ignore the call. It was Michael, his CIO/assistant, who, by sworn code, only called with important information. Torn between his natural instincts and call of duty, Nick was forced to make a decision.

Attempting to split the difference, Nick picked up the phone without breaking eye contact. His Bluetooth was connected, but the look of an important call was easier to communicate with phone in hand. The brunette's saunter was slow and teasing as she made her way near the front of his car, nearly halfway across the street. In a low tone, just shy of a whisper, Nick said, "Michael, you have three seconds. I'm staring at a fucking unicorn."

"Char Teague is on the line. You have a scheduled call with her."

Nick leaned his head back, took a deep breath, and exhaled mightily. Shaking his head, he winked at the unicorn, and offered a reluctant, but proud expression of, "Sorry, had to take this one." Nick tapped the pedal and let the engine scream briefly in salute. The confident brunette turned her gaze forward and sauntered the rest of the way through the crosswalk, ending their brief connection. "Put her through," he said and waited for the phone to click.

"Char, how's life in Raleigh? How are the hotels doing?" He asked the questions back-to-back as if they were synonymous. His tone was professional, almost somber.

"I'm good, and the numbers are good. You said you wanted to jump on a call?" she replied, never one for pleasantries.

The light turned green, and Nick rolled forward, instinctively peering off to the right to steal one last glimpse of his unicorn amid the office entrances tucked between retail storefronts, a futile effort to track her potential future whereabouts. "Yeah, I wanted to get your thoughts on the markets for these hotels." He craned his neck one last time; the confident brunette was gone.

"Well," Char said hesitantly. "Austin's picking up. Announcements every day. Tesla, Oracle, Dropbox, they're all locating there. Everybody's pumped about it." Though unnatural, she had developed a salesmanship ever-present in the hospitality industry.

"I read about that. That's great. Of course, that's going to take a long time to move the needle for Launch Pad, right?" he offered rhetorically. "What's the market occupancy month-over-month versus last year?" His line of questioning signaled a tougher conversation was about to ensue.

"Sucks compared to last year, but we're crushing where we were six months ago." Char was still selling the positive.

"And what about the other Launch Pads...how are they doing?"

"They're climbing, just like Austin. We're small compared to the competition...easier for us to gain occupancy. Gonna be in great shape for next year." She paused to breathe. "I just need everyone to leave me the fuck alone."

"Look, I know nobody wants to deal with the elephant in the room here, Char, but none of us knows if that will be the case, right? I mean, numbers could drop next year...could be another COVID scenario. Kinda changes the game a bit." Nick adjusted the tone of his voice and quality of his delivery, like a doctor delivering life-changing bad news. It was slow and deliberate, and lacked the authenticity needed to be comfortable.

"You're a piss-poor cheerleader," Char said, attempting to sprinkle in levity.

He instinctively shifted the 911 Turbo S into third gear as he barreled down South Congress attempting to catch the yellow light. "Char, you know I'm a fan of yours. You have an amazing product, but right now I'm struggling to tolerate the risk in my portfolio. We agreed on certain terms and metrics that needed to be met year one in order for me to renew my original position. It's nobody's fault here, but obviously you aren't making the type of gross profit we both anticipated. All of a sudden my investors are nervous about the leadership on this asset." Nick steered the conversation to his trusty, vague group of investors—a favorite move of his when the message was tough to swallow. He had picked up the tactic in the early days when his bravado escorted him into some highly charged conversations about exiting deals. If the investors were pushing him to make the move, it was simply less adversarial, and if he played his cards right, he could even be viewed as a cooperative problem solver.

"Leadership?" Char belted. "What do you want me to do? Was I supposed to develop a vaccine? This is bullshit, Nick. We're outpacing the market at all three properties. Nobody on earth is doing better right now. I'm making interest payments. What else would these assholes want?" Char apparently did not view his role as cooperative.

"They called me last week. You're actually thirty-five days behind on our priority payment. They want out. They want me to place the money in a more popular investment. Every jackass thinks that building a warehouse for the big boys is foolproof now." Nick elevated his ruse into an outright charge against his investor group—yet another well-practiced ploy.

His timing was flawless; he pulled into the subterranean parking deck below his South Congress office space and left the 911 Turbo S purring in his reserved parking spot right next to Michael's Honda Civic. The wall in front of him read "Boanerges Investments." He had five reserved spots, although he and Michael currently made up the entire company—a bit of future planning.

"So what does that mean?" Char said pressingly. "It's a five-year deal, right? You can't just pull the plug on me now. I've never been late before. It's crazy out there. We're partners, remember?"

Nick, now sitting idly in the parking spot, found the timing right to help...himself. "Okay, I know this puts you in a tough position. That's why I talked to them before this call and got some consensus. I don't want to leave you out in the cold here, Char. We have another way we could do this: If I leave my money in place and you give up 50% of the ownership of Launch Pad Austin." He delivered the blow and waited patiently for the response. Offers of this ilk elicited unpredictable responses. Nick found it best to simply throw the punch;

his victim would either fall to the ground or fight back hard. There was no middle ground.

"50% of my business? You piece of shit! You had this cooked up from the beginning, didn't you?"

Nick, now a seasoned deal pugilist, did not return in kind. He slowed his tone even more, attempting to smooth the situation. His bedside manner was impeccable. He couched the ideas as if they were inevitable, as if anyone in his position would have to take the same approach. Nick was between a rock and a hard place, and that's where he needed to be to get this deal done. "Char, I'm trying to help you. At this point, you aren't meeting any of the financial covenants in our agreement. As a matter of fact, you aren't meeting them for the bank either. Your cash reserves are gone, and the current revenues won't support our deal structure in Austin. I honestly don't know how you've made the mortgage payments up to now, but the fact that this payment is late has given everybody anxiety."

"You gotta lot of nerve, Nick," she said soberly. The trajectory of the conversation was taking its toll. "I'm not giving up ownership. Tell them I've got this under control. I'll find a way to make that late payment, but you gotta get these guys off my back."

"It's too late for that, but I do have a second idea. I know it's going to be next to impossible right now to find money to replace my investment. And, look, we both know you're also going to start taking heat from your lenders. What if I loan you all the money?"

"You're already loaning me what I need."

"No, I mean all the money for all the Launch Pads. The rate will need to be a little higher because of the risk, but I can do that, Char."

"How's that supposed to be better?! Jesus, Nick. I'm already drowning here. I can't take on higher debt payments."

"You know the math, Char. You don't have a lot of options here.

You can try to right the ship without the lenders breathing down your neck. I would replace the debt with my investors' money on all three projects. But I'm going to have to move quickly if we want to pull this one off. It involves a lot of politicking on my end."

Char was quiet. The chasm between the pretense of the phone call and the actual dialogue taking place warranted some immediate introspection. Nick was happy with the silence; silence meant she was contemplating. He would sit in his 911 Turbo S as long as it took, but he would much rather get an answer in the immediacy of the call than give her days to think about it. In the moment, there were only two answers to the equation, and he had supplied them both. Char was sharp and gritty, and if given enough time, she might find another solution that didn't involve Nick achieving what he wanted, or the resolve to fight him tooth and nail.

"I need to call you right back," she spoke up.

"Okay. How long?"

"Couple of minutes."

Nick hung up and grabbed his laptop from the passenger seat of the tiny sports car. It was a short walk to the parking garage elevators, which took him directly to the Boanerges Investment offices. By now, Michael should've digested the morning news and screened any early calls from investors hoping to catch Nick before the markets opened. Though Nick lived in Austin and kept only a small portion of the fund in stocks, he'd made it clear that the early trading hours were no time to bother him. Projecting a sense of busyness was strategic. His role was deliberately vague, and it served him well to appear constantly in motion, too busy to explain.

The investors played along. Their egos kept them from asking too many questions, and when they did, Nick's answers only deepened the mystery. They liked it that way—believing their "guy" was working behind the curtain on complicated investments they barely understood. After all, complexity implied intelligence. And intelligence meant their money was in good hands.

"Morning, Michael. Who called?" Nick said while approaching Michael's open office door on his way to his office at the end of the hall. As he passed, he saw his CIO/assistant was on the phone. Michael motioned with a pointing finger that he would be passing the call to Nick as soon as he got to his phone. Nick mouthed silently back, "Who is it?"

"Char," Michael mouthed back and then said audibly, "He's just walking in. I'll put you through." Michael, ever professional, paged Nick's phone. "Char Teague on Line 1."

Nick, still with his computer in tow, pushed the Line 1 button on his desk phone and said, "That was fast. So what are you thinking, Char?"

"I'm buying you out. Me and my new partner think your ideas are really shitty," she said with unfounded confidence.

"Really?!" Nick scorned. "And who is this partner?"

"His name is Will Powell, and you're not changing my mind." Nick found himself on the receiving end of a dial tone for a change.

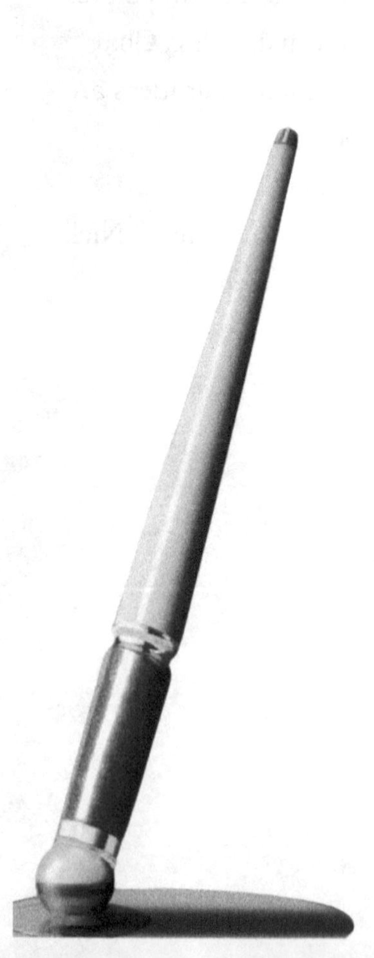

Chapter 27

—Yogi Berra

9 DAYS TO RFP

Will reached down and tied the laces on his neon-yellow running shoes outside of his home in Littleton. Will, inspired by Char's distant friends, decided running was an appropriate activity for what had been a relaxing Saturday. Today was particularly inspiring. Char had given him the news: she had chosen one of his options with no renegotiation, thanks to Dex, and the only appropriate action seemed to be a long, celebratory run to clear his mind.

Will eased back up, shook out his legs, and gave his AirPods a gentle push to ensure they were properly planted. A quick scroll through the music app on his phone started an all-too-familiar playlist of songs. His eyes closed briefly as the intro to "November Rain" by Guns N' Roses began playing loudly in his ears. The noise of dogs barking and cars rolling down his street gave way to the melodic piano intro against the synthesized raindrops. He exhaled deeply and began to jog slowly west into the setting sun; it was time to decompress. The work was paying off and the pieces were beginning to finally fall into place. Maybe Julian was right. Maybe it was as easy as following a process.

The playlist was structured, each song leading to the next in a deliberate order. Kirsty had curated the list for him; she knew his favorites. He hadn't listened to them in a while—long enough they almost felt foreign. Running wasn't second nature to him, but maybe it could be. His best ideas always seemed to come near the point of exhaustion, when his mind was clear and distractions faded.

He should do this more often.

This would be the headspace he needed to develop the first steps in taking stock of Launch Pad. Julian would no doubt be ecstatic. It was his vision, after all. And Dexter might owe him a drink after the deal was signed and sealed. Of course, that felt perfunctory following Char's willingness to accept their investment. Maybe they'd discuss Dexter's new software company, RevMax, over that drink. Char would surely love to hear the upside potential of some easy additional revenue ginned up by the click of a button. For a guy who had felt lost only a few weeks earlier, this moment felt amazingly right.

He picked up the pace as "Walk This Way" by Run-DMC began to deliver a beat that demanded physical reaction. Thanks, Kirsty.

Ten minutes into the run, the music paused. "Call From: Boenerges Investments." Siri obviously did not respect the musical lyricism of Run-DMC. He instinctively said, "Answer," with little regard for what would happen next.

"This Will Powell?"

"Yeah," Will said, allowing his fast-paced gait to slow evenly to a brisk walk. He could pick the pace right back up as soon as he shook the call. "This is Will."

"You got some balls."

"Excuse me?" Will said, his heavy breathing audible to the listener.

"Catch you at a bad time?"

"Actually, I'm just trying to get in a quick—"

"Good. You know what tortious interference with a contract is, Will?"

"Who is this?"

"It's a pretty sloppy play. You might not know it. A lot of rookies don't understand you can't simply break up a fucking contract."

"Nick? Nick Spencer?"

"Great. You know who I am. That's not a good sign, Will. That means you knew Char and I had an agreement. You knew she was late on her payment, which means she's in default and I'm exercising my rights. Shouldn't have copped to that. I would've played dumb there, if I were you."

Will's brisk walk slowed to a standstill. He was in unfamiliar territory, but taking verbal abuse from a stranger was not in the cards. "Listen, asshole. I'm not a rookie. And I don't know who you think you are, but you aren't just going to call me up and—"

"I'll do whatever the hell I want," Nick interrupted for a second time. "Look, I'm sitting on a $100 million portfolio. You think they're going to be happy if I don't close this deal? And I gotta say, it's a pretty sweet deal for me."

Will stood silently. The barrage had been swift and he was flat footed, now squinting into the sun. His heart raced, kickstarted by the jog and exploding into palpable rhythm by the immediate onslaught at the hands of Nick Spencer. At that moment, he did not know the cards to play. Julian would have an answer for this, but Julian wasn't there to coach him. He quickly ripped through the mental list of rules. Nothing seemed to fit his current circumstance; craft and process alluded him. Adrenaline was at the wheel, and his reversion to old habits was unavoidable. And adding to the aggravation was the intense Denver sunset. The sunset...empathy...interest. Julian's parable danced through his mind.

"Why are you calling me, Nick?"

Silence.

Will continued, "What do you want? I'm listening."

Now Nick was briefly silent. "I want my deal," he said coolly.

"You want your deal?" If you have nothing, repeat what they say. Let them talk.

"Yeah, I need to put this money to work. You're screwing that up for me, Will."

"How much money we talking?" Will continued, hoping if he kept Nick talking some shred of useful evidence would start to present itself.

"That's none of your damn business. But a lot."

"I thought you loaned a little over $2.5 million on Austin."

Nick belted out a sinister laugh. "You think this is about my mezz loan in Austin?"

"Isn't it? What happens if we just pay you off in Austin? I can do that quickly, Nick, and all this goes away."

"You should've read my agreement instead of skimming it. The Austin loan was just a down payment. She's in default based on our terms. I can step right into her shoes. I'm taking the whole fucking portfolio, Will, and you can't do shit about it."

Will paused, collecting his thoughts and allowing a level head to prevail. "So is that the deal, Nick? Do you really want Launch Pad, or do you just need to place a ton of cash?"

"They don't pay me to sit on piles of money."

"Who's they?" Will asked.

"They are a bunch of guys who will own your ass if they want to. We're done here," Nick said, frustrated. "I've got an agreement with Char. If you try to get in the way, I'll steamroll you. The takeover docs are being drafted now. I'd suggest you back out by tomorrow. If not, I'm going to start the process of filing suit with the attorneys." The next sound Will heard was a click. Then silence. Then Run-DMC returned without prompting.

Run-DMC gave way to Survivor's "Burning Heart"—Kirsty would

not have made a living as a DJ. His yellow shoes now eased into the cadence of the beat. It was a subconscious effort. The lyrics didn't register, just the rhythm. His blood was pumping now, almost enough to stem the anxiety produced in the quick exchange with Nick. With his first quick steps toward home, rivulets of sweat were starting to work their way down his forehead. His pace was fast. The endorphins were releasing, and the euphoric feeling of being both exhausted and clear-minded was setting in. Though he was proud of the way he handled Nick, Nick was now a major problem. He needed to talk to Julian.

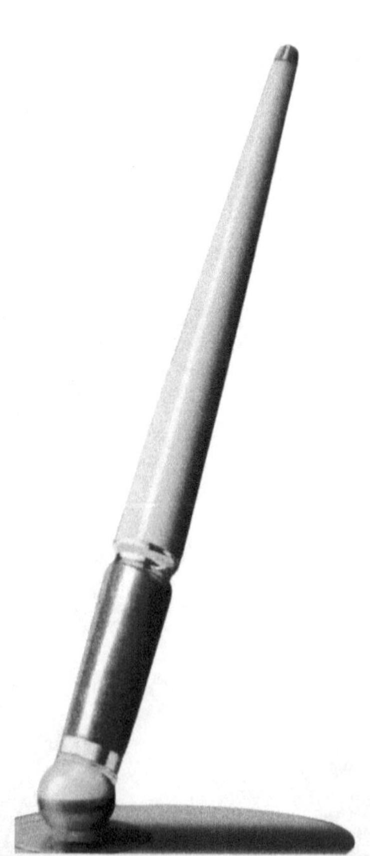

Chapter 28

"The soul never thinks without a picture."

—Aristotle

7 DAYS TO RFP

The deep tones of Julian's doorbell resonated throughout the glass house.

Curiously, Vince greeted Will at the door. "He's in the office," Vince offered. Will, though puzzled at the driver greeting him—or being in the house at all, for that matter—said thanks and worked his way through the living room to Julian's office. Julian was seated at the desk in anticipation of their prearranged meeting. Will hurriedly plopped down and rubbed his hand back and forth along the arm of the cognac leather chair; the anxiety was audible as the oiled leather croaking with each rub of his palm. "Her equity partner doesn't want to be bought out. And, Julian...I'm telling you...he's a real piece of work. This guy's going to screw up our deal. He's not walking softly here."

"Is that his decision to make?" Julian asked, reaching for his notebook and golden pen, unfazed by the lack of salutations. "This equity partner, what is the impetus, I wonder, for him to take over Launch Pad?" The calm with which he delivered both questions stood in contrast to Will's demeanor. Julian's ability to separate the emotion from the problem was not natural. It was discernibly learned, drilled into the fabric of his being to a point that all problems seemed to appear as mere puzzles on his desk.

"He's a shark. I talked to him myself. He said that Char's in default because of her late payment, and he has the right to step into her shoes under their agreement. He's going to send me the doc they signed. This asshole's been angling at this from the beginning."

"Step in her shoes?"

"Yeah, take the whole thing over. Apparently, he thinks he has the right to kick her completely out of the deal."

Julian looked up from his desk. "Remind me, which hotel is he involved in again?"

"Austin," Will said curiously—Julian should've known that fact. "He's in Austin."

"Perhaps he's doing her a favor. Austin seemed like her first mistake."

"No, I mean he can kick her out of ALL of them." Will reproached. "I offered to buy him out of his Austin position, and he wasn't interested. I know he's full of shit, but he didn't bite. He says he's going to make arrangements to prepare the takeover docs."

Julian looked down at his calendar. "Unfortunate. The RFP is in seven days, Will. This is late notice." He reached over and started flipping back and forth through pages of his notebook, shaking his head, as if the answers were already transcribed before him. His desk was predictably tidy as usual: pens standing upright in a sleek wooden stand, a metal box of paper clips, rubbers bands, a staple remover, and that one mysterious picture facing him at an angle. But the room around him was chaos, his purposefully jumbled books still stacked and shuffled about in an order only Julian could discern. Will sat quietly, still unable to piece together the pattern—not alphabetical, not by genre. It was as if Julian's mind was on display in printed form around him. "Perhaps I was unclear with my prior rule. Did I not stress the importance of controlling the offer process?" Julian asked.

Will clenched the ends of the chair, frustrated and white-knuckled. "If I had more time, I could flip this guy. But he's sharp, and he's tough. I don't want to push too hard, or he'll use my lack of time against me."

"Perhaps he could just as easily use your lack of testosterone against you."

"What did you just say?" Will puffed up his chest in defiance.

"It appears you don't have the stones to call him and tell him he won't be buying Launch Pad as long as you're involved."

Will's shoulders pulled in close to his body as he crossed his arms. "Julian, you ever call my manhood into question again and I'll—"

"Perfect. That's the spirit," Julian cheered. "Do you see how easy that was? You're a reasonable person, and yet, how much harder would I need to push for you to make an obvious mistake? Now realize how much easier it would be to get to that level of excitement with a pernicious character like this Nick. And if the conversation escalates to that level, you lose. First things first, he's attempting to squeeze your timeline, which is a prototypical move from a narcissist. The best defense for this is to simply ignore it. If there's a real timeline, you will know it. His language will be very direct and conclusive. Any softness in his statement...any hint of 'probably' or 'getting ready to' statements ensure the timelines are fictitious. They should be ignored, not argued."

"If all that's true, then this guy's definitely bluffing on the timeline," Will offered. "He was posturing. I should call him to the carpet."

Julian placed his elbows on the desk, interlacing his fingers. "And therein lies the craft. If you simply pick a fight, you'll both ultimately lose. Two dogs ejected from the park. And you'll both regret it."

Will stood up and began aggressively pacing the room; he was visibly working himself up. The thought of going toe-to-toe with Nick Spencer was enough to get the blood flowing. "So then what are the next steps?" he said while gesturing with an outstretched arm, inviting Julian to start talking.

"For starters, calm down, Will. That's step one."

"I'm serious."

"As am I," Julian said tersely. "Narcissists and bullies like to elevate the energy. They feed on emotion. You need to cut off that food supply. Calm is their famine."

"So be calm," Will said mockingly. "You're really bringing the goods tonight. Very helpful."

"Calm is always an objective. With Char. With this Nick character. It doesn't matter. Calm projects control. And remember you need to—"

"Control the offer process," Will finished Julian's sentence. "I got that part. Now tell me, how are they different? If you're going to tell me there's a one-size-fits-all approach to dealing with Char and Nick, I'm about to lose interest. Char is awesome and she wants to work together. Nick Spencer's a bully. He'll burn the house down to get what he wants. You weren't there...you didn't hear him talk."

"You're right, I wasn't," Julian replied, unprovoked. "Yet, I've dealt with him many times by another name."

"So how do I deal with Nick?" Will asked feverishly.

"Rely first on the rules we've discussed. You must realize your value, and you must regain control of the offer process. Above these two, you need to understand his interests. Don't forget, sharks have interests, too. Perhaps start with the notion that he and Char share at least one common thread...they're human, just as you are. Ask yourself how different you are from them both. And me for that matter. We are all entrepreneurial by nature, driven by two things: greed and the necessity to carve our own way. We are, of sorts, unemployable, unwilling to bend to the will of others. By our very nature, we are then influenced by vision of the future and fear of loss. These are a common interest in every negotiation and can be our Achilles' heel. I'm confident this confrontation with Nick has escalated past visioning, but we all maintain a fear of loss." Julian's wry smile showed on his face. "Fear has affected Char, and I suspect it will have greater impact on Nick Spencer if aimed correctly. He wants to win at all costs, and perhaps more than you, he wants to look good doing it. But be sure of this: none of us wants to lose."

Will stopped pacing, his shoulders slumped as he sighed heavily. "How the hell am I supposed to feel better about dealing with a guy who will win at all costs?"

Julian continued smiling. "Because someone who will win at all costs is deathly afraid of losing. Even more so than Char Teague. You don't need to mine for that information. It's encoded in his DNA. The craft is in showing him the prospect of failure. And if the opportunity presents itself, a path to look good by not failing. It's only when fear of loss becomes a real threat that the negotiation can continue and you may regain control."

"His agreement gives him the right to take the properties," Will offered in defeat. "It's pretty cut-and-dried."

"Irrelevant."

"Hardly," Will shot back.

"If he chooses to act, has success been preordained? Don't look at this in such binary terms. You have to be able to show him the potential of loss either way. The Nick Spencers of the world want to prove they have all the power to choose, so let him choose freely. You simply need to know the choice he wants to make. The bigger a bully, the more obvious the choice. He's already threatened it, correct?"

Julian was staring off at the books again as if speaking to the entire room, laser focused. He then trained his gazed directly on Will, who nodded in agreement. "When you calmly convince Nick that the choice, or action, he wants to force upon you has great potential to create a loss for him, the balance shifts. And now you have leverage." Julian's smile reappeared. "And you can feel it in the marrow of your bones. It's euphoric."

Will began pacing the room again. Julian's description, though eloquent, presented a sinister lust for winning that Will had not yet seen from the silver-haired gentleman. "So how do I convince Nick Spencer that he's making a mistake...that he could suffer a loss?"

"Perhaps you could tell me? What would your next step be?"

Will continued pacing and began to think out loud. "He won't see my value. It doesn't mean anything to him. And I can't tell him what to do."

"It appears you are ready for another rule, then," Julian straightened his two pointer fingers from his interlaced hands and rested them in the crook between his lower lip and chin.

"RULE NUMBER FIVE: SPEAK FROM YOUR AUTHORITY. NO PERSON IS THE AUTHORITY ON ALL SUBJECTS."

"Man. We're back to this again? Authority?"

"We will always be back to this."

"Well, you should know Dex basically told me the same thing."

"Then maybe the hippie and I are more alike after all."

"And what is my authority?"

"It's whatever his isn't."

"Again with the cryptic speak," Will groused, his pacing now relegated to the back-and-forth directly in front of Julian's desk.

"If you're not the absolute authority on the subject, then change the subject," Julian said with utter simplicity. "You can't be the authority on Nick's business, but perhaps real estate is your subject to own, or hotel operations, or Char Teague herself. Each party always has a subject of which they are the authority."

"Dex says you have to acknowledge their authority first before showing them yours."

"I see you've given it some thought. Excellent. There is merit to that theory, so long as the focus is centered around your authority over theirs. That is absolutely critical. If you haggle with a homeless man, he is the authority on surviving a cold night. And if merely surviving is the focus of your dealings, he will dictate the narrative." Julian paused. "Your friend Don Andino is no doubt a master at this concept. You said it yourself. He took the city's narrative and turned it into a discussion about winterization." He chuckled. "He made that word up for all I know. It's a different scenario, but the craft is identical. He changed the conversation to focus on something about which he has absolute authority."

"Now we're talking about Don Andino? You're all over the place, Julian."

"I most certainly am not. It's universal. The rules are the rules. Do you remember the day we met? The auction? You were there to buy real estate, and I wanted you to enter an RFP on the Telemark Building."

Will looked at Julian, waiting for the punchline. "Yeah, I remember."

"So why then did I choose to be the authority on auctions? Could it be that I knew I was the authority on the subject? Interesting that you did not second-guess the correlation between the auction and the task

I required of you. But I gathered you would assume, rather erroneously, that you were the authority on real estate. Therefore, I chose another indisputable authority. These pieces are universal...activity, finding interests, controlling the offer process, finding your authority. The craft lies in the spaces between. Char and Nick are both unique, but in a sense they're generic. They're the two poles, the north and south. When you recognize the traits, you'll run into these two people by a different name over and over. The Char Teagues of the world respond positively to their interests, which can be cultivated with thoughtful questions. This Nick...Nick..."

"Spencer...Nick Spencer," Will filled in.

"Right, yes, Nick Spencer," Julian said with disdain. "The Nick Spencers will hold their interests close to the vest, wrapped up tightly so that no one may see. Ironically, their fear of sharing reveals their fear of loss. But either must respect your authority."

Will, still pacing, turned and cocked his head, "And how do you know what he's afraid of losing?"

"It will be written on the hammer he tries to crush you with." Julian pushed his notebook aside and stared again at the notes in his calendar, appearing to land on a date with his finger. He maintained his nonchalance and even tone as he said, "Perhaps it's time I paid this gentleman a visit."

"Wait, why you and not me?" Will asked.

"You're not prepared."

"In what way?"

"In the way we're having this conversation now, and this cannot be left to chance."

Will stopped pacing, stood squarely in front of Julian, placing his hands on the desk, almost knocking over the picture that faced away from him. "And why are you the white knight here?"

"Do you understand what he's afraid of losing?" Julian asked.

"No," Will replied. He looked down for a moment before saying, "Well, maybe. Nick said he had to place a ton of money. That's gotta have something to do with his plan."

"Interesting," the silver-haired gentleman responded. "And do you know why?"

"No, do you?"

"I will before I see him," Julian offered. "And I'll understand where my authority lies. You can count on that." He returned his finger to the calendar, tracing through the days. "I'll go on Wednesday. That gives us a few days to resolve the matter."

"It's Monday. He lives in Austin." Will said.

"Unfortunate," Julian said with a look of disappointment. "I'll find my Stetson and designer boots." Julian placed his pen down on the legal pad, shifted the pad to the center of his large-format calendar, and walked directly past Will's chair as if he was not there. "Vince," Julian said loudly as he exited the room, not knowing where Vince might be located in the vast space outside the office. "I've got some homework to do. Please make sure to change the oil in the Town Car."

***

Will stood up and started to leave. As he turned, the back of the picture on Julian's desk caught his eye. Though he was in no mood for childish sleuthing, his curiosity was getting the better of him—a single inspiration atop the desk of an indisputably complex creature. He had been reminded of it when he almost knocked the picture down earlier. Will slid between the bookshelf and the corner of the desk, leaning out over his left foot to catch a quick glimpse in case the silver-haired gentleman returned.

He reached out for the picture frame, extending his torso passed some imaginary line, which seemed slyer than simply edging up to the desk. As he leaned forward the word, "*Will*," caught his eye on the calendar. There it was, "*Will*," over and over again in perfect penmanship. The large-format calendar, set to October, was chock-full of notes in the first seven days—foretelling that every day to come would surely follow suit. His name appeared consistently in each square: *Will meeting with Char, Will at home office 6:45, Will and Dexter flight #7144 to Raleigh*. He reached over and opened the notebook with one hand, again looking over his shoulder to make sure no one was lurking. The notes were in jarring detail. Every account fastidiously recorded as if Julian were taking them for someone else. The revelation almost completely redirected his focus from the picture and his initial curiosity.

The picture.

It was the picture that lured him into sneaking in the first place. For a moment, he turned his attention away from the troubling mass of notes on the calendar. Will twisted the frame to face him. His eyes widened. He turned again quickly to ensure he was alone. Julian would not appreciate the reconnaissance, especially not this particular mission. Will turned back to the picture for confirmation. He stared at the image, investigating each detail until he was absolutely sure of what he saw. A warm rush of anxious blood surged through his body. "Oh, shit."

Chapter 29

"The supreme art of war is to subdue the enemy without fighting."

—Sun Tzu

5 DAYS TO RFP

The October wind whipped through the open windows of the 911 Turbo S as Nick Spencer barreled down a short section of I-35 toward the South Congress exit. Changing lanes with the deftness of an Indy driver, he pinned the accelerator to the floor and wove around the slow-moving vehicles lacking his ever-present sense of urgency. The opposite side of I-35 was jam-packed with well-dressed professionals funneling into the city, but Nick, heading southbound, enjoyed just enough vehicle separation to dominate his morning commute.

Fifteen minutes later, he was easing the sports car into the underground parking deck of his office building. A few right-hand turns led him to the five spaces designated for Boanerges Investments. Michael's silver Honda Civic was reliably nestled in the far left. However, a rather large black sedan with Colorado tags had carelessly parked across the dividing line, and now occupied two of Nick's remaining four spots. The freshly polished bumper protruded into the drive aisle; the black Town Car seemed fully grown among a collection of expensive children—notwithstanding Nick's 911 Turbo S.

"Jackass," Nick said, as he forcefully pulled the hand-stitched leather steering wheel and whizzed into one of the two vacant spaces. Upon further inspection, the large black sedan was still running, and the olive-skinned driver was focused straight ahead like an automaton. He appeared to be scratching letters onto a crossword puzzle in a newspaper with a tiny pen. Nick rapped on the window with his knuckles. The diminutive driver turned his head slowly, appraising Nick from head to toe, and rolled down the window.

"Hey, asshole, you can't park in these spots," Nick said, skipping any morning pleasantries.

"Take it up with him." The driver delivered the message with no emotion and an obvious lack of regard for Nick's authority.

"With who?" Nick demanded, still holding on to his bravado.

The driver furrowed an eyebrow and moved his hand to the door controls, pushing the metallic button that slowly raised the window; a high-pitched whine emanated from the glass as it closed in Nick's face.

"Open the window!" Nick shouted.

The driver flashed an empty smile. He returned his focus to the newspaper and was again scratching letters into the crossword puzzle. Nick, assessing the driver's lack of regard, turned with an audible huff, grabbed his computer, and headed toward the elevators leading to his office.

Upon entering the glass door marked "Boanerges Investments," he headed toward Michael's office and began to shout. "Hey, did you see that fucking guy parked—" He cut the statement short as he noticed a silver-haired gentleman sitting with Michael, calmly enjoying a sip of coffee.

"Nick Spencer, I presume." Julian stood and offered a hand to shake. "Julian Darrow."

"Your driver parked in my spot," Nick posited as he shook Julian's hand.

"Oh, Vince? My apologies. He's a poor substitute for a driver. I keep him around for the conversation." He walked around the chair. "Shall we?" Julian gestured to the hall as if he were the office tenant.

"Julian, did we have a meeting lined up? If not, I'm busy today." Nick feebly attempted to regain control of his environment. He was not a fan of being handled, especially when Michael was around to witness it.

Julian started walking toward the door, putting his hand on Nick's shoulder as he passed. "I'll just take a moment of your time." Julian eased into the hall as Nick started to pull Michael's door shut behind them. With his head still inside the doorway, Nick mouthed "You're dead" to his unwitting protégé.

Nick, now in the hallway alone with Julian, seized on the moment before the silver-haired gentleman could speak. "You got thirty seconds to tell me what we're meeting about or I'm walking through that door." Nick pointed at his personal office.

"I believe you have a vested interest in Launch Pad Hotels," Julian said plainly. "And perhaps, in the short time I have, we can engage in a productive conversation."

"Not much to talk about there," Nick said as he started to head toward his office. "If by vested interest you mean I'm about to own the entire fucking thing, then you're right, I have a vested interest."

Julian looked quizzically at Nick. "That's correct. Exactly the way I understand it. Char Teague is noncompliant due to her inability to make her payment this month. And in your loan documents, that is a technical default, giving you the ability to step into her shoes, as it were."

"Yep." Nick's face was triumphant. To hear someone else articulate the genius deal he had composed was satisfying. Far too many had underestimated him as a smooth-talking salesman, a money raiser. Salesmen didn't craft intricate equity deals that left them holding all the cards.

"Unfortunate," Julian said. "For her."

"Yep," Nick said, relishing his accomplishment.

"Do you know the smell she'll miss most, Nick?" Julian rubbed his chin and gazed right past Nick's head, looking as if he were conjuring up the answer in the distance.

"What's that?"

"The vomit," Julian said with a slight wince. "It's rather overpowering the morning after a night on the town. And it's stubborn...it won't simply wipe up once it's dried. Often times you have to scrape it off the edges of the toilet with your fingernail. Of course, you don't want to do it, but it can be the most expedient way, I'm told."

"She owns three hotels worth millions. I don't think she cleans the toilets."

"Not as her daily occupation. But I assure you, Nick, the smell of bile mixed with cocktails is etched in her memory. It's a particularly pungent aroma. The variety of smell you can feel, a byproduct of the business she built."

"I hope this is headed somewhere quickly, Julian." Nick walked through the door of his personal office and plopped down at his desk. He motioned for Julian, who was already approaching. "She won't be cleaning toilets when I own the hotels. Char is too talented for that. She can dream up the next project, and the next one."

"Do you like cleaning toilets, Nick?"

"Again with the fucking toilets?" Nick said, his aggravation intensifying.

"It's a messy business. When the housekeeper calls in sick at the last minute. It won't be Char Teague cleaning them. You will have taken that sort of passion away from her. She will be too jaded to see the genius of your deal. She'll only see a man that stole her business." The silver-haired gentleman took his seat directly opposite Nick and continued. "Entrepreneurial spirit doesn't employ well. It doesn't fall in line...especially when there's resentment." Julian seemed to stare directly through Nick's head, out over the bustling South Congress scene. His casual demeanor further intensified the young portfolio manager's ire. "The issue is with your logic. It assumes this business is a commodity, a widget; when, in fact, it is not. If you move forward with this Launch Pad takeover, you aren't buying a revenue stream, you're buying question marks. And no price you'll pay will afford you the woman that started it."

"I have P&L statements that say differently. And I can bring in a management group to run it if I have to."

"I would suggest interviewing them quickly, then. That's another game all unto itself, I'm sure. But that game isn't for me. I know very little about hotels. I'm into simpler ventures."

"Simpler ventures, huh?" Nick refuted with an expression of disbelief.

Julian tilted his head and softly smiled as he spoke. "You strike me as a sophisticated man, one who understands his business," Julian said. Nick nodded in agreement. "And what business are you in exactly?"

"I invest money for a return. It's that simple," Nick replied. "My investors trust me to find the right deals. I don't have any bullshit rules around it. I see opportunity and I make a move."

"And this type of investment. This type of corporate arbitrage, if you will. Is that how you afford those cufflinks?" Julian looked down at the large white folds of Nick's cuffs, a shiny pair of gold cufflinks standing in stark contrast to the brilliant white.

Nick leaned in over his elbows. "How about we get to the fucking point? You didn't land in my office unannounced so we could dissect my business and talk about my cufflinks. You obviously have some interest here. Let's get on with it, Julian."

"Very astute. I can see you are a man not to be trifled with. I shall cut to the chase. I'm here to keep you from making a mistake, son. There's a reason Char Teague is in default. Launch Pad Hotels is on the verge of collapse if Char Teague does not restructure its debt. Perhaps we can both agree that is an objective reality."

"That's a short-term problem. The hotel market is on the way up. It will be normalized by Q4 next year."

Julian pulled his chair closer to Nick, resting his elbows on top of the desk. As he went to fold his hands together, Nick thought he saw his name, "Nick Spencer," curiously written on the inside of Julian's palm. It was quick, and he wasn't absolutely sure, but for a man that prided himself on processing information at rapid speed, he was more confident than not he saw his name scribbled on Julian's palm in red ink—as if his name were so insignificant it was hard for Julian to remember.

"You're buying someone else's obsession. That's not a viable business plan. Char Teague's hotels outperform every market they're in. Why is that? Is it because of the product, or because of the person agonizing over every detail of her precious business? You tell me, Nick. Because one is scalable, and the other is flammable." Julian paused for effect and looked squarely into Nick's eyes. "But that isn't the point here, is it? I couldn't put my finger on why you would act so aggressively, and then it hit me." Julian pointed his finger directly at Nick and winked with one eye. It was a mix between pointing at him and shooting him. "You're in a predicament."

"How do you figure, old man?" Nick said, engaged, pissed, and unconvinced.

"I do not know your business. But I shall hasten a guess. I suspect you're sitting on a sizable pile of money that needs a home, but you have nowhere to place it. Is that your predicament? It's at least a daunting thought, I'm sure...a pile of money collecting zero return, or close to it." He paused, allowing the thought to simmer with Nick. "There are a host of numbers scarier than zero, Nick. At times, in my own dealings, I would've begged for zero." Apparently confident he had explained himself enough, Julian eased back into his chair. "I know you understand me, Nick, because we see things similarly. And your investors? They're mainly oil money, I presume...boom and bust. Undoubtedly, they comprehend that zero is no more or less than middle ground. Your current path will surely put the money to work, but the reward?" Julian paused and shook his head. "Is the upside high enough, son? Because you're risking becoming something you're not."

"And what's that?"

"A toilet cleaner." Julian paused, taking a deep breath. "A small business operator. A man who now busies himself with the humdrum tasks of managing operations instead of investing in them. You're too talented for that. Your lending position in Launch Pad...that was sharp. It's your willingness to own it that baffles me. Surely that isn't your angle here. How about we focus on your true interests, rather than the unenviable decision to own something you don't understand?"

"Are you making me an offer?" Nick questioned. " 'Cause this business history class is cute, but I have shit to do."

"Brass tacks. Excellent. We are more similar than I gave you credit for. I'm offering you perspective, my good man. Daring greatly is admirable...only not with other people's money."

"You don't know me," Nick said tersely.

"I've *been* you. Perhaps you don't know yourself. What is it you want, Nick? If the world would give it to you, what do you desire to have?"

Without hesitation Nick replied, "I will have a billion under management."

"Good. Your goals are clear. Then here's the part you'll grow to understand. You're not in the business of taking risk, you're in the business of collecting clients. If you bury their money underground and give it back to them in ten years, you'd be doing them a great service. Keep your variables to a minimum and your risk measurable. You obviously understand debt at a high level. Play in that arena. Stick with your strengths. If issuing debt is your game, then issue it. You seem to know a great deal in that department, much more than I do. Don't be a hero by taking it a step further. You're creative enough to find opportunity without risk."

Nick, absorbing Julian's points yet growing impatient, leaned in and said, "I can do both. That's what you don't get, old man. I can add clients and take risk."

"You shouldn't try. You have a knack for deal structures that's impressive. I might say superior to mine. But, Nick, I've had a long run on this earth fueled by investors' money. This is a subject I know intimately." The old man paused, deftly displaying his authority. "Shiny things are fun to play with until they cut you deep enough to bleed. Unfortunately, in this business, you bleed alone, son." Julian stared at Nick as the message sunk in. "But, to the point, shall we?" He changed his tone instantly. "You need to put money to work, and I need a better debt structure at Launch Pad Hotel. You really did a number on Char Teague with that debt. 15%? You should be both commended and sentenced for that one," Julian said with a smirk. "Indeed, you have talent, Nick Spencer. Her blended interest rate over all the hotels is almost 8%. Most of that debt is with banks, which do not involve you. Lower your 15% mezzanine loan to 10% and take all the banks out of their positions on all three Launch Pads at their current balances. Between the three hotels, you'll put over $20 million more to work. We'll blend the interest rate on the original loans to 7%. I'll give you a personal guarantee on top of the properties, which you'll hold as collateral."

"Why the hell would I reduce my mezzanine interest from 15% to 10%, and put a bunch more out at 7%?" Nick challenged.

"You've crafted a wonderful deal, Nick. But please do not dig into that singular position. What I'm offering you arrives more at your key interest. You can explain to every investor in your portfolio that you're a genius. You solidified your $2.55 million...the riskiest tier of the loan...with me as a cosigner and a personal guarantee in lieu of a calamitous deal fraught with risk. And then you put an additional $20 million from your fund to work at 7%, which appears to be preferable to zero. Your total return on Launch Pad will triple. Tell them you twisted her arm."

"I don't loan money at 7%, Julian. What if I considered 10% on the mezzanine loan, and 8% on the $20 million?"

"7%. If you find a better investment within two years, Char will refinance the portfolio with my help if needed. After two years, you can exit anytime, and so can she. Does that satisfy your needs?" Julian paused again. There was little doubt who was controlling the offer.

"How solid is your personal guarantee?"

Julian did not speak. His soft smile answered Nick's question.

"Seems a bit manipulative."

Julian looked at Nick through narrowed eyes. "You know the difference between manipulation and persuasion? We are smart enough to know the line is blurry. The difference, son, is talent. One satisfies your needs alone, the other satisfies both parties. You are too talented to be a manipulator."

Nick was lost in thought. He enjoyed pondering any scenario where he looked brilliant, yet he brimmed with mistrust. "Wait. So, on one hand you're making the argument the hotels are in jeopardy, but when it's time for me to lend them money, they're worth a fortune, right?"

Julian's eyes narrowed. "You're forgetting the Char Teague factor. She only sticks around in one scenario. And, Nick, you have until Friday."

"Why Friday?"

"I have rather important business to take care of next Monday," Julian said.

"You're pressing me," Nick charged.

"Not at all. It is your decision to make, not mine. I'm simply offering you an alternative. One that benefits us both."

"I'll consider it," Nick said. "What happens if I say no?"

"You'll own a question mark." Julian's smile shifted to a devilish grin. "But fear not. I have contacts at the Small Business Administration."

"What the fuck does that have to do with anything?" Nick said, annoyed.

"I hear they're making loans to struggling small business owners...even toilet cleaners." Julian stood up, pushed his chair back enough to create walking room, and proffered his hand. Nick looked at him, leaning aggressively forward as he stood and keeping his hands planted firmly on his desk. "Get out of my fucking office."

"Think it through, son. That's all I ask. You have until Friday." Julian replied as he turned and walked out the door. Nick watched him leave before plopping down into his chair. He rubbed his chin repeatedly with his thumb and forefinger. After a moment of thought, he pressed the paging button on his phone.

"Yes?" Michael said attentively.

"Is the old man gone?"

"He just left."

"Find out who that asshole is."

Chapter 30

"…If truth and honesty are stamped upon her face
all will be attracted to her."
—Eleanor Roosevelt

3 DAYS TO RFP

The fifth-floor RiNO condo welcomed the early Friday sun, warming their faces. At 6:15 a.m., Dexter stirred, his head still foggy, and turned to see his black T-shirt slipping from her bare shoulder, revealing a brightly tattooed arm. The quiet thrill of waking up with a beautiful woman beside him never completely dulled, but at nearly fifty, the flicker of boyish energy that stirred in his chest was something he hadn't felt in a long time—at least not since those rare mornings when everything used to feel whole. He shifted slowly, careful not to wake her, and leaned over to find Char deep in sleep, her breathing slow and steady, far from waking.

The vintage black-rimmed glasses she wore were neatly folded on the nightstand, her garments in a pile on the floor. Somewhere in the closing moments of the night before, Char managed to pilfer his black T-shirt and claim it as her own. Dexter kissed her on the back of the head so gently and quietly that she could not have perceived it; it wasn't meant for her enjoyment. Then he raised his feet up gradually and eased them over the edge of the bed.

Dexter used both hands to pull back his long black hair and reached for a hair band on the nightstand. He stood up, slipped on his jeans, and headed to the kitchen to brew some coffee, as was the ritual. A short while later he reemerged with two steaming Americanos from his wall-mounted espresso machine.

Char rolled over, and in a soft, raspy tone that can only be struck after a night of drinking, said, "Is that coffee?"

"Yes, it is."

In a still groggy voice, she said, "It's early." She started to sit up and lean her back against the plush suede headboard. Char looked down with heavily squinted eyes to notice she wasn't wearing a bra. She immediately wrapped her arms across herself modestly and then, while keeping her left arm about her chest, extended her right hand slowly to grab the clean, white coffee cup.

Dexter handed it to her while smiling. "I had a great time last night, Char. There's something about you I can't figure out, but I like it."

"I have to pee," she said, with a look of urgency. Char rolled out of bed, gathered the hem of Dexter's shirt in both hands and disappeared into the Carrera marble bathroom. "I DON'T DO WELL WITH VODKA TONICS," she said loudly from the bathroom as the unmistakable sound of urine began to splash. "BAD DECISIONS WERE MADE," she added. Dexter grinned as he raised his trusty yellow Breckenridge coffee mug and took a sip. He stood there as Char reemerged, still crossing her left arm over her chest, and leaned down to grab her brassiere. She popped back in the bathroom for a few seconds and then reappeared with her arms at her sides. Dexter's black T-shirt hit her just above mid-thigh. He stood silently, taking in the image. There was something unique about her aura, charmingly at the intersection of confident and uncomfortable with the situation.

"I can't see shit," she said. "Hand me my glasses."

Dexter grabbed the thick, black-rimmed glasses, walked over, and attempted to slip them onto her face. She awkwardly intercepted them with her free hand before he could finish. "Thanks, but I can handle it."

"Fair enough," Dexter replied. "I'm going to head out on my mountain bike. I usually ride in the mornings."

"I usually don't wake up in an older man's house. Not really ready for coffee. My head's killing me." She walked toward the bed and set the white cup on the nightstand.

"Okay. Just make yourself at home. If I'm not back when you leave—"

"You do you, and I'll do me," she said, interrupting him. The "morning after" exchange was noticeably foreign to her. "I'm going back to sleep. Got a ton of work to do this afternoon. Go ride your bike." Char climbed back in bed and rolled up in the thick comforter. She exhaled slowly and sunk into the bed. "Don't have sheets like this in my apartment."

Dexter—heeding his bed partner's wishes—walked softly to the closet, grabbed his mountain biking clothes and his keys, and quietly dressed for the outing. He emerged from the closet on a beeline toward the master bedroom door. Something within him created the urge to exit the scene. The situation, though marred with déjà vu, felt different, almost uncomfortable. He turned briefly on his way out to see Char rolled up snugly in his comforter—her back facing him. He could not help but manage a slight smile. Dexter headed to the kitchen and prepared a water bottle. Then he grabbed his bike and rolled it out the door.

***

A few short minutes later, Dexter was barreling down I-70 West toward the foothills of the Rockies in his sticker-covered Range Rover.

The windows were cracked, letting in the cool, dry October air, and the snow-capped peaks in the distance were starting to accumulate their winter white. He pushed the button on his steering wheel. "Play AC/DC, 'Back in Black'," he said aloud. The anthem was reserved only for celebration. The sound of the mountains gave way to electric guitars and a dependable drumbeat. As far as Dexter Mathis was concerned, there was no better commute on earth.

In twenty minutes, he pulled into Matthews/Winters Park and was greeted by the sound of gravel under his tires as he pulled into the parking lot. After grabbing his helmet and water bottle, Dexter pulled the bike from the rack, clipped his bike shoes into the pedals, and headed off. A few short yards into his ride, Dexter's music soundtrack paused and the agitating sounds of his ring tone began. "Will Powell" appeared on the phone screen cradled between his handlebars.

"You're playing with fire, man. I'm about to dominate this ride."

"Julian talked him into it," Will said.

"What?"

"The guy, Nick Spencer. Julian talked him into getting out of the way for Launch Pad. The RFP's due in three days."

"How'd he pull that off?"

"You know how Julian is. He said something about understanding Nick's interests...then some shit about speaking from his authority. But whatever he did, it worked. Nick called him a few minutes ago and said he would completely rework the loan terms. He's going to take all the banks out of their positions and lower Char's overall interest rate."

"Damn, man. Julian's good. But what's that mean for me? If this Nick guy lowers the rates, I don't need to pay him off, right?"

"Right. But Char's gonna love this once I explain it. This Nick guy's going to loan her over $20 million—take out all three lenders on her hotels. We can work on her numbers and refinance the whole portfolio within the next two years. And you can provide the rest of the equity for the Launch Pad in Golden. That is, if you're wanting to really scale this thing." Will paused. "This is going to be good, man. I need to call Char ASAP and let her know."

Silence.

"Dex?"

"So what's all this cost you?" Dexter questioned. "You thought of that? Julian's in this for a reason, dude."

"I know he is. But I can't care about that right now. Apparently, you didn't hear me. The RFP's due in three days, man."

"What do you mean, you can't care about that?" Dexter pressed. "What do you know?"

"I don't know anything. I saw something on his desk. I'm getting there." Will said. He was still struggling with the image he had seen in the picture. "Anyway, I need to call Char and let her know." The excitement in Will's voice was palpable. "This is big. I was starting to think I was screwed."

"Alright, but Char's asleep, man," Dexter said with no sound of remorse.

"It's not that early. She might be up. She's on East Coast time."

"Just trust me on this one, man," Dexter said, deadpan.

Silence.

"You dipshit!" Will exclaimed. "Please tell me you didn't. That's my partner now."

"Technically mine, too," Dexter said, a grin popping up in the corner of his mouth as he said it—Char still likely lying in his bed at that very moment. "Will, I'm not going to get into this, but you can't ask me to stay away from her. It's not cosmically right. She's something else."

"Ah man," Will said. "This is getting weirder by the minute. Why the hell is she in Denver?"

"I kinda invited her. She texted me for the address in Golden. Think she was gonna sneak in here and look at it. Maybe she's excited too, dude. Look, I know it's a little messy, but you gotta admit she—"

"Dex, save the excuses. I can't think about you and Char right now, but you hit the nail on the head about Julian. There's something going on. Something he's not telling us."

"What is it?" Dexter asked.

"I'm piecing it together. Can't talk about it right now."

"Is it going to mess up our deal...with Char?" Dexter asked.

"No, man. We're good there, I think. Let me figure it out."

"Alright, I obviously trust you, man. But take my word for it, give Char a few hours before you let her know."

"Geez," Will said. Dexter envisioned Will shaking his head. Will only uttered the word "Geez" while shaking his head. "I'll give it a little while before I call her...you son of a bitch."

"For what's it's worth, I like this girl."

"That's not worth much to me, Dex. You and I both know that."

Chapter 31

*"Alone. Yes, that's the key word, the most awful word
in the English tongue."*

—Stephen King

3 DAYS TO RFP

An hour later, Dexter pulled into the garage of his RiNO condo. His endorphins were surging from the ride. He uncharacteristically left the bike locked into the rack on the SUV as he headed toward the elevator, a mode of transportation he only took after a workout. Though Char was likely long gone by now—as most of the women in her position had been—he found himself stepping more quickly. He slid his key into the front door; with a simple half-turn he realized it had been left unlocked. Upon opening it, he could hear the television playing. As he moved through the condo, on course to the master bedroom, her smell caught his attention. It lingered in the space like a gift. He caught himself inhaling and remembering the night before, and the morning after.

He turned the corner to find the bedroom door open. The television wall came into view first. A rerun of *Friends* was on; the two main characters Joey and Chandler were tossing a ball back and forth and pretending to be aggravated with each other while a prerecorded audience found much more humor in the situation than Dexter. As he entered farther into the bedroom he startled her, which startled him.

"Oh shit. Thought you'd be gone longer," she said, straightening her slouched posture while holding a large white bowl of cereal. Char was propped up against the headboard, staring at the old episode of *Friends* and scrolling through her phone. She was still wearing Dexter's black T-shirt. She patted the spot next to her on the bed, inviting Dexter to join her. "Come on in. This is how I spend my mornings. Lose the bike shorts first though. Not comfortable with those."

"Thought you'd be gone," Dexter said, immediately sensing by her reaction that the comment was obtuse.

"Subtle," she replied. "Look, I can get my stuff."

"No, no, I didn't mean it like that. I just thought you'd be gone."

"You're right. Should've left. What kind of fucking cereal is this?" She harassed him while churning through the bowl slowly with her spoon, as if investigating the contents. "It's like cardboard. I put sugar on it, but that made it worse. Next time, how about some Cocoa Puffs?"

"Next time?" Dexter said.

"Maybe next time...IF you burn those bike shorts."

Dexter walked into his closet, slid on some long jogging pants, and eased in next to Char in his bed. He looked her in the eyes, and she gave him a moment of focus from the television and her phone. "Look, Char, I realize on paper this is a disaster waiting to happen. But I don't put much stock in what's on paper."

"Good, because I can't put myself down on paper. Know what I mean?"

Dexter grinned. "I sure do."

"I'm leaving when this episode's over." Char regained her focus on the television and reengaged her bowl of cereal, holding the spoon in a childlike full fist. Her phone emitted a quick vibrate, signaling a text. Dexter paid it little attention, distracted by the moment. She reached down and held the screen at mid-distance, squinting through her black-rimmed glasses at the small text. A troubled look of surprise came over her. She gasped and immediately dropped the phone on the bed, pushing back against the headboard abruptly—as if staring at a bed full of spiders.

"What is it? You okay?" Dexter said, frazzled by her physical reaction to the text message.

"It's from Nick. He wants to know why I sent a guy named Julian to his office. Please tell me this is bullshit...and please..." She looked up at Dexter with piercing eyes. Her arms were now fully outstretched against the mattress, pushing her tighter against the headboard. "Please tell me he isn't talking about Julian Darrow."

"You know Julian?"

Char's glare was answer enough. Her face puckered deeply as if she were trying to swallow hard.

"What is it, Char?" Dexter said with concern.

"I've got a horrible taste in my mouth," she said, fighting back tears.

***

The Lincoln Town Car had returned from its lengthy Austin commute after several expected pit stops for caffeine, snacks and Julian's seasoned bladder. He now sat in his office, the rare rush of adrenaline coursing through his aged body. Playing in the shadows was a foreign construct for the silver-haired gentleman. His deliberate and necessary encounter with Nick Spencer awakened a vibrancy that had been missing lately.

Perhaps his vested interest in Will Powell was too little too late. After all, Julian's plan was threading a series of needles. Was he foolhardy in assuming Will could pull it off? The stakes were increasing as time dwindled, and the pleasure he felt on the journey home from Austin further buttressed the idea that this scheme needed a confident leader. This scheme needed Julian Darrow.

"Vince, please join me in the office," he said into the microphone of his desktop phone. Within seconds, the driver appeared in the doorway.

"You understand the significance of this latest endeavor, correct?"

Vince nodded.

"You've met Will Powell."

Vince nodded.

"The table is set, yet I have no seat. Am I burdening him with too tall a task?"

Vince inhaled slowly as he pondered the question. "I don't think you're asking me."

Chapter 32

—Sir Walter Scott

It was October 22, the Tuesday after the RFP was due. The moment was fraught with uncertainty. Char Teague had effectively disappeared over the weekend. She had not answered any of the multiple text messages from Will or Dexter. Dexter had informed Will of Char's mysterious link to Julian Darrow, though the specifics eluded him. And Will's attempts to reach Julian for details about Char were unsuccessful. Doubt plagued all of the above.

If Char was unwilling to move forward, Will's RFP would surely fall apart, even if he was the lucky winner. And further adding to the stress was his lack of confidence in the city's decision-making. The interested parties—Sharon and Don—had prior relationships with the City of Golden on their side. That thought haunted him now as he waited.

Will sat in his home office pretending he could muster the levelheadedness to busy himself with monotonous tasks until the RFP news sprung. His phone was ready on the desk. Would they call? Would they email? He kicked himself for not paying more attention to the instructions in the initial meeting. In any event, the city's decision would surely take a few weeks. He knew that; it was a multi-million-dollar investment, and worth deliberating over. Still, he caught himself glancing at the phone's screen every few seconds on the off chance a notification would pop up. And even though he knew it was excessive, he refreshed his inbox repeatedly...nothing.

Will had given himself one hour to knock out the first task. In times past, he could spend the morning buried in the undertaking. It was the same thing every time, vendors' small innocent errors in invoicing: an extra item here, a minor per item price adjustment there. The curious thing was they never seemed to work in his favor, not a single time. In a mathematical anomaly, every error was 100% in favor of the vendors. Previously, it had agitated him. It was the guile of people thinking they could sneak something past him—or hoping that he was too lazy to review it—that would itch under his skin as he worked through them. Still, as he thumbed through each invoice, thoughts of the RFP outcome loomed overhead.

The busy work kept his attention just enough to not go crazy. Pairing invoices with budgets was a finite chore, like mowing the grass. Today it didn't matter that the plumber obviously overcharged for the vanity installs or that the landscaper billed a month ahead. It was expected and therefore encapsulated in the simple task of the job at hand. He methodically moved through the corrections and logged them into the accounting software. With fifteen minutes to spare, the task was almost done. Nearing the last data entry, an email notification popped up in the top right corner of his screen.

From: Jessica Dews
Subject: Telemark Building RFP
final selection

Instantly, his body warmed and his hands tingled. Though he should've clicked immediately on his inbox icon, he hesitated. That was fast. Maybe too fast, he thought. All the work, Julian's rules, unpacking Char Teague and Nick Spencer, Dexter's approach to life, the universe, and everything, had led to this simple moment in time: his fate unveiled in a standard, impersonal email. He knew he should check the email, but Will couldn't bring himself to do it. He entered another vendor invoice, though any error short of $100,000 would have surely slid past his wandering attention.

It should be different. Some things warranted an email: Sela's soccer practice being rescheduled, that was worthy of a simple email. However, this? The relentless pace this RFP created over the past six weeks should trigger a personal phone call at the least, but the quicker than expected correspondence would have to suffice. He moved the cursor over the message and clicked.

Dear Respondents,

We thank you all for the proposals issued for the former Telemark Building located at 1148 Ford Street. The ideas and creativity of our citizens never cease to amaze us. In total, we received four project submittals of varying size and scale. All four showed merit and a fundamental understanding of the development process. It was a very difficult decision to choose a single developer from this talented group. In the end, it is our distinct privilege to award the project to Sharon Peyton of Golden Partners Holdings. Ms. Peyton has been a trusted member of our community for several years and has a proven track record in successfully developing projects in Golden, Colorado. Ultimately Ms. Peyton's vision aligned most with our goals for the future of the Telemark Building.

Golden is constantly striving to move forward as a community. There will be many more opportunities to help us improve our great city. We appreciate all of you who participated and sincerely hope to see you in the future when the next opportunity presents itself to further the mission of Golden, Colorado.

Sincerely,

Jessica Dews
Deputy City Manager
Golden, Colorado

Will stared blankly at the screen for several minutes. He could feel the acid creeping up the back of his throat. The initial exhilarating surge of adrenaline gave way to an internal pang of dissonance. The dissonance gave way to shame. Everyone had tried to tell him. Paul Tollison told him. Don Andino warned him. Sharon Peyton herself explained expressly that she would get the deal. It was all obvious in hindsight; however, something was amiss. As he mentally kicked himself, a notification buzzed on his phone. It was Farrah Parks from Grand Bank Colorado.

> Need to catch up with u on Westminster

> Why?

> Payment late. Trying not to charge u late fees.

> ???I'll take care of it. Thx.

Will found the text interesting. Aimless Action LLC, funded by Julian Darrow himself, made the two prior payments without concern for Will's oversight. He hoped it was a mere coincidence that this tardy payment surfaced the moment of the RFP—or more accurately, he prayed. The negatives were flooding in faster than he could process, and the photo he saw on Julian's desk was compounding the problem. In light of this current RFP debacle, the image was haunting him. Will began to weave together a narrative; a narrative he hoped was not accurate.

***

Sharon Peyton read the email on her phone while driving to a condo appointment in the Denver Art District, often referred to as the Golden Triangle. The aptly named Museum Residences were a smattering of high-end condos adjacent the Denver Art Museum. She scrolled through Jessica Dews's email and shuddered at the words "Golden Partners Holdings". "The Peyton Team" would have been much more suitable for public relations. She would surely be speaking to the city before any press releases.

There was little reaction other than that. The RFP, it seemed, was a foregone conclusion, just as Terry Branson, the city manager, had hinted when she first met him about the project. She had fifteen minutes before her condo showing and she opted to close the loop on the RFP conversation while the news was fresh. A seasoned professional at operating a phone while navigating downtown Denver traffic, she squeezed the side button, initiating the audible command function. "Call Julian Darrow." Three rings later, a familiar voice answered the other line.

"Ms. Peyton. I presume the RFP is official?"

"Yes, I got it, just as I said I would. But it wasn't easy."

"No?" Julian asked.

"You were right about Don. Just had to call him and pretend he could be my contractor. He's going to be furious."

"Don Andino deserves his fate. Nothing short of furious would bring me joy. Be sure to drop my name to him when the deal is signed with the city."

"I understood about Will, but why go after Don? He was probably going to lose to me anyway." Sharon questioned.

"I deal in certainty, Sharon. This had to be a two-horse race. I simply had my money on both horses."

"Well, Don was easy. But I had some convincing to do with Paul

Tollison, he was enamored with your boy. Had to explain why my project was the only viable one. Nice pick, by the way. Will Powell called me directly the other day...daring move. Anyway, I told Paul he could never pull it together."

"Ah, a liar's lie. You know better than to question my tutelage. Will was prepared, no doubt."

"Doesn't matter, does it?" Sharon coldly stated. "You knew I would win. Hang on a second." She wheeled into an on-street parking spot on 12th Avenue just past the main entrance to the Museum Residences. She sat in her red Jeep while it idled.

"I was hopeful, never certain," Julian remarked. "But it is done. The Telemark Building is yours, which leaves me the other site in Golden. I'll send the agreements over this evening." Julian did not need to go into detail. The details had been laid out on the front end.

"You're a troubled soul, you know that, right?" she said rhetorically. "What will you do with the other site in Golden?"

"That's for me to ponder." Julian paused for a moment. "Unfortunately, I'm not playing with a lot of time here, and I need to see this thing through."

"I can appreciate your position, Julian," she replied. "I really can. But you need to hurry with that paperwork. We have an excited client to please."

"Indeed, we do," Julian said as he hung up the phone.

Chapter 33

"The opposite of love is not hate, it's indifference."

—Eli Wiesel

Will stood under the streetlight at 6:45 a.m., the October morning's chill sinking into his bones—whether from the cold or the weight of the RFP announcement, he couldn't tell. His breath danced in the glow, dissipating like the restless thoughts gnawing at him. He should go inside for a jacket, but instead he paced, his mind circling back to Julian's desk. The notes. The picture. They were burned into his memory, feeding his unease.

Headlights cut through the early morning haze. The black Town Car rumbled closer, its exhaust curling into the dim light. Vince was on time, as always. Will stepped forward, opened the door, and slid in beside Julian. No greeting. No glance. Just the quiet rustle of a newspaper, a green folder balanced in Julian's lap. The interior light was on—he'd been preparing. For what, Will wasn't sure. But he would find out soon enough.

"There's a coffee for you in the cup holder," Julian said, skipping the salutation. Will sat stoically, peering toward the back of Vince's head.

"Okay," Will responded, expressionless.

Julian raised his head with a single nod, which signaled Vince to start the drive.

"You set me up," Will said, looking forward, not granting Julian the dignity of eye contact. He grabbed Vince's headrest, still settling into his seat, and moved his head slightly from side to side as if busying himself with the traffic before them. "A nine-letter word for 'item from one's past'. I couldn't get it. I knew all your other stupid words immediately, but that one stumped me. You strung me along. You made me think you were some kind of marked man...like your name couldn't be whispered in Golden. I didn't care. I played along. I trusted you. I didn't know why I had to be the face, but I put all that aside and just went after the RFP." Will stopped and shook his head slowly as he said, "I saw the picture on your desk and all those crazy notes. Rolled it around in my head all night trying to make sense of it. You've been laughing at me the whole time, you piece of shit. The little girl. She had a scar on her cheek." He peered down to his right, but not far enough to see Julian's face; he still couldn't look at him. "That was Char in the picture. CHARLOTTE...nine letters. Item from one's past. From that first car ride...the crossword puzzle. CHARLOTTE was the answer, right? Why the hell are we doing this? This isn't a game to me. You knew I needed the money. And now I've been screwing with this for over a month, letting everything else go to shit. My hotel's coughing up blood, the apartments are a disaster, and now you're telling me this was all some kind of stunt. I trusted you to put all that aside, and I don't have a plan B, Julian. I want an answer right now. Why are we doing this?"

"Unfortunate," the silver-haired gentleman offered while lowering his chin. "That's a complicated answer you seek. And I'm not convinced it will bring you any solace."

"Try me. Is she your daughter, Julian?"

Julian folded the newspaper into its original form, laying it atop the green folder in his lap. He turned onto his left hip and placed his hand down on the seat next to Will, facing him. "No." He smiled at the absurdity of being labeled a father. "I have no children. Charlotte was my business partner's daughter. Though I cared for her very much. I suppose that's an important piece of the equation for you now," he said almost emotionlessly. Julian then returned to his prior seated posture and took a sip of coffee, almost intimating he expected the conversation to cease at that point.

"What do you mean *was* your partner's daughter?"

Julian was silent.

"He's dead?" Will prodded.

Silence.

"Tell me what's going on," Will pleaded.

"It cost him everything."

The silver-haired gentleman wet his lips with the tip of his tongue, as if preparing them for the words they would form.

"Five dollars per foot."

"What?"

"Long story."

"Tell me, Julian. Did you have something to do with his death?" Will's voice cracked with emotion.

"As I said, it's complicated. He took his own life."

"So what the hell do you mean by 'five dollars per foot'?"

Julian inhaled deeply, placed his hands flat over the paper in his lap, and locked eyes with Will.

"It was an amazing building. In all my wildest dreams, I never thought I'd have a chance to own it. Completely covered in mirrored glass. You should have seen it. Remarkable." He fashioned a regrettable smile. The pain was evident in his tone.

"It was a home run. A high-rise downtown. The dot-com bust in the early 2000s emptied nearly all the tenants, but I had connections— attorneys, developers, accounting firms. I was filling the building one by one, and I was going to own half of it when I was finished. Charlotte's father saw the potential, too. He had been a small partner for years, though our deals had been much smaller. I was completely out of money, tapped out from overextending myself in various projects at once. Sound familiar, son?"

Will did not answer.

"Her father stepped up, no questions asked. Handed me $200,000 to preserve my position and keep the deal going. I didn't realize it was all the money he had." Julian paused and swallowed hard. "Perhaps I was too greedy to ask."

"You couldn't get the tenants?"

"It's a curious truth in real estate: you can be making a fortune and still go broke. I had to pay $50,000 a month to keep the agreement in place. That was my piece. I negotiated for that. It was foolproof. We kept 50% of the new leases, and they were big leases. But I made a misstep."

"What was that?"

"I had a major tenant teed up. They wanted a third of the entire building...eighty thousand square feet. It was the piece to put us over the top—to make the whole deal profitable. I turned down several smaller tenants to keep the footage in place. After five months of negotiating a deal I thought was ironclad, it dissolved over five dollars per foot in lease rate.

"I had plenty of backup tenants by then, but the building owner lost faith in me. He demanded I keep making the monthly payments. When her father's money was spent, I scrambled to put together the backup tenant deals—but the offers dried up faster than I expected.

"And there was Don Andino...not a villain, but far from a savior."

Julian exhaled slowly, rubbing his fingers together as if trying to wipe away something invisible.

"He was my contractor, my closest ally in the project. I trusted him to keep things steady—to buy me time, to keep the owner from panicking. But instead of reassuring him, Don started hedging his bets. He had contacts everywhere, and when it looked like I might not pull through, he whispered to the owner behind my back. He didn't exactly sabotage me—he simply stopped vouching for me. And when the owner asked him, point-blank, whether I could hold the deal together, Don hesitated.

"In those moments, hesitation is death.

"The owner pulled the plug, told me he wanted his money, no more delays. Don stayed on as the contractor for the next group—the investors who swooped in the moment I was out."

Julian looked down at his hands. "Don's intentions weren't malicious. They were self-serving."

"He acted in his own self-interests?" Will questioned, parroting the rule.

"I was foolish to expect anything else."

Julian continued, "But Charlotte's father...he entrusted me with everything he had. And I lost it all. I had to look my partner in the eyes and tell him I failed." He turned toward the window, his voice barely above a whisper. "The next morning, I found a note on my office chair. No mention of blame, no semblance of remorse for handing me his very last penny. He thanked me for being his partner and asked that I watch over his daughter." With a quick turn of his head toward Will, he said, "It is a request I shall not dismiss at any cost."

"So where does that leave me?"

"Right where you were."

"You lied to me, and you're making me out to be a fool." Will now trained his sights on the traffic ahead. His only alternative was to look Julian in the eyes, which just didn't seem possible. The morning light was gaining full advantage over the darkness, the snow-capped mountains glowing ahead of the distant rising sun. Julian's crossword puzzle caught an amber glow through the window. Though the penmanship was razor sharp, there were fewer words filled in than last time. Something else was keeping his attention.

"Why drag her into this now? It doesn't make sense. If you wanted to win the RFP, why complicate all this with your personal baggage? And, newsflash...I'm assuming Char wants nothing to do with you, right? That's why you're hiding yourself from her. I'm guessing she's going to lose her mind when she finds out about this." Will paused, took a breath, and then lashed back out. "You lured me in with this nonsense about changing my mindset, and the whole time you were trying to take control of Char's business. For what? That's not my cross to bear. You're a sick bastard."

Julian pretended to read the section of visible newspaper in his lap. "Are you finished?"

"What? Am I finished? No, I'm not even close to finished. Like I said, here's the part I can't square up...the RFP...you didn't care about the RFP, did you? If you did, you wouldn't complicate it with Launch Pad. The timing doesn't make sense. You're too smart. And I'm assuming it's no coincidence that my banker texted me about my late payments, the payments you've been making. Here's what I think. I think you're still screwing with me."

"Vince, keep it in the right lane and keep it slow," Julian said abruptly. Vince immediately flipped on the blinker, obeying his command. "I'll do the talking now," Julian said sternly. "The payments on your loan, those are an investment, son. You don't get to exit today simply because it's convenient. I will make them whole, but their delinquency is a reminder. We are inextricably linked. I've watched Charlotte from afar for years. And I kept my distance all those years because it was best for her. She blames me for her father's death. That's understandable. I can deal with that. What happened between her father and me was complicated. But when a friend called me a few months ago and explained that Charlotte was involved with this…" Julian's face molded into a look of disgust. "…this piece of filth from Austin." He stopped, visibly frustrated, and gathered himself. "You must understand. She's different from us. Even as a little girl, I could see she was different. She's idealistic. She's creative. She stands alone. By not requiring my assistance, she compels me to act. She's a star. But she's not built to see the deceit that lurks around every corner. I had to intervene. Watching her be victimized was not an option." The silver-haired gentleman froze for a moment. "It was a coward's way out." His statement was marked with fresh contempt. "But he asked me to look after her…to promise she would be okay. And I intend to keep that promise. Will, I trust you can appreciate the circumstances. If Sela was in trouble, you would—"

"Stop right there," Will said. "Don't try to paint us with the same brush. And don't try to act like your chivalry made you set me up. Are you kidding me right now? Are you seriously going to sit here and pretend you didn't try to screw me? This is unbelievable…even for you."

"Is that how you see this?" Julian responded defiantly. He reached for his coffee and took a deliberate sip. There was no sign of angst or concern in the nonchalant pace of his movements. The tension was gone in his voice, as if he eased back into business mode. "Use you…possibly. But wrong you? In what way have you been wronged?"

"I put everything aside and trusted you. Now I'm a casualty of your game. You're killing me, Julian."

"I'm saving you from yourself."

"I don't need saving."

"You do, or you wouldn't be here. You wouldn't have agreed to the deal!" The silver-haired gentleman accused Will with a raised voice;

the conversation had stayed emotionally charged for too long.

"Jesus, this is rich. You can't stop, can you? This is the part I'm struggling with the most." Will turned and leaned in toward Julian. "Why even go through the RFP effort? You could've skipped all that and gone straight to the part where you asked me to buy a part of Char's company. The part where you leave me looking like an asshole. This whole circus wasn't necessary."

"Your memory fails you." Julian said, deftly absorbing the blow. "I never asked you to buy a part of Launch Pad. But, congratulations, you've led me to Rule Number Six."

"What? You have to be kidding me. Now?" Will grilled.

"You signed up for this class," Julian said, unfettered. "Did you not think we'd leave the schoolyard on occasion?" He took another slow, calming sip of coffee. "Rule Number Six?"

"Be my guest." Will breathed through his nose with lips tight together. The exhales were forced and more audible, bordering on the line between involuntary and accusatory. Julian, oblivious to Will's irritation, continued in an even tone:

"RULE NUMBER SIX: GOOD IDEAS BECOME GREAT IDEAS WHEN YOU GIFT THEM TO OTHERS."

Julian continued, "It was Dexter's idea, if you'll remember. Did I hand him the file and plant the seed?...possibly. But I did not force any decision on him. He's an investor and I offered him a platform to invest."

Will shook his head and placed his hands around the back of his neck, as if to rub out the tension. Slowly, and with his eyes closed, he said, "Dex...Dex?!?...Shit. Him, too?" Julian was silent. "You had me invite him. So you're telling me he was in your sights from the beginning?" Julian did not answer. Will continued, "You played him."

"I set my ego aside and led him to water," Julian sparred. "Even your precious Dexter Mathis is not immune to pride of authorship. Take this to heart, Will. Ideas are in the ether. They aren't owned. There's no merit in being the one with the idea in hand. Gift them to others. Pride of authorship is dangerous and powerful. If you tell them your idea, you have a shot at making a deal. If you create the environment to let them arrive at the idea, you simply need to spell your name correctly on the contract. The investment had to be a joint effort. I simply handed him the file."

"He's going to pull out, you know. He won't be happy about being played. You can kiss this whole thing goodbye. And frankly, you deserve to see it crumble."

"Was it a bad idea?" Julian asked.

"Stop it."

"Answer me. Do you think Dexter made a poor decision?"

Will was silent.

"Play this out, son. It's in his best interest to do the deal. And interests will rule the day."

The Town Car eased up Highway 121 toward I-70. Julian sat sipping coffee and rubbing his fingers together in a rhythmical pattern, deep in thought. Will still peered forward over Vince's shoulder, watching the traffic move. As the vehicle reached the westbound I-70 exit, Vince sped onto the interstate. The increase in speed seemed to aid in the resurgence of discourse. "He won't back out because he wants to see the deal through," Julian said, breaking the silence. "He's underwritten the numbers, and they work. You see, to Dexter, this is more his deal than yours or mine. That's the power of owning the idea."

"Dex won't see it that way after I'm done talking to him."

"It doesn't have to end this way."

"As far as I'm concerned, it's already ended."

"Don't be so shortsighted. I never wronged you. This is your deal to do. The fundamentals haven't changed. The Austin investor has agreed to restructure all the Launch Pad loans, and Charlotte..." he paused to correct, "Char is willing and able to enter into an agreement. This is still the deal I approached you about from the beginning. This is why I agreed to pay you and to help you hone your craft. I can't be the messenger on this one, Will. I need you to get her across the finish line." Julian reached over and placed his hand on Will's shoulder. "I need you to finish what you started."

"What I started?" Will asked rhetorically. He looked down on his shoulder at Julian's sharp hand. "And why on earth would I go after that now?"

"Why wouldn't you? The RFP was never your prize...it was the process. Your prize was Launch Pad and a new development, correct? Your interests are still aligned with Char's, whether you want them to be or not. Launch Pad is the business deal. And, Will, you can search for years and not find a deal with this much potential. The RFP was just the vessel in which to deliver it to you."

Will looked Julian square in the eyes for the first time that morning. "You've got a lot of nerve, Julian. And, if she hates you as much as I think she does, insinuating Char would even consider this deal now is downright pathological."

"Is that so? Interesting. Let me ask you a question, son. Suppose you were her. Suspend all you know and believe right now, and pretend you are Char. If you had a lifeline to completely change the trajectory of your business, but it came with a little baggage, what would you do?" He turned and stared at Will, who did not offer any cues that he was entertaining the idea. "Humor me. Take a second. Put yourself in Char's shoes. Understand her interests here. Do you think her main interest is to despise me now? That ship's been sailing for years. She has a lifeline to rid herself of a wretch of an investor, who would surely take Launch Pad away from her. She has two people she has grown to trust. My interference in the matter is ancillary to the deal at hand. I'm a bit player. Char needs...or better, she deserves, to thrive in her business with a solid foundation around her. I sought you and Dexter out because you, son, have the grit and talent to make the tough decisions and Dexter has a background in scaling companies. She's talented enough to see that."

Will shook his head. "She's going to resent me just for knowing you. And the trust I built will blow up when she finds out what's going on. I'm not going to pretend like I don't know. That's not fair to her. What if she wants nothing to do with anything your hands have touched?"

"That's a position she will most definitely take. I know Char's situation well enough to know that will happen. So, build trust again. Tell her everything. The onus then falls on you to allow her to see her interests are more important than a trivial position."

"Here's a novel idea," Will said while reaching forward to the headrest and turning toward Julian. "Maybe she doesn't need your help. You ever consider that? She built three hotels by herself. Maybe Julian Darrow jumped the gun on his partner's dying wish and underestimated her ability."

Julian stared into the middle distance, as if envisioning her. "Yes, she is impressive, and rare, and she's built a superb portfolio." Just as Will thought Julian was about to agree with him, Julian continued, "And that portfolio will be owned by the hotshot in Austin within twelve months if you don't perform. If not him, another will come as her portfolio grows. Don't be naive."

"I don't know what the hell to say to that. And, honestly, I don't know what to think right now."

The silver-haired gentleman put his hands in his lap. He was now the one facing forward, avoiding eye contact. "Boil this down, Will, and ask yourself a simple question."

"What?"

"Have I helped you?"

"You're an animal."

"That may be. But if I've served your interests, if I've helped you, who I am is of no consequence. One day, you'll understand that."

"I'll never be you."

"Let's pray that's true. It does not alter the question: Have I helped you?"

Will was silent.

"If that answer is 'yes,' then take a minute to consider what I'm asking you to do. If the answer is 'no,' then bring your payment current with the bank and walk out the door."

"You're boxing me in."

"I need you to finish what we started." For the first time in their short relationship, Will heard the emotion in Julian voice. He looked at his sullen eyes and thought he indeed detected the slightest hint of emotion.

"You're playing me."

"This is not a game to me, son."

Will's eyes narrowed. "Then why not go tell her yourself and make this happen? And why'd you let Dex put up the money?" Will said, exasperated.

Julian turned, pressed his lips together and squinted dismissively. "She would never accept my money. Our relationship is..." he paused, "...complicated. But I've taken care of Dexter's investment in the short run. It will not be necessary until it's time to refinance the entire portfolio. As I've told you, Nick Spencer will restructure his loan to something more accommodating, which will not require any capital to be invested for now."

"Right. You told me that. And somehow you're the white knight?"

"Not to worry, you and Dexter can take credit for the move. I know my place in this arrangement." The silver-haired gentleman's words trailed off at the end. "Consider it a gift."

"A gift," Will repeated in a low tone. He now found himself in the unchartered territory of pitying Julian. "I'll speak to her. I'm not saying I'm in, but I'll speak to her." He cocked his head to the side to see Julian clearly, "But you need to understand, I will tell her everything. She'll understand your role."

"That's your decision. Consider it wisely."

Will grabbed his coffee from the cup holder and took a swig. His throat was dry with emotion. He rubbed his forehead as he sat quietly, digesting the information and the task at hand. Will looked up to see they were nearing the exit to his home. Seeing his time was drawing to a close, he offered, "There's one more thing. You didn't answer me about the RFP. Did you know we would lose?"

Julian did not answer.

"Does that have something to do with all the notes?" Will looked at the silver-haired gentleman and waited until he made direct eye contact. "Are you in trouble, Julian? Is that why you've played me? Who's really boxed in here? You or me?"

Julian looked at him sheepishly. "It's been a long day. I think it's time you went home."

"Answer me."

"Let's just say I'm running out of time," Julian said flatly.

"Who are the notes for?"

Julian raised his eyes to the rearview mirror and glared at Vince, a gesture he had given once already to end the trip, this time with slightly more fervor.

Chapter 34

"In any negotiation there exist realities that are hard to change."

—Roger Fisher

The proverbial dust had settled on the Julian Darrow news in Dexter's RiNO condo. Dexter had spoken to Will before finally receiving a text back from Char. She had been hiding out in a Denver hotel for the past few days, trying to make sense of it all. He pleaded with her to come to his condo before she left; unpacking her ties to Julian was on his agenda.

Char reluctantly took him up on the offer, even if to simply say goodbye. "I'm not sure what to say." Char stood just inside his door. "This is some twisted shit."

"What happened?" Dexter's question stopped her cold.

"What do you mean?"

"With Julian? I saw your face, Char. There's something behind that name for you. More than just being your father's business partner."

"Define partner," she shot back, then paused. "Wait. How'd you—"

"Will told me," Dexter interjected. He had been running through the events leading up to Char's call in his mind, and the eventual reality that Julian Darrow did not seem capable of doing her harm. In fact, as far as Dexter was concerned, his elaborate ruse was ostensibly a pathway for him to help her. But for Char to have such a visceral reaction to the name Julian Darrow meant Dexter was missing some critical details.

"He fed my dad to the wolves," Char responded. She turned back toward Dexter in a gesture that ensured there was a longer story. "My dad gave Julian every dollar he had. Julian was his fucking hero."

"A lot of deals go south, Char. What's it about him that rips at you?"

"He had a black briefcase." She looked at Dexter and started to fight back emotions. "He showed up with it a few days after Dad…" Her voice trailed off. "Came right into our living room. I was nine years old. Supposed to be in bed. It was late. Mom and I would keep each other company. I think neither of us wanted to go to sleep alone." Char shook her head as the memory seemed to sear her brain. "Funny, don't even know which project they were working on, but I remember the briefcase. Had big brass buckles on it. Full of cash. He tried to give it to Mom, like that would make everything better, like he could wipe his hands clean."

"You were in the room for all that?" Dexter asked.

"Yeah, just listening. The nine-year-old me knew Mom wouldn't take it. I'm sure we needed it, but there was no way in hell she'd give him the satisfaction, especially not in front of me. Then he looked at me." Char stopped. She was trying desperately to hold back any tears, but the gloss in her eyes was evident to Dexter. "He looked at me with big fucking tears in his eyes. And then I knew…I hated him. He walked over and kissed me on the head, and said he was sorry. Then he walked out the fucking door."

"Jesus, Char. That's terrible."

"Yeah, I mean he didn't disappear," she consoled herself. "He would call and check on us every once in a while. But the older I got, the less he called. And then when I went off to college, I decided I could forget about him. I could forget about how much I hated him. But I couldn't. My dad was my hero. He took my hero from me."

"Does your mother have the same feelings?"

"She did," Char said. "She passed away six years ago…breast

cancer." Char began to rub under her dry eyes. She had spoken long enough for the emotion to run its course and a faint shamed smile began to form as she recoiled into herself.

"Hey, you don't have to be embarrassed." Dexter said, in a natural display of empathy, even had a bit of glossiness in his own eyes. He considered walking over and hugging her; but realizing he was somewhat embroiled in the saga, he thought better of it.

"When he found out about her being sick, he started sending money. We honestly laughed about it, me and her. Don't get me wrong, we needed it, and we kept it. And this sounds fucked up, but I hated him for being able to give it to us." She took a deep breath and pulled back her shoulders, regaining her posture. Then she exhaled quickly through her nose in disgust. "That asshole had the nerve to come to her funeral. That's the last time I saw him." She stopped, bit her lip while raising her eyebrows, and then somehow snapped right out of the story, as if she'd dealt with the feelings around the subject matter enough to compartmentalize them.

"Char, I hope you know I had no idea Julian was tied to you like that."

"He's not tied to me," she replied. "I believe you...because if you did know and didn't tell me, you'd be a first-class asshole. I'm going to get out of here, though. Overstayed my welcome. I can't be in this city."

"I'd rather you stay longer than never come back," Dexter replied.

Char turned and grabbed the door lever. Just before leaving she said, "I gotta get back to Raleigh. I had fun before all this started, Dexter. I just can't do this. It's too much."

"I could get some different cereal," Dexter said, trying to add levity.

Char wiped her eyes and fashioned a smile in an effort to show no blame. She then turned and left, pulling the door behind her.

***

The Denver Central Market was an eclectic food hall on Larimer Street in RiNO. Unlike many of the generic food hall concepts throughout the metro area, the Market offered a unique mix of well-executed, yet reasonable, cuisine. It was common to see white collars and red hoodies in line behind each other, pining for charcuterie plates, grain bowls, fine cuts of steak, craft pizza, or Will's favorite: fresh fish from Silva's. It was a place you could eat in anonymity and feel connected to a sea of people enjoying the same.

Char walked into the Market that evening at 5:15 p.m. in a pair of ripped-in-the-knee faded jeans and an argyle sweater; her eyes, behind her signature thick, black-rimmed glasses, were scanning the space immediately. She was fresh off an impromptu work session at the coffee shop down the street after the unscripted, and rather emotional, visit to Dexter's. Will raised his hand from the communal table where he sat, realizing immediately that this Denver food hall was the exact type of establishment that might elevate Char's anxiety. There were people milling about in several directions, producing the exact type of buzz that food halls hoped to create. She offered a nod of recognition and headed toward his table. He was just starting to enjoy a creatively named craft beer from the Curio Cocktail Bar, though admittedly he preferred Miller Light.

"Thanks for meeting me here," Will said. "Dex told me you…" He paused. "…you were in town. I know you were about to fly out, so thanks."

"Yeah, I needed the stress relief. All fun and games until my equity guy, Nick, texted me."

"Ex-equity guy," Will said.

"Ballsy," Char replied while commandeering Will's glass. "You owe me this beer, considering the circumstances. Just spent the last four hours drinking coffee and wondering exactly who the fuck was on my side. And where do you stand, Will Powell? Have you been in on this Julian thing from the beginning? You're the one who kept reaching out to me. He had to be behind it."

"He was behind it. I'm not going to dispute that, but I had no idea you two were connected."

"Yeah, everyone keeps saying that."

"It's the truth. Dex and I had no idea."

"Then how'd you find out?"

"He had your picture on his desk. It has been there since I met him, but it was always facing his chair. A few days ago was the first time I actually saw the photograph. You were a little girl, but I could tell it was you. You had a pink cowboy hat on, and you were on top of a bull."

"H-Huh," she stammered.

Will looked up and, though she showed no emotion, he could see the memory in her eyes.

"That was my birthday." She let out a quick breath, just short of a laugh, and took another sip of beer. "I wanted a cowgirl party, and Julian stepped in and threw it. He bought me the pink cowboy hat. Bastard probably spent Dad's money on it. Went all out, too. Showed up with a ranch hand and a real bull...a longhorn. A real fucking bull...Big Bully. That was its name," she said in almost a chuckle.

"Well, he must have been fond of that party. I think it's the only photograph in his house. Tell you what, I'm going to grab a beer, since you stole mine. When I get back, I want to talk about where we are with Launch Pad." He stood up, and Char grabbed his arm as he passed.

"We don't need to talk about that. I'm not doing shit that he's a part of."

"I'm going to go grab a beer. In the meantime, clear him out of your mind for a minute and let's talk about business." Char released his arm without responding.

Five minutes later he was back with two fresh glasses of beer.

Char looked at him steely-eyed. "Not enough beer in this joint for you to change my mind, Will."

"What's the concern?" he said. She looked at him quizzically, as if any buffoon would know the answer. "No, really, what is it? Julian was an asshole for keeping everyone in the dark, but honestly Char, he just led Dex and me to the water. He's not a partner in this. He never asked to be. I think he knew you'd be out the door in a heartbeat. I don't know what went down between you two, and I really don't want to get into that, but he knows where he stands with you."

"My concern? My concern is he gets closure by being involved," she said.

"I don't think you heard me. He has no part of this deal."

Char shook her head as she took a rather large swig of beer. "Not into Launch Pad...into a relationship with me."

"Would that be so bad?" Will questioned.

"Not going to happen."

"Okay, then. So are you saying you'd rather stay on the hook with this Nick guy in Austin and risk losing your business than do a deal with me and Dex, just because somehow Julian found a way to pull this deal together without getting involved?"

"He went to Nick's fucking office, Will. That's involved, right? He's not out in the fringes. He's manipulating everything. He'll get what he wants, like always. Can't you see that?"

Will sat in silence. He looked down at his hands while he rubbed the condensation of the cold glass with his thumbs. Without looking up he said, "I supported his idea to visit Nick Spencer."

"Huh. Well, you made a fucking mistake," Char replied.

"Did I? I didn't have the answer for Nick. I tried to talk it through and leave Julian out of it, but Nick is a supreme asshole, and he had the upper hand. You can say what you want about Julian, but that guy can get a deal done."

"I can think of one big one he didn't," she said, staring down at her beer. "And this deal is my business...the business I built with my own two hands. He didn't give a flying shit about it until it was big enough to notice. Now he wants to wedge his way back in. No fucking way."

"I don't think that's what he wants, Char."

"Really? And what is it you think he wants?"

"He wants to see you succeed." Will leaned into the table and crossed his hands in front of his glass. His elbows now rested heavy on the table, forcing his shoulders to shrug upward. "This is going to sound shitty coming from me right now, but I read your financials, Char. Your company's in jeopardy. If you want to know what I think, I think he's just trying to make sure you get to see this thing through. Nothing else makes any sense to me."

Two men sat at the communal table near Will and Char. Though keeping their appropriate social distance, they were easily within earshot. Will instinctively leaned into the table and took the posture of someone who might speak in a softer tone going forward. Char, lacking the requisite social norms, stayed completely erect and took another sip of beer while leaning back slightly. Will offered them the obligatory nod. Char did not.

Will said in a volume marginally above a whisper, "If I'm being honest, he didn't have a lot of options here. There's no way he could have come to you directly. In his own way, I think he's trying to keep a promise to your dad."

"A what?" Char charged.

"He told me your dad left him a letter asking him to promise he'd take care of you if you needed it."

As if the two men were invisible, Char said aloud, "If I'm being honest, I don't really give a shit that he used you and Dexter. That was his only move. He knows full well I would've shut it down if he reached out to save my business. I don't care what my dad asked him to do before he…" Her voice trailed off just as it had with Dexter.

"So does your business need saving?" Will asked.

Char sat quietly staring at him. She didn't have to speak; he could see the acknowledgment in her face.

At that moment, he knew he had struck a chord. In seeing her expression, he ironically found himself going through the short list of rules Julian laid out. Her interests were clear: Char needed to save her business, she wanted to run the show, and she did not want Julian within a million miles of it. It was time to control the conversation. He realized in the moment, for the first time in his short tenure as Julian's disciple, his ability to look objectively at the situation while in the heat of the discussion seemed natural. He was divorced from the emotion and tapping into his internal operating system in real time. It was the flow state of dealmaking. And though he would have preferred different circumstances, he liked feeling it. "Look, we both know that it does. Why don't we talk about what it would look like for us to work together? I don't want to run your business. I want to create a space where you can run your business without all the background noise. I can take care of the noise. I can't create the music, Char. Only you can do that part."

"I did not realize you were a fucking poet," she said.

"And then there's Julian. If I can get Julian to move aside, do we have a deal?"

Char snickered. "You get Julian to disappear, and we can talk about what working together might look like. Right now, I'm gonna grab some food. I'm starving." She pulled her leg up over the bench at the communal table with an awkward tug.

Will smiled. The ball was now in his court.

Chapter 35

"Walking with a friend in the dark is better than walking alone in the light."

—Helen Keller

To: Will Powell
From: Julian Darrow
Date: Monday, October 21, 2025, 6:16:20 MDT

Subject: Pick you up today at your house 4:00 p.m.

Will read the subject line and sensed something was off. Julian had cemented 6:45—in the morning or the evening—as the only acceptable meeting time. The email curiously read 4:00 p.m. Still, Will found himself at the window a few minutes before, anxiously watching for the black Town Car to ease up the block. A light dusting of snow fell, far gentler than the storm that had hit during one of their previous meetings.

Now every encounter with Julian carried more weight—especially since Julian had stopped covering the mortgage payments. The financial pressure hummed beneath everything, making even a vague calendar invite feel like a test.

Right on time, with windshield wipers swiping, the black Town Car rolled into view. Will grabbed his light jacket, phone, and wallet, and walked outside into an expected brisk breeze. He buried his hands deep into his jacket pockets as he noticed the car exhaust showing faint signs of dark smoke against the ethereal white flakes, so sparse they danced against the exhaust as they disintegrated and turned to mush behind the tire. Will opened the door to the Town Car and immediately knew something was wrong. Julian was not inside.

"Where is he?" Will said to Vince as he climbed into the car next to the empty spot where Julian should have been. Vince did not respond but waited for Will to grab the freshly polished chrome handle and pull the door shut before he put the car in gear and headed down the street. "I knew it. Julian would have said six forty-five. He always does. Is something wrong with him?"

Vince's head never moved as he shot his eyes up at the rearview mirror briefly, making eye contact with Will, before instantly returning his focus to the road. "In the pocket in front of you," he said.

Will leaned forward, scooting enough to reach into the large pocket on the back of the passenger seat. After digging his hand deep into the pleated pocket, he pulled out a single pill bottle—though he felt a second beneath it. He turned the label toward him and read the name: donepezil. Vince's eyes darted up at the rearview mirror again, egging Will to continue his investigation. He returned to the pocket and produced the second bottle: memantine. He kept them in his palm as he eased back into his seat. Cocking his head to the side, so that he had the most direct line of sight to the rearview mirror, he said, "This doesn't mean anything to me. Are you telling me Julian's sick?"

"Donepezil is an enzyme blocker. Memantine is a receptor antagonist," Vince said while staring straight ahead. "Starting to forget stuff if he skips the pills."

Will looked into the mirror again and said coolly, "I suppose you're more than his driver?"

"I'm whatever he needs me to be."

"What's wrong with him?" Will asked.

"Long list," Vince smiled pityingly. "But he's fading."

"What?"

"Alzheimer's. If he skips the pills, you can tell. Kinda screwed up, right? Have to remember to take pills for remembering things."

Will released an audible "huh" as he sat rolling the bottles in his right hand in a circular motion, like a set of Chinese Baoding balls, while looking out the window. The brown and green bases of the mountains were starting to give way to the leverage of the white caps as they flexed their muscle in the early snowfalls. "How long has he known about this?"

" 'Bout a year," Vince responded. "Packed up shop as soon as he figured it out. Called everybody he worked with."

"He told them about it?"

Vince glanced into the rearview mirror. His eyes squinted in disbelief. "You think he told them?"

Will did not answer. The current revelation explained Julian's abrupt disappearance, the one that spooked Kirsty in her early investigation. "How bad is it?"

"Not bad yet. But it will be soon. The paranoia's first. That's what the doctor said. Every time a car cuts us off he thinks they're out to get us. If a stranger gets too close to him, it freaks him out. That's not him, it's the sickness. And the notebooks. He started writing down everything in notebooks. I heard you ask him about the notes. They're not for someone else. He is the someone else."

"I had no idea."

"That's the plan," Vince continued. "He only takes phone calls in his office. You know why? Because he writes down everyone's name, and what they talked about, on the big calendar on his desk. If somebody calls, he can read enough to keep up. Your name's all over the calendar, because he talks to you more than anyone else."

"Pretty smart, I guess," Will conceded. "Sad...but smart. The old bastard is thorough."

"He's paranoid. If he has a meeting, he writes their name on the inside of his palm in case he forgets."

Will shook his head, remembering his name scribbled on Julian's palm in their first encounter.

"It's sad shit," Vince continued. "And the crossword puzzles. Kills me with those damn things. He thinks they'll slow this down, give him an extra six months," Vince said, shaking his head in the rearview. "He read that in some bullshit article a few months ago. When I get bored, I fill in some answers. Took me a while to write like him. He writes real sharp."

"Why are you telling me this? I'm assuming Julian doesn't want it getting out." Will quizzed.

"Nobody'll ever understand him...I don't understand him. But you need to know where he's coming from. He's got nobody to tell."

Will was quiet for the next few minutes of the drive. He had never heard Vince utter more than a few words in a sentence. The pill bottles rolled around and around in his hand as he took the time to digest the news and its impact on the current events with Char and Dexter. "You're a good friend, Vince."

"Friends don't get paid."

"Well, you're the closest thing Julian has to a friend."

The olive-skinned Italian looked into the rearview with weathered eyes—no nod or smile, just eyes that understood. "I think that's you, kid."

Chapter 36

"Truth—more precisely an accurate understanding of reality—is the essential foundation for producing good outcomes."
—Ray Dalio

Julian Darrow looked flawed when he answered the door with Vince at his side. He was clean-shaven, donning an expected cashmere sweater, no hair out of place on his head, but he was flawed.

"How you holding up?" Will asked as the silver-haired gentleman stood stoically in the doorway of his home.

His eyes, squinting intentionally, threw daggers at the younger man. "What type of infantile question is that? I'm holding up as I always have."

"Okay, but I need to—"

"Save your dignity. Vince apprised me of your ticketless ride in my car. For the record, I knew you'd been in there." He stepped aside, allowing Will to enter as he continued, "Vince has been squirrely, and the back seat reeked of betrayal." He maintained his cold demeanor as he walked ahead of Will toward the office. Vince followed on this visit. Will noticed the room was substantially similar to the last time he saw it; books were haphazardly lined and stacked in the shelves, and in the center of the room was the large round coffee table and the deep cognac leather chairs. But this time, he saw Julian's favored items through a different lens—the heavily used legal pad with copious notes and ink-filled pages folded over the back, the oversized white calendar on his desk, and the single framed picture he now knew to be Char. It was all marred with pity. Vince's presence, as a guardian of sorts, only added to the feeling.

"Why did you call me to meet, Julian?"

"Rule Number Seven," Julian said with no inflection.

"Come on, we're not really still doing this, are we? You didn't invite me here for a lesson. And if you're not going to admit to tanking the RFP, then I'm not interested."

"Should I share the final rule, or not?"

"You're a spectacular asshole," Will said. "I'd love to hear the rule that somehow applies to this exact situation."

"RULE NUMBER SEVEN: PREPARE MORE THAN ANYONE ELSE IN THE DEAL."

"What good is that for me now?" Will said with a scowl. "And isn't that basically the same as Rule Number One? Be active?"

Julian paid Will's insult no attention. "Activity creates opportunity. Preparation capitalizes on opportunity. Those who can't parse the two are sentenced to a life of aimless activity."

"Are we going to pretend this meeting is about rules? I don't believe that's why you called me here."

Julian took a deep, slow breath, ignoring his pupil. He then launched into a soliloquy, "Dealmaking is a game, and the others know a lazy set of rules...a tit for tat, appearing just in time to play. They press their suits, comb their hair, and polish their shoes—and then what? They rely on intellect, experience, and bluster alone. Their egos mock a more thorough craft. They wear their lack of preparation as a badge of honor." Julian pointed directly at Will with a fatherly candor. "Prepare more than them, son. You're free to move the pieces about before the game begins. And if you find yourself disadvantaged, turn the lights out and prepare more fervently while they foolishly choose to sit idle. Deals are conceived, coddled, manipulated...all in preparation. Relationships are formed, allies are employed, it all happens in preparation for an end result. The bigger the deal, the more preparation transpires throughout the process. In the end, you're tasked with discerning how to strengthen both sides. The best deals— the deals expertly conceived—leave no one diminished. Preparation is not support for craft; it is craft." Julian rolled his chair back slowly and slid the shallow center desk drawer open. The hand that appeared from below the desk was now holding a tri-folded group of papers. He held them out for Will.

"What's this?" Will asked, taking the documents in hand.

"A deed. I've been carrying it around with me from the beginning. I assumed you'd come to understand Charlotte was my aim at some point, though Vince's enlightening you of my medical misfortune was unforeseen. Regardless, it's another part of the plan...a function of my preparation. You see, son, both sides must settle on an earnest deal. That's the essence of dealmaking."

Will scanned the top paragraph of the first page stating the listed address and ownership. He read under his breath, "415 Ford Street, Golden, Colorado. Owner: Golden Partners Holdings LLC." He turned to Julian, brows furrowed in anticipation of a tough question. Will had seen that company name before. "Why are you showing this to me?"

"You don't recognize the address?" Julian said, feigning surprise. "You tried to buy it once before."

"Is this the parking lot...from the auction?" Will said. "I thought you said Sharon Peyton would end up with it."

"It is. And I said she'd buy it," Julian responded. "Retaining it was not a foregone conclusion."

"What do you mean?"

"Sharon owns 10% of Golden Partners Holdings LLC. That company owns the parking lot in Golden, and in some glorious stroke of good fortune—or possibly preparation—that same company just won the RFP on the Telemark Building."

Will sighed. "And let me guess who owns the rest."

"Indeed," Julian said with a devilish grin.

Will's head instinctively cocked back, as if a jolt of electricity shot through his spinal cord, straightening his entire upper torso. The feeble Julian Darrow was not ready to be feeble. "Wait. So the company you own is the holding company that won the RFP and the one that owns the parking lot?"

"Yes," Julian replied laconically.

"I was going up against you this whole time?"

"Again, you ask binary questions. The answers don't fit into proper boxes."

"Answer the question, Julian," Will demanded.

Julian inhaled deeply. "He's really going to make me spell it out, Vince," he drawled, casting a mock-pained look toward the silent driver. "I can see why you prefer the quiet." He grabbed his coffee cup, taking a long, deliberate sip before inching back in his chair. Rolling it snugly under the desk, he propped his elbows on the table, folded his fists together, and delivered the details with the air of a man reluctantly indulging a slow student. "The Telemark Building. I had the client for it. The one Sharon Peyton's now representing...he's a friend of mine, tired of Denver, and wanted to move his operation to Golden. It started that innocently. I deduced the city would be looking for a new user immediately." He paused and took another sip. "I became aware of Charlotte's predicament somewhere along the way. Predictably, the city had no interest in negotiating directly with a single private developer—far too sensible, I suppose. Instead, they embarked on the folly of a six-week RFP process. Six weeks, mind you, to assemble a proposal for a project of that scale. Can you fathom such short-sightedness? Only a handful of suitors would even entertain moving at such an absurd pace. Bureaucracy at its finest." Julian shook his head, with the posture of a parent watching a child jump in mud puddles. "The thought occurred to me: I needed to find someone. I needed to find someone capable of action, adept enough to court Charlotte's business interests, and yet hungry enough to go along."

The statement landed hard on Will. He had not seen himself as a target. The thoroughness with which Julian was presenting his case left little doubt he was indeed just that: a target. That lingering thought could not be left unsettled. "How'd you find me?"

"How did I find you?" Julian smiled. "More preparation. The auction for the downtown Golden site was in the newspaper...turns out there's more in there than crossword puzzles. The article described a $25,000 deposit needed to enter the room. I made a few calls and established the roster of qualified bidders. You, Will, were the only one in the group with the drive—and perhaps the hunger—to pursue the Launch Pad deal."

"Wait...why partner with Sharon, then?"

"She wanted the Telemark Building with or without me, and she's connected with the city council." Julian sat back in his chair and folded his cashmere-sweatered arms in satisfaction. "I could not fix the race, son, but I could bet on two horses."

Will, trying desperately to find holes in the story, said, "What about Don Andino? What if he outbid Sharon?" Julian scrunched up one side of his face, obviously holding back. Will, catching on to the facial cues, said, "He was in on this, too?"

"Not at all, that's flirting with collusion," Julian winked. "Sharon disposed of him quickly. He knew he'd be the contractor on the

Telemark Building when she won. Outbidding her would have been...well...bad for business." Julian tilted his head to the side, giving Will a look of fulfillment. "And I owed him one."

Will shook his head in disbelief. "Okay, back to me. You picked me just because I was young and hungry?"

"Will, perhaps you might give an old man more credit. As I said, I researched you. I saw the development deals you were doing. I did the math. You were young and borderline broke. I knew I could help you."

"You've got an interesting way of helping. You said the RFP gave you the idea. Why?"

Julian smiled and said, "Time. Their contrived ticking clock. Let me ask you, when the auctioneer was spouting off numbers in Golden, in the heat of the moment, did you stretch your bid?"

"I stopped at $3 million."

"That's not what I asked. Did you stretch your bid? Did you intend on stopping at less than $3 million?"

"Maybe."

"Of course you did. That's why auctions and RFPs exist. By design, they control the offer process. They expedite the timeline and force irrational decisions. If I gave you an infinite timeline to deal with Charlotte, would you have approached it the same way?"

Will took a deep reflective breath through his flared nostrils. "No, probably not. I probably would have done more due diligence."

"You probably would have talked yourself out of it, son. Over time, the idea would have lost its luster. Tight timelines make fools of us all. We are enamored with the ordinary and want to win at all costs. You may not like it, but you lost focus, and you allowed me to take control, just like we've discussed."

Will did not fight back. He wanted to return fire, but there was little ammunition to use. The statement was accurate; he knew it. And even though it was evident Julian Darrow spent his waking hours attempting to gain leverage at all costs, the reality was humbling. "Was all this really necessary, Julian? Did it have to be this over the top?"

"Perhaps an edited version would have sufficed," Julian said, his sharp chin now coming to rest on the point of his fingers as he uncrossed his arms and leaned forward. "But I suppose I needed the challenge...a swan song. And this is why I need you to finish this. In this unforgiving state I find myself, Charlotte's success is my only measure of value, and you know my time is waning."

Will extended the folded deed with a steady hand. "Here you go. Nice move, Julian. I'll give you that."

Julian didn't take it. He just tilted his head, half a grin playing at his lips. "So that's how this ends? You hand me back the deed to the very parcel you once eagerly chased? All that preparation, and somehow, no appetite left for the prize?"

Will glanced at the deed, then tucked it under his arm. "That's right."

Julian smiled, shaking his head. "Funnier still—I always envisioned it as the next Launch Pad. More frontage, better exposure. Frankly, I expected you'd see it, too. Perhaps even fight me for it."

Will shrugged. "Still not interested."

Julian rounded the desk, hands behind his back, amused now. "Sleep on it, son. I'll draft generous terms that put your newfound wisdom to work."

Will was already moving. "I doubt it," he said, halfway out the door. "I know you too well."

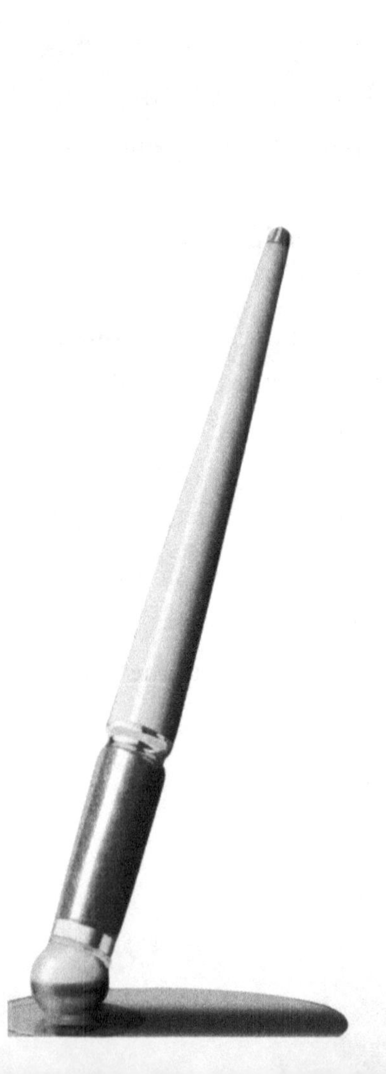

Chapter 37

"The course of this conflict is not known, yet its outcome is certain."

—George W. Bush

It was a cold dinner at Will Powell's house. Not the food—the salmon was cooked to flaky perfection—but Dexter, Kirsty, and Sela could all pick up on Will's uncomfortable state. The topics, ranging from the weather to the economy, were meant to distract from an obvious conversation needing to be had. Kirsty, sensing Dexter's invite was to discuss something more pressing, gathered the plates and glanced at Sela with a stern stare to join in the effort. Dexter piped up, "Wait. Let me help you, ladies."

"Thanks, Boo," Will said to Kirsty. "Let them clean up, Dex. I want to catch up with you in the other room."

"Let them clean up?" Kirsty reproached, sending a displeasured stare across the table. Sela picked up on it too and sneered.

"I think I'll take some more wine," Dexter said, lightheartedly, slicing through the tension.

Will reached for the bottle and poured two overly generous glasses of cabernet. "I need to tell you something," he said as they both moved toward the pair of royal blue chairs. Dexter sank into his, casually pulling one knee up onto the cushion, his snakeskin boot hanging off the edge. The posture, like his clothes, said nothing could rattle him—least of all whatever Will was about to say.

"I got you into a mess," Will admitted.

"How so, man?"

"Julian played me."

Dexter gave him a look—one part concern, one part curiosity. "You told me about Char. And I already talked to her, dude."

"Yeah, I know. And, Dex, I shouldn't have said anything about you and Char." Will swirled the wine in his glass, avoiding Dexter's eyes. "It wasn't my place. Whatever's happening between you two...it's not for me to say. What you had with my sister—that chapter closed a long time ago. You both tried to make it work. It didn't. She's happy. You're happy. And I'm over it. That's got nothing to do with Julian's bullshit."

Dexter didn't say anything, just nodded.

Will went on. "Man, there's more to this than you think. Julian never cared about the RFP on the Telemark Building. That was just the bait. It was all about getting us into Char's company—to block Nick Spencer from taking over."

"Can't really fault him for too much for that...now that I know about his partnership with her dad."

"But, Dex," Will said, leaning toward him with an apologetic tone. "He wasn't just targeting me. He handed you the financials hoping you'd join in the fun."

Dexter sat quietly, appearing to recall events in his head as he sipped from the behemoth glass of wine. After a few minutes—and what seemed like an eternity to Will—Dexter smirked. "He tell you that?"

"Yep."

"Well, if I'm being honest, man, I kinda figured that," Dexter said casually, as if the concept were not the least bit bothersome.

"How?" Will questioned him with a look of amazement.

"The documents he handed me. I didn't catch it at first, dude. His little trick worked on me, I gotta admit. He asked me for help, stroked my ego, and I took it hook, line, and sinker. But I thought about the docs after." Dexter pulled back in his chair and grabbed the front of his shin. "First off, you don't get private company financials out of the blue. They're not public knowledge. He had to work to get them. Second, he was too smart not to know. That's the part that stuck with me. The info was all there, and I guessed he knew it."

"Why didn't you say anything?"

"He was right. I knew there was a good investment for me. Also, Will, you've asked me more questions in the last two months than you ever have. This guy lit some kinda fire in you, man. I couldn't put my finger on it, but I thought it was all coming from a good place. Julian was coaching you."

"You saying you jumped to help me?"

"I'm not into charity, man. I'm saying I thought it was good for both of us. And I'm a big boy. I could get out when I wanted. Did find one thing odd, though."

"What?" Will asked.

"Why now? Why did Julian come out of the woodworks now to help out Char? That's the answer I didn't believe. I don't think this Nick Spencer guy was enough. I think that's an excuse."

Will stood quickly. "Damn, Dex. You're beating me to the punchline. I asked myself the same thing when I figured out about his connection to Char. Get this," Will said, raising his hands and folding them behind his head as he leaned back. "I didn't see it at all, the notebooks, the crossword puzzles, the vacant stares. The old guy has Alzheimer's. This is like his last hurrah, or something."

"How'd you figure that out?"

"Vince had to tell me. Julian would've died before he let it out."

"That son of a bitch," Dexter said, a small smirk reappearing in the corners of his mouth. "If it's bad, he's pretty good at hiding it."

Will, puzzled by the response, said, "That's it? This is a game to you?"

Dexter sent his gaze jaggedly around the room, never looking directly at Will, practically ignoring him. He shook his head. "All the pieces were there the whole time...so obvious."

Will stood quickly. "What the hell, Dex? I trusted this asshole. You aren't pissed?"

Dexter took another slow sip of wine. "Of course, dude, I don't like it. But here we are. He didn't twist my arm. And he didn't give me cooked books." He continued to stare into middle distance. "Honestly, Char's numbers were scary." Dexter shook his head again. "He did something way more dangerous than trying to force me...he asked me for help. He let me be the smartest guy in the room, and then he asked me for help. That old bastard handed me a puzzle to solve and stroked my ego."

Dexter's fascination with Julian's tactics were visibly agitating Will, who shook his head violently from side to side. "You don't get it, Dex. The deal's blowing up."

"It is?" Dexter said curiously. "Why?"

"She can't stand the sight of him, and he's got his fingerprints all over this thing. You tell me."

"Do you want it to end?" Dexter asked.

"Don't go Julian on me, Dex. He lied to us."

"Yes, he did." Dexter sat with that statement in brief silence before continuing, "But now it's our choice, right? We can fold our hand. If so, Julian and Char are in trouble. Or we can do this on our terms."

"Char's gonna bail, Dex. She hates Julian."

"Maybe it's time for Julian to get out of the way."

Will rubbed the top of his head with his folded hands, slowly releasing rows of hair that fell forward. "I don't think he wants to."

"Then let's convince him to get out of the way," Dexter said plainly.

"Easier said than done," Will said. "He's got an obvious interest here, and he's in total control. He's slick, Dex. And the only thing Julian truly respects is authority."

Dexter flattened his lips in thought. The two men sat silently, each taking a sip from their glasses, looking for answers. "Authority's a funny thing. There's an angle in here somewhere. You just gotta exploit it."

Will quieted. He sat slowly shaking his head and looking down, searching for the answer. Finally, he looked up. "Got any ideas on how to do that?"

Dexter cocked his head to the side, staring straight into Will's eyes. "Sounds like he needs a friend to shoot him straight. Are you his friend?"

***

Later that evening, Will found himself in bed, eyeing the shadows cast along the ceiling. Dexter's question lingered in his scattered thoughts.

"Can't sleep?" Kirsty asked, lying next to him. She reached over and grabbed his hand. Rolling over to face Will, she said, "What is it, honey?" She was wearing one of their vacation T-shirts and uttered the words in a flirtatious tone. The simple gesture would typically dissolve any concerns Will had and reduce him to other more basic thoughts.

He inhaled slowly through his nose and sighed. Her efforts could not shake his trepidation. He shifted his head back on the pillow away from her, creating enough room to talk. "You were right about Julian. He played me."

"Are you in trouble?" she pivoted. He was clearly unmoved by her common attempt at physical affection.

"No. Not like that. Everything's good. But this whole RFP thing was a sham. You saw it coming, and I didn't listen."

"Where's that leave you?" she consulted.

"I think I can still put the Launch Pad deal together. Honestly, I couldn't have done it without him."

She scooted closer to him in the bed, now cupping his hand between both of hers. "Been there. Men have a way of hiding things," she said flatly.

"What's that supposed to mean?"

"I know why you trusted him. You had to, right? He was your best option." She moved her knees up against his legs before continuing. "Does this have something to do with the late payments on the apartments? They called me looking for you."

"What?!" he said abruptly. "Why didn't you say anything?"

"Why didn't you?"

Will remained quiet for a moment. Though they were lying face-to-face, his newfound shame did not allow him to hold her gaze. "Were you just never going to bring this up?"

"I never questioned your intentions, Will. People act in their own self-interests. They always do." She paused, pulling his hand up to her mouth and kissing it. "It's how they treat the ones involved. That's what tells you who they are."

"So you just didn't say anything?" he said.

"I trusted your intentions. I always will."

Will looked up, their eyes reconnecting. "Hmmm," he breathed, marveling in the simplicity of her wisdom.

"I read that in one of my books." She smiled. "If you and Julian weren't so hellbent on hiding your intentions, maybe the world would be an easier place."

"Maybe so," Will responded. Finding comfort in their openness, he pulled her closer to him.

"So is he screwing you over?" Kirsty questioned.

"I don't think so, Boo. I think he's really trying to help me...in his own messed-up way."

"I don't understand men."

"Me neither," Will said, pulling her hands up to his lips, kissing them in appreciation.

"Well, he has to want something. What is it?"

"He wants me to finish what he started."

"What's keeping you from doing it, then?" she said, now so close to him that their noses touched.

"Right now, he is."

Will gazed into her eyes. The darkness gave the blue irises a look of transparency. "I'm sorry...for not telling you about the payments."

"Okay. Then next time don't be so stupid," she said playfully, as she nuzzled in tighter. "But I guess this means you owe me one."

"Anything," he said as he moved his hand behind her head.

Kirsty leaned in and kissed him slowly. Her lips were warm and soft and full of meaning. She finished the kiss and tilted her forehead until it rested on his. "Go out there and finish what you started."

"Can I finish this right now?" he asked, now wrapping his arms completely around her.

"Yeah," she said softly. "If you want to owe me again."

"Deal."

Chapter 38

"You should run your life not by the calendar but how you feel, and what your interests are and ambitions."
—John Glenn

"You're screwing up," Will said as he found himself in Julian's office the very next day. Vince's presence in the room had no impact on his candor.

"Oh?" Julian responded, ending the single syllable with a slow, dramatic uptick in pitch. "I'm screwing up. Forgive me if I'm not roused to action by your words. And remind me, please, did we have an engagement set, or have you simply grown comfortable dropping in unannounced?"

Will walked a serpentine path through the deep cognac chairs and stood a few feet away from Julian's desk. "You're breaking your own rules."

"Excuse me?"

"I've been struggling with this, Julian. I don't know why. You lied to me and kept me in the dark since the day we met. But ever since Vince told me about your condition, I've been struggling with how I can help you finish this. I should let you fail. I know I should, but I can't. The truth is, we've both broken the rules. Every single one of them. You were right—they aren't easy."

As Will continued to talk, Julian slid his elbows onto his desk and interlaced his fingers. "Okay, then, amuse me."

"The thought occurred to me. I couldn't see it before, partially because I was pissed at you, but Launch Pad is exactly the type of business I need. I wouldn't want it without Char's passion and Dex's...well, whatever the hell Dex does. But you were right, the RFP doesn't mean anything to me. Growing Launch Pad with talented people around me, that's my interest. I wouldn't have seen that without you."

"Good then. However, I'm afraid Charlotte's interests may not align with yours at the moment," Julian said.

"That's just it. They absolutely do. But her position is firm, Julian, and that's where you're screwing up."

"This is fascinating," Julian said as he eased forward, resting his sharp chin on his interlaced knuckles. "Go ahead, son, fill me in."

"Char has a decision to make, but as I see it, the decision is really yours. And what did you tell me about interests on our first car ride? Sometimes our positions are incongruent with our interests."

"To the point," Julian pressed, now growing agitated at the trajectory of the conversation.

"I believe your interest is to see Char succeed. It's your duty, right? And it eats at your insides to think you could have coupled her talent with your wisdom...that she despises you, and you may not get to celebrate this final win...that there's no parade at the end for Julian."

"Just a damn minute," Julian barked, rising abruptly from his chair, which tipped onto its back legs and caromed off the wall behind him. "You haven't the faintest idea what you're talking about. I have a duty—a responsibility—to her father."

"You killed her father!" Will belted.

"His cowardice killed him!" Julian said, slamming the desk with his hand. "My lack of craft drove him there, but I don't own his blood. That selfish coward left a villain for his daughter to blame. I'll regret the position I put Charlotte in until the day I die, but I have no interest in listening to these...these ill-conceived mutterings. My past is not an academic exercise. Tread lightly with what leaves your mouth next."

"Calm down, Julian," Will pleaded. "Look, I don't know a tenth as much about negotiating as you do...not a tenth. But when it comes to people's daughters, you don't need to teach any courses. For once, I'm asking you to listen to me." Will took a breath and waited for the tension to leave Julian's face. "When I married Kirsty, Sela was nine, just like Char was when all this went down. She was headstrong and smart. We went through a funk there at the beginning. I wasn't foolish enough to try to be her dad, but I wanted us to have a real relationship. I played every sport growing up, so I thought we could enjoy working on soccer together. She had a trophy from each year since she was five in a row on her dresser. I knew she loved it."

"Son, I'm getting a bit old for anecdotes." Julian's tone returned to the controlled levelness he had mastered. "I appreciate you're finding your authority. Well played. But should I not be somewhat immune to my own tactics?"

Will paid him no attention and continued, "I screwed up at first. Tried to teach her some better fundamentals. She shut down. We did it for a week. I was going to show her I wanted to put in the time. At the end of the week, I had to force her to go out in the yard with me. That weekend, she had a game. She was brilliant. She scored three goals. At the end of the game, I was so proud of her, and I was proud of myself for teaching her. I gave her a high five and said, 'You were great.' She looked up at me and smiled. And with a shit-eating grin, she said 'Thanks, Will. Told you I was good. Can you just come to the games from now on?'"

Julian, setting aside his annoyance, smiled at the story. "She sounds like a firecracker."

"She definitely is. But here's the point," Will offered. "You have conflicting interests, and you need to decide which one is more important today. Is it to force her to see the impact you're having on this...to forgive you...to rid yourself of guilt? Or is it to keep your promise to her father and see her succeed? You can't do both at the same time, and I know your situation well enough now to know which one matters most to you. It's always been your interest. You saved her from the one poor business decision she made. The guy in Austin...she knows it was you who made that asshole cooperate. But if you want to achieve your interest, to see her succeed, then you need to give Char some space, the same space you've given her for years. Maybe she'll forgive you. Maybe she won't. Maybe you just need to forgive yourself. I'm not a shrink. But your name doesn't get cleared here, Julian. You'll always be the villain in her eyes. You need to let that go. Launch Pad is her game, and you need to respect that. So if you want to give her a gift, if you want to see her succeed, back the hell up and give her space. Stay a thousand miles away from Launch Pad and let me and Dex close this deal. You've done your part. That's what you wanted all along, right?"

Julian stood silent for a moment. The piercing look of rage with which he began the conversation had softened to a melancholy stare. He leaned over, as if the weight of the decision were physically pulling him down, bracing himself with his fingertips against the smooth soapstone desktop. Then he picked up and held the childhood picture of Char in the pink cowboy hat—a warm, approving smile returned, building in his cheeks, tears welling in his eyes. "You've made your point. I don't know how long I have left to act. Six months? Two years? Trivial, isn't it, what priorities surface when time is running out. I barely know her, but I can't force this image from my every thought. Let me ask you, son, what assurance do I have that she'll succeed?"

Will waited until Julian raised his gaze from the picture. "None. But you've seen what she's done so far. Do you really have any doubts? Your interest is to see her succeed. Forgiveness is another chapter, and you're not even giving her the chance to write it."

"Perhaps you're right," Julian offered.

"And another thing that's eating at me," Will said. "You've asked me all these questions...to arrive at interests. I'm supposed to gain all this knowledge from the other party. But you...you can't share your interests at all. You completely conceal what you want. You can't tell Char about your Alzheimer's. Why? What's the point? If she understood where you were coming from, maybe all of this would end up differently. But you act like everything is one-sided."

Julian stood up, walked around his desk, and placed his hands on each of Will's shoulders. "Stick with what you know."

"I don't know shit. I haven't figured out how that makes any sense at all. But I do know this: Char doesn't want you anywhere around Launch Pad Hotel. She needs the autonomy. She needs to know she built it without you. If you give her that, you might have a chance at forgiveness later. But you need to fill her in on what's going on. Otherwise, all of this comes out of left field, and you might as well forget she exists."

Julian leaned back against the desk, facing Will from just a few feet away. He removed his hands from Will's shoulders and crossed his arms. "You say that with such conviction."

"I'm telling you the truth."

"Telling me?" Julian glared at Will with a look of acceptance, a tight-lipped smile formed curiously on his face. He released a slow sigh and said, "Then so be it."

"That's it?" Will questioned, shaken by Julian's capitulation.

"That's it." The silver-haired gentleman conceded. "But Will?"

"Yes."

"This will be our last meeting. Continuing your tutelage is unnecessary. Perhaps today is proof."

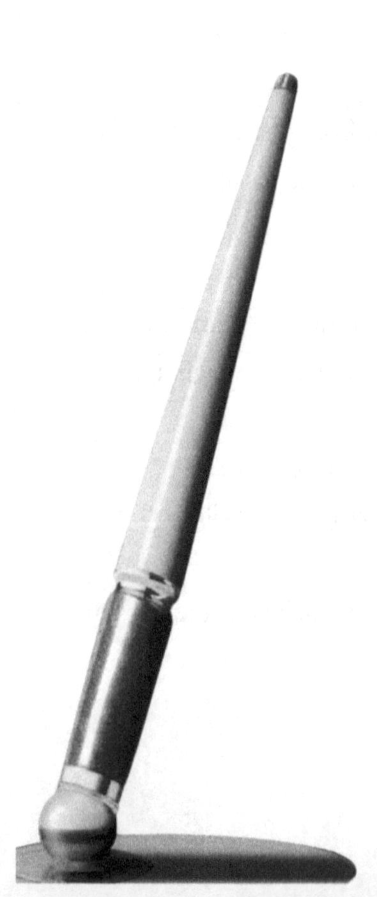

Chapter 39

"What wound did ever heal but by degrees?"

—William Shakespeare

The box was nondescript, medium sized—too big for a pair of shoes and too small for a printer. It was sitting on her office chair when she arrived at Launch Pad Raleigh. Char had not consumed her coffee yet, and thus the special delivery stirred nothing in her, just a box. She walked closer to see the return label, beautifully scribed by hand. The sender's name was at the top: Julian Darrow. "Humph," she mumbled as she left the box there, en route toward the smell of freshly brewed coffee at the wet bar in the hall. Upon her return, she placed the box gently on the floor by her desk and began to check emails. The box was lighter than she expected. She would have guessed it empty except for the slight tap of the shifting contents when she moved it.

Julian's box sat next to her as she sorted her screen's inbox, pretending to herself that she did not want to rip it open. Twenty-five minutes passed until her silver insulated mug banged against the desk without a drop remaining. She stood to refill it and saw his name again, just short of calligraphy. She slid the shallow center drawer of her desk open and grabbed the scissors, opening them fully until she brandished a single scissor blade in her hand. With a few long slashes, the tape was split, and the flaps opened.

Inside, beneath a small gathering of tissue paper, was a child's cowboy hat. She pulled it from the box and immediately recognized the pilled pink felt, the authenticity validated by her name scribbled in smudged marker inside the silken bucket. A note was tucked inside the hat on a single white cardstock:

For the ride. It's your show. Should you ever need me, I'll be in the barn where I belong.

"Humph," she uttered again, her lips softening, almost quivering. She held the cowboy hat close to her face, and with eyes closed, rubbed it against her cheek. Tears began to stream down her face, darkening the pink felt as they landed. She moved the hat down tight to her chest, the taste of cotton candy sizzling in her mouth; it had been over twenty years since she tasted cotton candy. She wiped her eyes on the hat before resting it on her desk.

Returning to her computer screen, Char pulled up the latest Launch Pad weekly report. Things were looking up. Week-over-week and month-over-month growth confirmed what she had quietly trusted all along: the brand just needed time to settle into itself. Growth took patience, and now it was showing up. Her early doubts about whether people still sought connection were giving way to something steadier: the belief that community was a basic human need. And she was ready to meet it. Julian Darrow, she had to admit—though rightfully demonized for much of her life—played some bit part in her current ability to dream.

"Fuck you for helping me," she whispered as she picked up the cowboy hat and held it close to her heart.

***

Dexter Mathis set the grocery bags in the corridor. It was his second trip from his SUV, toting numerous bags chock-full of identical goods. There were forty-two in all: every last one he could find in the three stores he visited. He carried ten bags, which followed the eleven he had lugged the trip before—each making their way to his pantry. It would be his most significant art installation, and he was giddy at the idea.

He stopped for a moment, realizing he hadn't even sampled the goods. He tore open a box and dumped its contents into a plain white bowl. The light, air-filled balls of puffed corn bounced as they hit the bowl. The sound was foreign to him; nonetheless he over-poured the milk until the cereal floated. He didn't know why he poured so much; it just felt natural to fill until the balls floated in the bowl. With a heaping spoonful he crunched into it. Truly, it was too sweet to eat for breakfast as far as Dexter Mathis was concerned, more a dessert. But he couldn't stop smiling as he crunched into it. The milk, eroding the artificial chocolate sheen of the individual puffs, was already losing its battle to remain a creamy white. Still, Dexter continued to eat it and smile.

After finishing the bowl, he grabbed each brown box and stacked it neatly on the shelf, shoving the current contents of his pantry back against the wall. The boxes needed to be front and center, concealing any other items. Side by side, he placed brown box after brown box until the levels of shelves all displayed the cartoonish image of a nonexistent bird—a creature so out of sorts it could only be satiated by abnormal quantities of chocolate. Dexter stood back, with phone in hand, until he could see the entire pantry in one image. There it was, a brilliant display of forty-two boxes of Cocoa Puffs, expertly arranged and filling every last inch of space. The gesture was overtly childish, unmistakably silly, and unbelievably foreign to Dexter's pattern of action with respect to the women in his life.

He did not know where the Launch Pad saga would end, and in that moment, his business dealings with Char were far from his mind. Will currently held those cards, and they were continuously being shuffled. This was simpler, natural, and unmarred by any acts of skill or persuasion. He steadied the phone's camera until he was sure he captured every box, and with a quick tap of his thumb, the image sat frozen on his screen. He then tapped the send icon and selected Char's name from the contacts. Beneath the image he typed the sentence fragment: *For next time you're in Denver.* And there it was, his first shot at a second act.

Chapter 40

"I saw the angel in the marble and carved until I set him free."

—Michelangelo

Knock...Knock...Knock. A quick triplet of heavy pounds startled Kirsty on Saturday morning as she sat reading on the blue couch. The heavy-handed knock rattled the windows. She uncrossed her legs and begrudgingly made her way to the door.

Kirsty peered through the sidelight as she approached, looking to see who might have banged so forcefully: nobody. As she pulled the door open, she saw an olive-skinned driver climbing into a black Lincoln Town Car with the engine still running. The driver noticed her, waved, and nodded, a vague gesture suggesting that successful delivery of the parcel was part of the job.

His delivery was nondescript: a thin green folder concealing a number of legal-sized papers. The folder had the name neatly penned on the front: Will Powell. "Will!" Kirsty called loudly. "You have a special delivery." Will emerged from the kitchen, holding a fresh cup of coffee and wearing a pair of tattered slippers, a T-shirt, and flannel pajama pants. "Did you get me something?" she said, facetiously, still standing in the open door. "A present?"

"You never know," Will replied. He hurried to the door, unsure of what awaited him. As he noticed the green folder, the penmanship caught his eye.

"Hand delivered," Kirsty said with eyebrows raised, watching the Town Car turn off their street. Will pulled the contents from the folder.

The top sheet was crisp, though the subsequent pages had obviously been forced from their previously folded shape. With squinted early morning eyes, he began to read the cover page.

"What does it say?" Kirsty prodded.

Will shook his head slowly, enjoying the moment of suspense. "Give me a second." The formality of the document was obvious. He read the short cover letter silently as Kirsty hovered behind him, urging some expediency. It read:

Dear Will,

Success cannot be measured by a single event. It is a culmination of great effort, a product of craft.

I appreciate our dealings more than you will ever comprehend. For now, I shall sit idly by, knowing full well the next steps are yours to take. I respectfully request that you accept this deed to the land in Golden, free and clear. There are no strings attached. You earned it. I have selfishly decided your position to reject the deed was incongruent with your interests. Your stubborn disagreement is futile in the matter, as my signature is affixed and the deed is fully recorded.

Should you proceed with Launch Pad, I trust you will send a picture from the Grand Opening. My desk is in dire need of a new photograph.

Sincerely,
Julian Darrow

As he finished reading the cover letter, Will could feel Kirsty's presence; her weight pressing against him. "What does it say?" she pressed him.

"That bastard," Will replied, biting his lip and attempting to swallow his emotions. "He's good."

"What is it?"

"It's the deed to the Launch Pad site in Golden," he continued. "Julian says I own it now."

"Wow. How much do you owe him?"

Will turned to her, clenching the papers firmly in both hands. "More than I'm willing to admit."

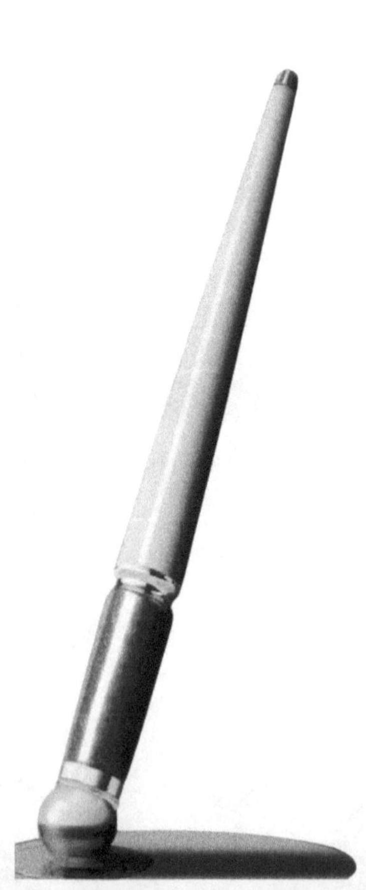

The Seven Rules of Julian Darrow

1. Be active…and take action.

2. Everyone is self-interested. Serve their interests to achieve yours.

3. Know your value. Your value makes the deal unique.

4. Guide the offer by understanding the role of price.

5. Speak from your authority. No person is the authority on all subjects.

6. Good ideas become great ideas when you gift them to others.

7. Prepare more than anyone else in the deal.

Acknowledgments

Writing this book was no solo act; the foundation was laid long ago by mentors and adversaries whose influence defined my early career in real estate. And turning those lessons into a story worth reading required a dedicated crew. They rooted out the flaws, sharpened the story's edges, and made sure the result was worthy of a page turn.

Special thanks to Amie Norris, whose sharp editorial instincts and attention to detail made the prose stronger on every page. To the tireless proofreaders—Lori Alden Holuta and Cameron Berry—thank you for catching the details that everyone else missed. To Brandon Gratton, whose patience and creative persistence delivered a cover that perfectly reflects the book's spirit (and my apologies for the countless rounds of redesign it took to get there). My sincere thanks also to Kristen Gilligan and Len Vlahos for their encouragement, belief in the story, and willingness to help see it through. Every comma, word choice, and design element was made stronger by your work, and I am grateful for the care and professionalism you each brought to the process. This book is simply better because of you.

And finally, thank you to my family, who indulged me in this escape from work and allowed me to fulfill a childhood dream. The result is The Dealmaker's Will—a finished work you can read cover to cover…or just set your drink on.

About the Author

WALKER THRASH is a seasoned real estate developer, entrepreneur, and the managing partner of Vertikal, a company focused on public-private partnerships in real estate development and construction. He is also a founding partner of the Origin Hotel brand. His businesses are built on the belief that successful projects begin with bold ideas—and the right partners to bring them to life. Throughout his career, Walker has developed and constructed real estate across the United States, with projects spanning hotels, residential, restaurants, mixed-use, and community-focused developments. His team at Vertikal is known for blending strategic vision with on-the-ground execution—often bringing together public-private partnerships and structuring complex financing solutions that include tax credits, federal and state grants, and layered incentive programs. Walker has built a reputation for solving tough development challenges with creativity, discipline, and a deep understanding of how to align design, capital, and construction. His focus on urban infill, and catalytic community projects reflects a belief that development should meet real needs—and that great ideas are only as valuable as their execution. As an author, Walker brings that same mindset to the page: practical, direct, and committed to results. His writing distills decades of hard-earned experience in dealmaking, leadership, and building things that matter—with the occasional dose of humor to keep it honest and relatable. Walker lives in Louisville, CO with his wife, Katie, and their four children: Annabelle, Marie, Lizzie, and Turner.

About the Publisher

LEFT FIELD PUBLISHING–where creativity meets collaboration. We're a forward-thinking publishing company created to combine the best attributes of traditional publishing with the best attributes of independent publishing. We exist to help authors bring their work to market in a cost-effective way while allowing them to retain control over their writing projects.

Our vision is to reimagine what publishing can be—bold, collaborative, and purpose-driven—by amplifying genre-defying voices across fiction, non-fiction, YA and kids books. Because great books aren't defined by a category.

Visit us at www.Left-Field-Publishing.com.

Connect with us!

Facebook: /leftfieldpublishing
Instagram: @leftfieldpublishing
TikTok: leftfieldpublishing
YouTube: @LeftFieldPublishing-m4g
LinkedIn: Left Field Publishing

Join the
Left Field Publishing
Readers Collective!

Where passionate readers become part of the publishing revolution

- ✦ **Adopt an Author**
- ✦ **Participate in Left Field Book Clubs**
- ✦ **Join a Street Team**
- ✦ **Influence What We Publish**
- ✦ **Read & Review**
- ✦ **& More!**

JOIN NOW @ www.Left-Field-Publishing.com